SCHOOL OF ADVAN
Institute of Gei

MW01199468

Terrorism, Italian Style
Representations of Political Violence in
Contemporary Italian Cinema

igrs books

Established by the Institute of Germanic & Romance Studies, this series aims to bring to the public monographs and collections of essays in the field of modern foreign languages. Proposals for publication are selected by the Institute's editorial board, which is advised by a peer review committee of 36 senior academics in the field. To make titles as accessible as possible to an English-speaking and multi-lingual readership, volumes are written in English and quotations given in English translation.

For further details on the annual competition, visit:
http://igrs.sas.ac.uk/publications/IGRS_books_2011.php.

igrs books
Volume 3

Volume Editor
Dr Katia Pizzi

Terrorism, Italian Style
Representations of Political Violence in Contemporary Italian Cinema

Edited by

Ruth Glynn, Giancarlo Lombardi
and Alan O'Leary

SCHOOL OF ADVANCED STUDY UNIVERSITY OF LONDON

Institute of Germanic & Romance Studies
2012

Published by the

Institute of Germanic & Romance Studies
School of Advanced Study, University of London
Senate House, Malet Street, London WC1E 7HU
http://igrs.sas.ac.uk

Cover image

Set photograph from *Attacco allo stato* (dir. Michele Soavi, 2006),
courtesy Taodue.

First published 2012

ISBN 978 0 85457 228 1

Contents

Acknowledgements

The editors wish to thank the following for their help with the preparation of this volume: Reena Aggarwal, Pierpaolo Antonello, Richard Churchill, Rebecca Green, Donatella Saroli, Barbara Spinelli, and the management and staff of the Agriturismo Iacchelli for providing a congenial working environment.

Our gratitude is also due to our respective institutions – the University of Bristol, Arts Faculty (Glynn); the University of Leeds, School of Modern Languages and Cultures (O'Leary); the College of Staten Island, CUNY and the PSC-CUNY (Lombardi) have all lent their financial support both for the production of this book and to subsidize travel for editorial meetings.

The cover image from *Attacco allo stato* (Michele Soavi, 2006) was generously provided by the production company Taodue.

Finally, thanks are due to Katia Pizzi, Naomi Segal and Jane Lewin at the Institute of Germanic & Romance Studies, as well as to the IGRS internal and external readers for the very many readings of the drafts of the manuscript.

Note

Throughout this book, all translations into English, unless otherwise attributed, are by the contributors or editors, and reference is given to the original text. Further references to a cited text will appear after quotations; passages without page references are from the last-cited page and page-numbers without specified text are similarly from the last one named. Unless otherwise stated, all italics are the authors'.

List of Contributors

Leonardo Cecchini is Associate Professor and Head of the Department of Italian at the Institute of Language, Literature and Culture, University of Aarhus. He works on Dante and the Italian Middle Ages, as well as modern and contemporary Italian culture and literature. His publications include: 'Rappresentazioni degli anni di piombo', in *Atti del VII congresso degli italianisti scandinavi* (Lunds, 2005), 299–310; and, with Francesco Caviglia, 'Narrative Models of Political Violence: Vicarious Experience and "Violentization" in 1970s Italy', in *Imagining Terrorism: The Rhetoric and Representation of Political Violence in Italy 1969–2009*, ed. Pierpaolo Antonello and Alan O'Leary (Legenda, 2009), 139–52.

Ruth Glynn is Senior Lecturer in Italian at the University of Bristol. Her research interests lie in late twentieth-century Italian culture and include representations of the *anni di piombo*, postmodernism and the historical novel. She is currently writing a monograph exploring how women's active participation in Italy's experience of political violence and terrorism in the *anni di piombo* is articulated as trauma in memoir, fiction and film. Her publications include *Contesting the Monument: The Anti-Illusionist Italian Historical Novel* (Northern Universities Press, 2005) and articles on cultural representations of Italian women terrorists and on literary works by Consolo, Eco and Malerba.

Max Henninger is a freelance translator and independent scholar in Berlin. He is the editor, with Angelika Ebbinghaus and Marcel van der Linden, of the volume *1968: A View of the Protest Movements 40 Years After, from a Global Perspective* (Akademische Verlagsanstalt, 2009), and coordinating editor, with Peter Burke, of the journal *Social History Online*.

Giancarlo Lombardi is Professor of Italian and Comparative Literature at the College of Staten Island and at the CUNY Graduate Center. In 2002, he published the monograph *Rooms with a View: Feminist Diary Fiction, 1954–1999* (Fairleigh Dickinson). He has also published a number of articles on contemporary women writers, television studies, Italian cinema and cultural studies. He is currently working on a volume on the rhetoric of fear in Italian serial drama of the 1960s and 1970s.

Nicoletta Marini-Maio is Assistant Professor of Italian at Dickinson College and works on twentieth- and twenty-first century Italian literature, theatre, and film, particularly in the intersections between politics, performance, narrative modes, and collective memory. She is completing a monograph on the representation of terrorism in Italian film and theatre, and coediting a critical translation of *Corpo di stato*, by the Italian playwright Marco Baliani. She is also interested in the pedagogy of Italian language, and technology-enhanced language learning, and has coedited the scholarly volumes *Set the Stage! Teaching Italian through Theatre* (Yale, 2009) and *Dramatic Interactions: Teaching the Foreign Language, Culture, and Literature through Theatre* (Cambridge Scholars Press, 2011).

Ellen Nerenberg is Professor of Romance Languages and Literatures and Feminist, Gender, and Sexuality Studies at Wesleyan University. She is the author of *Prison Terms: Representing Confinement During and After Italian Fascism* (Toronto, 2001), which won the Modern Language Association's Howard R. Marraro Prize for best book on an Italian subject published in the 2000–01 biennial. She has published essays on Alba de Céspedes, Pratolini, and Buzzati. She is completing a coedited translation and critical edition of Marco Baliani's *Corpo di Stato* as well as a monograph studying three post-1989 murder cases which is entitled *Making a Killing*.

Alan O'Leary is Senior Lecturer in Italian at the University of Leeds. His monograph *Tragedia all'italiana: cinema e terrorismo tra Moro e memoria* (Angelica) was published in 2007; a revised English edition was published in 2011 by Peter Lang. With Pierpaolo Antonello he is the editor of *Imagining Terrorism: The Rhetoric and Representation of Political Violence in Italy 1969–2009* (Legenda, 2009), and with Millicent Marcus of the annual film issue of the journal *The Italianist*. He coedited the special edition of *Italian Studies*, 'Thinking Italian Film', with Catherine O'Rawe (summer 2008).

Dana Renga, Assistant Professor of Italian at The Ohio State University, specializes in Italian film and twentieth- and twenty-first-century Italian cultural studies. She is working on a book called *Unfinished Business* on trauma, gender and mourning in Italian mafia films, and an edited volume entitled *Mafia Movies: A Reader* was published in 2011 (University of Toronto Press). She has published on Italo Calvino, Elsa Morante, Andrea Zanzotto, Federico Fellini, Roberto Benigni, Pier Paolo Pasolini and Lina Wertmüller, on contemporary Italian poetry, and on French and Italian Holocaust Cinema.

Rachele Tardi received a PhD in Italian Studies at UCL in 2005 with a dissertation entitled *Representations of Italian Left Political Violence in Film, Literature and Theatre (1973–2005)*. She has been a Research Fellow at the University of Leeds and is now working for the British Red Cross.

Mary P. Wood is Professor of European Cinema, and Head of the Department of Media and Cultural Studies at Birkbeck, University of London. She has written widely on Italian cinema and her recent publications include *Contemporary European Cinema* (Arnold, 2007) and *Italian Cinema* (Berg, 2005). Following her chapter, 'The Dark Side of the Mediterranean: Italian Noir', in Andrew Spicer (ed.), *European Noir* (Manchester University Press, 2007), her most recent research has been on aspects of Italian film noir, resulting in a chapter in Helen Hanson and Catherine O'Rawe (eds), *Cherchez la femme: The Cinematic Femme Fatale* (Palgrave Macmillan, 2010), and articles and conference papers on Italian political noir.

Introduction: Terrorism, Italian Style

Ruth Glynn, Giancarlo Lombardi and Alan O'Leary

The legacy of Italy's experience of political violence and terrorism in the period known as the *anni di piombo* [years of lead], c. 1969–83, continues to exercise the Italian imagination and that of its filmmakers to an extraordinary degree. The more recent resurgence of terrorist activity on the national as well as the global stage has contributed to a political and cultural return to the widespread, enduring political violence that culminated in two emblematic events: on the left, in the kidnapping and murder by the Brigate Rosse (BR) of Democrazia Cristiana (DC) president Aldo Moro in 1978; on the right, in the devastating bombing of the Bologna train station by a neo-fascist group in 1980.

In the cultural arena, cinema has played a particularly prominent role in articulating the ongoing impact of the *anni di piombo* and in defining the ways in which Italians remember and work through the events of the 1970s. Each year sees the release of one or more films addressing the atrocities and traumas of those years. The persistence of the cinematic return and the strength of feeling surrounding the reception of recent films addressing the events and legacy of political violence bear witness to the degree to which the *anni di piombo* are felt to impact on present-day conditions, and to the contentious nature of the representation of political violence.

The particular contribution made by the cinema has been recognized by a number of cultural commentators: Paola Tavella, for instance, has suggested that films addressing the *anni di piombo* allow us to confront issues which have never been adequately resolved in political terms.[1] Such claims, made in the cultural pages of the Italian media, are complemented within the academy by the recent work of Francesco Caviglia and Leonardo Cecchini who have argued that, in the absence of such a political process on the part of the Italian state, it is the cinema that has assumed the role and responsibilities of a Truth and Reconciliation Commission.[2]

Terrorism and Terrorisms in Italy

In order to discuss the cinema of terrorism, we need to retrace the violent events of the period known as the *anni di piombo*. The student protests of 1968 and the factory revolts of the *autunno caldo* [hot autumn] of the following year acted as the backdrop to the emergence of extreme political violence in the form of the bombing of a bank in Milan's Piazza Fontana in December 1969. This event inaugurated a long cycle of violence: according to official Interior Ministry figures, over 14,000 terrorist attacks were committed in the years between 1969 and 1983, resulting in 374 deaths and more than 1,170 injuries.[3]

Anarchists were initially deemed responsible for this first terrorist attack in 1969, but it soon became clear that a group of right-wing extremists had placed the bomb in Piazza Fontana, aided and abetted by the Italian secret services. Piazza Fontana was the first action of the *strategia della tensione* [strategy of tension] staged by the secret services through support of right-wing terrorist organizations as well as infiltration of their left-wing counterparts. Its goal, it would be revealed, was to pass off acts of public violence as the work of left-wing activists in order to undermine public support for the Partito Comunista Italiano (PCI), impede the party's ascent to power, and pave the way for the imposition of authoritarian or military rule. Although the *strategia della tensione* is usually said to be limited to the years preceding 1975, right-wing terrorism is held responsible for

1   Tavella is cited by Renato Venturelli, 'Intervista a Paola Tavella, coautrice di *Il prigioniero*', www.feltrinelli.it/IntervistaInterna?id_int=1193 [accessed 5 August 2010].

2   Francesco Caviglia and Leonardo Cecchini, 'A Quest for Dialogism: Looking Back at Italian Political Violence in the '70s', in *Constructing History, Society and Politics in Discourse: Multimodal Approaches*, ed. Torben Vestergaard (Aalborg: Aalborg University Press, 2009), 127–48.

3   The total number of attacks for the period 1969–87 is 14,491; the total number of deaths is 419 and 1,182 injuries. These figures are drawn from Alison Jamieson, *The Heart Attacked: Terrorism and Conflict in the Italian State* (London and New York: Marion Boyars, 1989), 19–21.

the crowning atrocity of the *anni di piombo*, the Bologna train station bombing of 1980.[4]

On the extreme left, certain militants chose to undertake what they referred to as an armed struggle, in part at least as a reaction to the *strategia della tensione*: groups like the Brigate Rosse, Prima Linea, and the Nuclei Armati Proletari disseminated anxiety and fear for over a decade. Although the violence was limited to a relatively small number of active extremist participants, passive support for left-wing violence was far more widespread. It seemed to many that the choice of armed struggle was a justified response to what was perceived as state-sponsored violence on the far-right.[5] Left-wing militants targeted the individual representatives of their capitalist adversaries – the large industrial corporations, the security forces, the pro-capitalist mainstream media and the Italian state – employing 'proletarian trials', beatings, kidnappings and shootings. The violence culminated in the BR's 1978 kidnapping and murder of the president of the DC, Aldo Moro, promoter of the 'historical compromise' between his party and the PCI, a compromise the kidnappers saw as the final selling-out of the left. During the fifty-four days of Moro's captivity, the major political parties in Italy articulated different opinions about the validity of negotiating with the terrorist organization in order to save Moro's life, even as the DC and PCI agreed on a stance of non-negotiation with his jailers.[6] The length of Moro's captivity, and the role played by the media in making the Italian public privy to the communications passing between the BR, Moro himself and the government, coopted the population in debates about whether Moro

4   The editors hold to the position that the Bologna station bombing was an act committed by right-wing militants, though we acknowledge that the entire circumstances have been inadequately explained. It should be noted that alternative explanations of this event have been suggested and have been taken increasingly seriously by judicial investigators and academics alike. See Anna Cento Bull, *Italian Neofascism: The Strategy of Tension and the Politics of Nonreconciliation* (New York: Berghahn, 2008), 21–22 and 26–27.
5   See Gabriele Calvi and Massimo Martini, *L'Estremismo politico: richerche psicologiche sul terrorismo e sugli atteggiamenti radicali* (Milan: Angeli, 1982), 122–33.
6   As Tobias Abse has pointed out, in a paper given at the 2003 conference 'Assassinations, Murders and Mysteries in Modern Italy' held at the Italian Cultural Institute in London, a peculiar detail of the Moro events is the lack of agreement between most Italian and most English-speaking writers as to the duration of the kidnapping. Italians, including Moro's jailers, tend to talk of fifty-five days, though a more conservative calculation yields fifty-four. No doubt we should not make too much of this – fifty-five is, after all, a more memorable number – but it may be that the exaggeration of the length of the kidnapping points to the sense of traumatic dilation in the event as experienced by public and protagonists subjected to its suspenseful permutations at the time.

should be saved at the risk of weakening the state. The subsequent death of the hostage thus implicated, alongside the BR and Italy's political leaders, the wider public and especially those members who had tacitly condoned left-wing violence until that moment.

Though left-wing terrorism persisted for several more years, the Moro killing alienated the armed groups of the left from a significant area of support that had previously sustained it. Moreover, the reorganization of anti-terrorist forces under the direction of General Carlo Alberto Dalla Chiesa and the criminalization and repression of the extra-parliamentary left following the Moro murder marked this event as the beginning of the end for Italian terrorism. Emergency anti-terrorist laws led to mass arrests in the late 1970s and early 1980s. Such laws increased convictions and sentences for common crimes committed by those the law defined as terrorists, while offering substantial reduction of sentences to terrorists willing to collaborate with justice and turn state's witness (the phenomenon known as *pentitismo*).

By the mid-1990s, most of the 5,000 people tried for terrorist offences began to re-enter society; at the time of writing only ninety-seven of those imprisoned are still in jail, twenty-six of them currently benefitting from the so-called Gozzini law, a legal provision which allows long-term convicts to work outside prison. However, just as the book on terrorism seemed to have definitively closed, a new chapter (or possibly an appendix) was opened: a group calling itself the (new) Brigate Rosse murdered two key advisors on government labour policies, Massimo D'Antona in 1999 and Marco Biagi in 2002. Subsequent arrests may or may not have dealt this organization a fatal blow.

Questions of Terminology: Terrorism and the *Anni di Piombo*

'Terrorism' is a contentious term. The epithet 'terrorist' always implies a negative judgement of the means and, by extension, the ends of the individuals or groups so described, and the word inevitably carries a sense of moral outrage. For this reason, the terms 'terrorism' and 'terrorist' are employed provisionally in this study (though we will now dispense with the scare quotes), their connotations always evolving so that the precise denotations are always deferred.[7] There is

7 Many of the contributors to this collection share our discomfort with the terms terrorist and terrorism, even though they, like us, may have been obliged

no satisfactory definition of terrorism – none that is both precise and widely accepted. Nonetheless, to evade the use of the term would be to risk bad faith. This volume is concerned with the representation of politically-motivated violence that is commonly, if tendentiously, known as terrorist violence, and it is neither our nor the wider scholarly community's normative understanding of this violence that is at issue here, but a more diffuse or nebulous set of perceptions at work, and in flux, in the wider Italian culture from the period of the *anni di piombo* to the present day.

From the perspective of a book on terrorism and film, it is significant that the phrase *anni di piombo* derives from the Italian title given to a German film. *Die bleierne Zeit*, directed by Margarethe Von Trotta and awarded the Golden Lion at the 1981 Venice film festival, tells the story of two German sisters who become politicized when confronted with the horror of images of the concentration camps and of the carnage in Vietnam, one of whom opts for armed struggle and clandestinity. Following its Venice festival success, the phrase *anni di piombo* began to appear in the Italian press, applied retrospectively to the period beginning with the Piazza Fontana bombing. According to Von Trotta, the film's title (literally 'the leaden times') was intended to refer to the 'leaden' weight of history; such an association is lost in the Italian translation (literally the 'years of lead').[8] In the metaphorical allusion to bullets, the term is suggestive of left-wing violence alone, because it appears to exclude the bombings characteristic of right-wing terrorism. Nonetheless, and as with the term terrorism, the common currency of the phrase *anni di piombo* means that we must continue to use it. However, it is intended here to refer to the whole spectrum of political violence in the period addressed.

Discourse and Memory

It has been suggested that most cultural or public discourse relating to Italian terrorism tends to concern itself to an inappropriate degree with the violence originating on the left.[9] A misplaced concentration

to use those terms. For the purposes of readability, however, we have asked them all to avoid the use of scare quotes as far as possible in the essays.

8   The title of Von Trotta's film is derived from a poem, 'Der Gang aufs Land' (1800), vv. 5–6, by Friedrich Hölderlin: 'Trüb ists heut, es schlummern die Gäng' und die Gassen und fast will / Mir es scheinen, es sei, als in der bleiernen Zeit' [Today the weather is torpid, the streets and paths are sleeping / and it almost seems to me to be like in the leaden time]. Friedrich Hölderlin, *Sämtliche Werke*, 6 vols (Stuttgart: Kohlhammer, 1965–66), ii (1965), 88.

9   See Tom Behan, 'Allende, Berlinguer, Pinochet … and Dario Fo', in *Speaking Out and Silencing: Culture, Society and Politics in Italy in the 1970s*, ed. Anna Cento

on leftist terrorist violence may misrepresent the balance of responsibilities for the atrocities of the *anni di piombo* and transmit a false memory of the period. It is certainly the case that the majority of the films dealt with in this study address the terrorism of the left, though Mary P. Wood's essay makes clear that a constantly renewed *filone* [sub-genre] of crime films has dealt with right-wing and state violence, albeit often scorned by respectable criticism.

The reasons that the majority of the films of this period deal with the terrorism of the left are complex. Left-wing terrorism represents a particular problem for left-wing political filmmakers, who have taken upon themselves the responsibility of articulating the meaning of terrorist violence practised by members of their own constituency. At the same time, political violence does not represent such a problem for the right. As Catanzaro argues, the extreme right 'conceives of society as being governed by violence; it does not propose to change this state of affairs but rather take it to the extreme'.[10] Furthermore, right-wing terrorism constitutes a formal as well as a political problem for filmmakers. If the representation of left-wing terrorism and terrorists lends itself to the intimist drama and family saga (as discussed below), right-wing terrorism, because of its obscure and spectacular nature, seems to require more extrovert means of depiction, typically in the conspiracy mode. The problem with this mode is that it confirms the extreme right's conception of society as ruled by violence, and implicitly validates the view that the effective exertion of authority and power is the only question of real importance. The conspiracy film might attempt to introduce questions of ethics, but these will inevitably seem 'unrealistic', in the sense that they are irrelevant to the 'real' questions of political survival and national strength.

One of the reasons that left-wing terrorism is so well-remembered is because of its practitioners' skill at self-publicity. The BR practised an effective demagogic politics, using a memorable symbol, catchy slogans and astute news manipulation to publicize their objectives and actions. To some extent, this material has proved attractive to filmmakers: the title of Gianni Amelio's *Colpire al cuore* (*Blow to the Heart*, 1982) marries two BR slogans to ironic effect ('colpirne uno per educarne cento' [strike one to educate one hundred] and 'portare l'attacco al cuore dello stato' [take the attack to the heart of the state]), and Marco Bellocchio employs the shock-value of a blood-

Bull and Adalgisa Giorgio (Oxford: Legenda, 2006), 160–71.

10   Raimondo Catanzaro, 'Subjective Experience and Objective Reality: An Account of Violence in the Words of its Protagonists', in *The Red Brigades and Left-wing Terrorism in Italy*, ed. Raimondo Catanzaro (London: Printer Publishers, 1991), 175.

red star, the symbol of the BR, painted inside a lift in *Buongiorno, notte* (*Good Morning, Night*, 2003). The employment of the *topoi* of the Moro kidnap is less ironic in *Il caso Moro* (*The Moro Case*, Giuseppe Ferrara, 1986) and *Piazza delle cinque lune* (*Piazza of the Five Moons*, Renzo Martinelli, 2003): for example, the iconic photographs of Moro seated before the BR star in the 'people's prison' are fetishistically reconstructed in both films.

Right-wing terrorism has proved more elusive for memory because of the obscure nature of the bombings carried out. Perhaps its most striking icon is the clock paused at 10.25 in Bologna station, indicating the time of the explosion on 2 August 1980. It is significant, however, that the stalled clock-face is the mysterious index of an event, retained by the city of Bologna itself, rather than the chosen symbol of a terrorist organization. In contrast to the *modus operandi* of left-wing terrorism, the perpetrators of the Bologna explosion elected to remain anonymous (though members of the neofascist Nuclei Armati Rivoluzionari were later convicted of the bombing). Unclaimed bombings were the norm, and right-wing terrorism in general was characterized by its anonymity and the frustrating invisibility of its perpetrators, a fact that has obvious consequences for memory – and forgetting.[11]

The Cinema of Terrorism

For much of the 1970s, it was the genres of the *poliziesco* or 'poliziottesco' ['cop film', 'Italian cop film'] and the *commedia all'italiana* [comedy Italian style] that addressed the terrorism of the *anni di piombo*.[12] *Poliziotteschi* such as *La polizia accusa: il servizio segreto uccide* (*Chopper Squad*, Sergio Mattino, 1975) and *L'istruttoria è chiusa: dimentichi* (*The Case is Closed, Forget It!*, Damiano Damiani, 1975) embedded social critique in their commercially exploitative portrayal of the corruption of state and security apparatus. The *commedia all'italiana*, in its capacity for social commentary, demonstrated a timely ability to respond to contemporary concerns, and thus to the phenomenon of terrorism, before either the *cinema d'autore* [auteurist cinema] or the *cinema d'impegno* [politically committed cinema], in films like *Mordi e*

11   This description of right-wing terrorism is necessarily reductive; small-scale violence and targeted assassination for which responsibility was declared were also employed by the right. See Marco Rimanelli, 'Italian Terrorism and Society, 1940s–1980s: Roots, Ideologies, Evolutions, and International Connections', in *Italy*, ed. Mark Donovan (Dartmouth: Ashgate, 1998), 236–52.
12   See the glossary for an explanation of these and the other Italian terms used in this paragraph.

fuggi (*Dirty Weekend*, Dino Risi, 1973) and *Caro papà* (*Dear Papa*, Dino Risi, 1979).

In the 1980s, a cluster of important films with a strong focus on terrorism appeared, among them *Colpire al cuore* and *Segreti segreti* (*Secrets, Secrets*, Giuseppe Bertolucci, 1984). In both films, victims are excised from the narrative while terrorists and their sympathizers are shown in relation to the family. Closely connected to the portrayal of the terrorist as family member stands the *topos* of *delazione* [informing on one's comrades], bearing its unspoken yet direct reference to the phenomenon of *pentitismo*. It is the figure of the terrorist as *pentito/a* that becomes central in these films, which devote much attention to the effects of *pentitismo* on the two social networks to which the terrorist belongs: family of origin and terrorist organization.

The watershed event of the *anni di piombo* was the kidnap and assassination of Aldo Moro in 1978. The first film to deal directly with these events, *Il caso Moro* of 1986, provides a minute historical reconstruction of the abduction and murder. Since *Il caso Moro*, the encumbering presence of the many victims of terrorist attacks, or that of their surviving relatives, continues to lie at the heart of the most important films on terrorism and its legacies. *Per non dimenticare* (*Lest We Forget*, Massimo Martelli, 1992), *La seconda volta* (*The Second Time*, Mimmo Calopresti, 1995), *Le mani forti* (*Strong Hands*, Franco Bernini, 1996), and *Vite in sospeso* (*Belleville*, Marco Turco, 1998) all choose to portray terrorism by giving direct or indirect voice to its victims. Viewed collectively, these films attempt the difficult task of bringing forth the victim while humanizing the terrorist. They refract and contribute to a wider political debate in late 1990s Italy on the possibility and morality of rescinding the sentences of incarcerated former terrorists.

Just as the return of left-wing terrorism in 1999 could be interpreted as the return of the repressed for a country that has never fully addressed the causes of social unrest, the simultaneous reappearance of films on the Aldo Moro kidnap identifies this episode as the locus of a trauma that elicits 'repetition compulsion'.[13] This is how we might read *Piazza delle cinque lune* as well as *Buongiorno, notte*, both released on the twenty-fifth anniversary of Moro's death. *La meglio gioventù* (*The Best of Youth*, Marco Tullio Giordana, 2003), on the other hand,

---

13   We borrow the concept from Freud, 'Beyond the Pleasure Principle', in *The Standard Edition of the Complete Psychological Works of Sigmund Freud*, ed. James Strachey in collaboration with Anna Freud and assisted by Alix Strachey and Alan Tyson, trans. by James Strachey, 24 vols (London: Hogarth Press and the Institute for Psycho-analysis, 1953–1974), xviii (1955), 7–64 [Jenseits des Lustprinzips (Vienna: Internationaler Psychoanalytischer Verlag, 1920)].

never mentions this event. Still, in Giordana's fresco of a generation of Italians who come of age in the late 1960s, much attention is devoted to the *anni di piombo*. The portrayal of the character Giulia's journey into clandestinity lies at the very heart of the film. Her abandonment of the family for the BR, followed by her partial reintegration at the end of the film, returns the depiction of the terrorist in Italian cinema to the modes of emplotment adopted by *Colpire al cuore* and *Segreti segreti*: the portrayal of Italian terrorism as a dysfunctional family affair.

Cinema that deals with historical events or circumstances eliminates the inessential from its version of the past, reworking it in order to enable it to be redeployed for the purposes of the present. *Romanzo criminale* (*Crime Story*, Michele Placido, 2005) lifts the two quintessentially traumatic events of the *anni di piombo* – the Moro kidnap and the Bologna bombing – out of their historical context and embeds them in a violent genre tale, apparently to express continued anxieties about the unaccountability of state and power in Italy. Conversely, another prestige production, this time made for television, *Attacco allo stato* (*Attack on the State*, Michele Soavi, 2006), seems designed to demonstrate the prowess of counter-terrorist forces while eliding the extent of the failure of the state to protect its servants, Massimo D'Antona and Marco Biagi. The film may best be contextualized in relation to the anti-terrorist rhetoric of the Berlusconi government, which was concerned to be seen to respond to the contemporary global security agenda.

Terrorism and Representation

Our assumption in this volume is that the study of cinematic and televisual texts can cast light on historical and ideological conditions, and on the topicality and legacies of terrorism in particular. We propose that events have a discursive as well as a phenomenal status, and enter into a field we may describe as representational or, better, refractional. No event exists as a fact outside a system of textual models; that is, no event can be independent of the context of its interpretation. Thus film, like historiography, exists along a continuum with events which allows it no autonomy and allows events no independence from their representation. Film reacts to, and in its turn impacts on, the social and political world and the interpretation of events.

Even so, it may be objected that cinema can only be a debased form of historiography and it inevitably simplifies events by turning them into 'mere' entertainment. Critiques of historical film tend to fixate upon issues of factual accuracy which are most often incidental: a positivistic factual accuracy is both beyond the means of the commercial film and rarely part of the intentions of filmmakers. To apply the criteria of a primarily written and document-based historiography to visual and commercial media like cinema and television is to misunderstand what it is that cinema and television 'fictions' are equipped to achieve. As Pierre Sorlin argues:

> If we were studying an historical text written [at a particular time], we would not compare it with the film version to see if it was true. We would instead try to understand the political logic of the account given in the book, asking why it emphasized this question, that event, rather than others. We should keep the same preoccupation in mind when analysing films.[14]

Terrorism, Italian Style

Scholarship on the cinematic representations of political violence in the *anni di piombo* is still limited. Apart from two dedicated volumes published in Italian in 2007, its critical reception consists primarily of a scattered body of film reviews, again mostly in Italian, and a limited number of essays treating individual films, thematic aspects and taxonomic considerations relating to the corpus as a whole.[15] Christian Uva's valuable edited collection, *Schermi di piombo*, affords an extremely comprehensive overview of the corpus of films, but

---

14   Pierre Sorlin, *The Film in History: Restaging the Past* (Oxford: Basil Blackwell, 1980), 32.
15   See, for example, Giancarlo Lombardi, 'Unforgiven: Revisiting Political Terrorism in *La seconda volta*', *Italica*, 77: 2 (2000), 199–213, and Marie Orton, '"Terrorism" In Italian Film: Striking the One to Educate the Hundred', *Romance Languages Annual*, 11 (1999), 306–12; both essays treat *La seconda volta*. For thematic aspects see Luca Bandirali and Enrico Terrone, 'L'Uomo che Sapeva Troppo', *Segnocinema*, 24: 125 (2004), 4–7, and Leonardo Cecchini, 'Rappresentazioni degli anni di piombo', in *Atti del VII Congresso degli Italianisti Scandinavi, Mémoires de la Société Néophilologique de Helsinki, LXVIII*, ed. Enrico Garavelli and Elina Suomela-Härmä (Helsinki: Société Néophilologique, 2005), 299–310. On relevant taxonomic considerations, see Maurizio Fantoni Minella, *Non riconciliati: politica e società nel cinema italiano dal neorealismo a oggi* (Turin: UTET, 2004), and Alan O'Leary, 'Film and the "Anni di piombo": Representations of Politically Motivated Violence in Recent Italian Cinema', in *Culture, Censorship and the State in Twentieth-Century Italy*, ed. Guido Bonsaver and Robert S. C. Gordon (Oxford: Legenda, 2005), 168–78.

holds back from providing an extensive theoretical analysis.[16] Alan O'Leary's *Tragedia all'italiana* deploys discussions of memory, genre and narrative modalities to help situate the corpus of films on the *anni di piombo* in its historical context.[17]

Terrorism Italian Style is the first English-language volume to offer a dedicated forum to scholars actively researching on cinematic representations of Italian terrorism. Building on the bibliography in both Italian and English, the range of critical perspectives adopted in this collection is broad. A comparative approach is predominant – i.e. most essays discuss two or more texts – and is complemented by theoretical frameworks absent from the Italian scholarship on the subject, such as gender studies and trauma theory. The authors in this volume have tended to focus on the cinema of *pentitismo* in the 1980s and representations of the Moro kidnapping, rather than on those titles released in the late 1990s which have already been extensively treated in the English-language criticism.[18] They have brought a renewed attention to questions of genre, and of course the most significant films of the new millennium are also discussed.

Genre concerns link the essays contained in the opening section, where Mary P. Wood, Alan O'Leary and Giancarlo Lombardi analyse cinematic and televisual representations of terrorism largely absent from existing critical readings. Wood tackles the police films and conspiracy thrillers of the 1970s, which work to uncover the complexity of unexplained and unpunished political crimes, resulting in films of unusual narrative and visual density. She sets out to establish links between the popular, low-budget and prestige auteurist versions of the genre, and identifies their stylistic legacy in more recent films. O'Leary asks why the mode of the *commedia all'italiana* was employed by Bernardo Bertolucci in his 'terrorist film', *La tragedia di un uomo ridicolo* (*The Tragedy of a Ridiculous Man*, 1981). He argues that it is the exhaustion of the genre which paradoxically grants it the capacity to characterize the position of the Italian intellectual perplexed and

---

16 *Schermi di piombo: il terrorismo nel cinema italiano* (Soveria Mannelli: Rubbettino, 2007), ed. Christian Uva.

17 Alan O'Leary, *Tragedia all'italiana: cinema e terrorismo tra Moro e memoria* (Tissi: Angelica, 2007). An English-language version of this book was published in 2011 in the 'Italian Modernities' series from Peter Lang.

18 See Orton, '"Terrorism"' and Lombardi, 'Unforgiven'; also by Lombardi: 'Virgil, Dante, Blade Runner, and Italian Terrorism: The Concept of *Pietas* in *La seconda volta* and *La mia generazione*', *Romance Languages Annual*, 11 (2000), 191–96; 'Terrorism, Truth, and the Secret Service: Questions of Accountability in the Cinema of the *stragi di stato*', *Annali d'Italianistica*, 19 (2001), 285–302; 'Parigi o cara: Terrorism, Exile, and Escape in Contemporary Italian Cinema and Theatre', *Annali d'Italianistica*, 20 (2002), 403–24.

impotent before the fact of terrorism. Lombardi's essay provides a fresh contribution and fills a void in scholarship by analysing the portrayal of political terrorism in primetime drama. He considers four Italian mini-series spanning twenty-five years: *Parole e sangue* (*Words and Blood*, Damiano Damiani, 1980), *Nucleo Zero* (*Nucleus Zero*, Carlo Lizzani, 1984), *Donne armate* (*Women in Arms*, Sergio Corbucci, 1990) and *Attacco allo stato* (2006). The essay combines content analysis with a discussion of the institutional practices in which such content is inscribed.

Family and gender motifs lie at the heart of the three essays written by Max Henninger, Ellen Nerenberg and Ruth Glynn. Henninger provides an ideological critique of *Tre fratelli* (*Three Brothers*, Francesco Rosi, 1981), *Colpire al cuore*, and *Segreti segreti*, interpreting the *mise-en-scène* of political violence as a translation of socio-political conflict into the terms of the family narrative. He formulates a hypothesis on the ways in which the family narrative reproduces the structural characteristics and conventions of the Italian public sphere in the 1980s. Themes of generational difference, typically cast in Freudian terms as Oedipal tension between father and son, characterize Italian films treating the subject of terrorism.[19] Nerenberg insists on the significance of Gianni Amelio's inversion of the classic positionality within the father-son dyad in *Colpire al cuore*. She demonstrates that the generational divide also subtends crucial formal properties in the film. Focusing specifically on *Segreti segreti* and *Diavolo in corpo* (*Devil in the Flesh*, Marco Bellocchio, 1986), Glynn explores the emergence of the violent woman in relation to the containment culture of *pentitismo*, instrumental in revealing the full extent of women's involvement in left-wing violence. She identifies a tendency in the films of that period to psychopathologize women's relationship with terrorism, by employing the twin motifs of the madwoman and the *femme fatale* to depict female perpetrator and female victim alike.

The third section of this book is devoted to the films on the Moro kidnap, the event which has come to represent metonymically the terrorism of the *anni di piombo*. Rachele Tardi examines three of the most visible feature films treating this subject – *Il caso Moro*, *Buongiorno, notte* and *Piazza delle cinque lune* – and explores how different genre conventions contribute to each film's rewriting of the event. She further considers how these rewritings provide important evidence of the boundaries of the social imaginary, by paying

---

19   Though identified in some earlier writings, Freud's concept of the Oedipal complex is first developed at length in *Totem and Taboo*, in *The Standard Edition of the Complete Psychological Works of Sigmund Freud*, xiii (1953), 1–162 [*Totem und Tabu* (Leipzig and Vienna: Heller, 1913)].

particular attention to the cinematic erasure of the political motives of the BR. Nicoletta Marini-Maio draws upon Jacques Derrida's politics of spectrality and Hayden White's notion of metahistory to show how the emplotment of left-wing subversive activity in the mode of the tragic palinode (the retraction of previous sentiments or actions) continues to assert the haunting presence of Moro and to enact a collective rite of mourning in the films discussed by Tardi, and also in televisual productions of both factual and fictional nature. The section closes with a close reading of *Buongiorno, notte* by Dana Renga, who argues that Bellocchio's cinematic reinvention of Moro and the female terrorist whose autobiography informs his film serves to indict Church and state rather than BR, and simultaneously engenders a form of martyrdom for the victim.

The book concludes with an essay in which Leonardo Cecchini considers the divided memory of the *anni di piombo*, focusing on Todorov's useful distinction between an ethics of conviction and an ethics of responsibility. He traces the workings of these distinct ethical systems in the portrayal of militants' decisions to take up arms portrayed in *Ogro* (*Operation Ogre*, Gillo Pontecorvo, 1979), *Piazza delle cinque lune, Buongiorno, notte* and *La meglio gioventù*.

This book has a variety of intended audiences. We aim to contribute to the study of Italian history, politics and society, as well as to the fields of Italian cultural and cinema studies. We hope the book will also be of interest to scholars beyond Italian studies, especially those researching the cultural representation of political violence in other contexts. Finally, we have tried to provide a useful tool for those involved in the teaching and study of the growing number of postgraduate and undergraduate courses devoted to the issue of film and terrorism. The title of this book is coined by analogy with the English translation of the term *commedia all'italiana*, or 'comedy Italian style', but it is not meant to suggest that a single genre of cinema exists which has dealt with terrorism in the Italian context. The title is intended to suggest, instead, that this is not a book on Italy's recent history, but a study of how the experience of terrorism has been refracted through more than three decades of its filmmaking.

Section 1
Terrorism and Genre

1. Navigating the Labyrinth: Cinematic Investigations of Right-Wing Terrorism

Mary P. Wood

Fictions of Uncertainty

There are many reasons for the proliferation of investigative fictions in Italian cinema, for the subsequent decline of the myriad sub-genres and *filoni* [cycles of films] and for the obsessive return to events of the 1970s in the films of the 1990s and 2000s.[1] The circumstances of the *anni di piombo*, the *strategia della tensione* [strategy of tension] and the political corruption of the 1970s and 1980s resulted in labyrinthine scenarios proposed and debated on television and radio and in the press in attempts to establish the causes and attribute blame. Cinematic narratives of police investigations were also part of this impetus to give concrete form to fears and anxieties, and to understand what was happening in society. As such they are pointers to the emotional trauma caused by apparently random terrorist attacks such as the Bologna station bombing of 2 August 1980, in which 85 people died and 200 were injured. The constant unexplained accidents, murders and atrocities which hit the headlines in the 1970s and 1980s proved difficult to assimilate into an image of a peaceful, modern capitalist state. The plethora of representations of violence and terrorism

---

1   Italian film genres are flexible forms and are more usefully identified as *filoni*, or cycles of films with related subjects and titles. The perennial crises in Italian cinema led to the practice of trend-spotting successful subjects, names and stars, resulting in the rushed production of similar films to exploit the trend for as long as it was popular at the box-office. See Mary P. Wood, *Italian Cinema* (Oxford: Berg, 2005), 11.

constitute serial attempts to build an acceptable picture of profoundly disturbing events in the past and the present.

My focus in this chapter will be on films which, however obliquely, attempt to investigate terrorist events and to identify and give a face to right-wing perpetrators. These films fall into three broad categories: the first explores the exercise of legal and illegal power, the second attempts to identify the class and capitalist interests behind right-wing terrorism, and the third deflects attention from those responsible for terrorism to representatives of social problems. In the films about right-wing terrorism examined here, filmmakers use the full resources of *mise-en-scène*, editing and camera work to generate multiple signs to interpret the misuse of power and responsibility for violence. These concerns occur in Italian films across the spectrum of quality from 'art' films categorized as the *cinema di impegno* [politically committed cinema], through well-made, financially successful, mid-budget films with police or detective heroes, to the low-budget examples of the *poliziottesco* [Italian cop film], which were equally successful at the box office, but critically despised. Each category tends to attract its own cohorts of directors, actors and creative personnel, reflecting the historical antecedents of each budget stratum. Italian political cinema proclaims its neorealist credentials in its use of realist conventions and agenda of uncovering a truth behind events, whereas the violent protagonists of the *poliziotteschi* rehearsed their performance style in the sword-and-sandal epics of the 1950s, and the 1960s spaghetti westerns. In his essay in this volume, Alan O'Leary suggests that the first cinematic response to terrorism was not provided by authorial *cinema d'impegno* but by popular genres. However, in the case of the explorations of right-wing terrorism examined here, the popular genre of the police investigation predominates, for reasons which will be examined (note that Italian authorial cinema can be considered as the intellectual and/or better funded end of national genre production).

Right-wing Terrorism and the Secret State

Films in the first category which explore the exercise of political power are interesting for the difficulties they have picturing those responsible for atrocities. In his essay in this collection, O'Leary attributes these to 'the disorientation of the intellectual confronted with the perplexing circumstances of the *anni di piombo*'. In the Italian case, the ability of the centrist party Democrazia Cristiana (DC) to cling on to power through a series of coalition governments until the early 1990s led to the sense that there existed secret alliances 'between private individuals and groups with shared class interests' resulting in greater access to powerful positions 'than their numbers would allow them in a participatory democratic state'.[2] The DC's instrumental mode of government lent itself to interpretation by conspiracy thrillers.[3] However, even if names are not named, right-wing terrorism in Italian films is linked firmly to the governing classes, the upper bourgeoisie, and to the capitalist interests it shares with illegal power networks, such as the mafia.

The number of films about the terroristic activities of the Italian governing class indicates a considerable interest from the cinema-going public and to a large extent the investigators of right-wing terrorism, whether honest or rogue cops, stand for the Italian citizen's desire for justice. Film producers at all budgetary levels of the film industry attracted the necessary finance to churn out large numbers of films on this subject. These 1970s films, and their successors, effectively offer a range of negotiated and oppositional engagements with the dominant, hegemonic viewpoint of the 'natural' ordering of society and, as Stuart Hall suggests, are therefore 'shot through with contradictions'.[4]

The corruption trials of the early 1990s gave fresh impetus to investigations of mysteries in Italian civic life, and a new cohort of hero figures in the shape of honest judges and magistrates. What unites films investigating state terrorism in the 1970s is their distinctive combination of cinematic realism and the conventions of Italian film noir. Moreover, the targets of these police investigations provide indications of where the trauma (the unassimilated problems) lies.

The use of realist conventions is significant. As Thomas Elsaesser has argued, trauma theory is less useful as a term which 'refers' to a catastrophic event than to 'the revised understandings of referentiality it prompts'.[5] Although, as Andrea Pergolari points out, few films about right-wing terrorism investigate actual, well-known events, they do encourage fresh perceptions about the preferred simple explanations proposed by the powers that be.[6] In the case of Italian

2 Mark Fenster, *Conspiracy Theories: Secrecy and Power in American Culture* (Minneapolis: University of Minnesota Press, 1999), xv.
3 Paul Ginsborg, *Italy and its Discontents: Family, Civil Society, State 1980–2001* (London: Penguin, 2001), 281.
4 Stuart Hall, 'Encoding/decoding', in *Culture, Media, Language*, ed. Stuart Hall and others (London: Hutchinson/Centre for Contemporary Cultural Studies, 1980), 137.
5 Thomas Elsaesser, 'Postmodernism as Mourning Work', *Screen*, 42: 2 (2001), 201.
6 Andrea Pergolari, 'La fisionomia del terrorismo nero nel cinema poliziesco italiano degli anni '70', in *Schermi di piombo: il terrorismo nel cinema italiano*, ed. Christian Uva (Soveria Mannelli: Rubbettino, 2007), 170.

cinema, the psychic investment of engagement with contemporary history is indicated by the constant references to the 'real' world of Italian politics or social life. Realist conventions such as location shooting, illusionistic detail, a typically European use of the mobile camera and intra-sequence long take are used to link diegetic events firmly to the world of contemporary Italy.

In effect, conspiracy theories and attempts to visualize and put a face to those responsible for atrocities represent a failure in the hegemonic process because they signal the inability of a power elite to impose its own view of events. The violence which is so graphically depicted in films of the 1970s (and later) represents a disruption to unproblematic acceptance of class hierarchies or social and political marginalization. Violent acts targeting investigators who get too close to identifying the misuse of power, or atrocities staged to discredit political factions seeking legitimate access to government, pinpoint the existence of alliances which are usually hidden. How Italian cinema tries to visualize terrorism and to link it to the dominant political class appears fraught with difficulties and ambiguities. Strikes and the student protests of 1968 played into the hands of right-wing politicians seeking to deflect responsibility away from themselves. In order to move the spotlight back to a corrupt political class, more positive representations of the Italian police had to evolve so that the investigating protagonist implicitly affirms the principles of law and order in the service of the people. In this respect cinema mirrored the process of democratic renewal taking place within the police force.[7] Police investigator figures had to demonstrate probity and democratic sentiments in order to provide a contrast to the political class usually found to be the instigator of terrorist crimes.

When identifying the individuals who were behind traumatic events, 1970s terrorism narratives had antecedents to draw on. Popular films like those of the Neapolitan comic actor Totò poked fun at the pomposity or venality of the powerful. Serious films such as *In nome della legge* (*In the Name of the Law*, Pietro Germi, 1949), and *Processo alla città* (*A City on Trial*, Luigi Zampa, 1952) depicted mafia collusion with state bureaucrats and the mechanisms by which power was maintained. *Salvatore Giuliano* (Francesco Rosi, 1961) used the death of the eponymous bandit to expose the collusions between political factions, the mafia and local institutions or interests. Sicilian

7   Maurizio Matrone, 'Police Film Festival: un festival per i poliziotti', in *3° Police Film Festival: anni '70. Il poliziotto tra fiction e realtà*, ed. Anna Di Martino and others (Bologna: Cineteca di Bologna, 1997), 6.

political separatists coopted Giuliano into their illegal army after the Second World War; Rosi shows that separatist elements included local politicians, businessmen and aristocrats for whom the bandit represented a convenient way of distancing themselves from crimes against their political opponents. Such crimes are represented by the massacre of a popular May-day procession at Portella della Ginestra in Sicily.

On the other hand, the conventions of American and European cop films and thrillers (on which all of these films draw) allow the source of the traumatic event to be expressed as a disruption which sets in motion investigations into the complexity of Italian society. Noir elements cohere around the disruption, drawing attention to the problematic nature of simple explanations by narrative and visual disorder, flamboyant visuals, ultra-violence, and by the use of yellow tones to indicate the presence of mysteries.[8] The conventions of Italian film noir reached their most codified form in the 1970s. Deriving from French and American film noir, they include the gradual uncovering of clues revealing why a crime was committed rather than who committed it, pessimism about the possibility of bringing perpetrators to justice, high-contrast lighting, shadows, unusual camera angles and low-life *milieux*. These conventions are inflected by the creative use of *mise-en-scène* and cinematography in a manner typical of the Italian cinema tradition. Investigations of mysteries and crimes are concerned to link the story events of films to the micro-context of personal ways of being in Italian society, and to the macro-context of the exercise of power in the Italian state. Insistence on realism is part of their politicized agenda.

Visualizing Disruption

Investigative fictions provide filmmakers with templates for moving from the disruptions of murders and crimes to possible explanations. In *Cadaveri eccellenti* (*Illustrious Corpses*, 1976), Francesco Rosi adapts Sciascia's *Il contesto* [*Equal Danger*] but sets it firmly in the reality of contemporary Italy. He repeatedly uses the conventions of the cinematic thriller to identify the true sources of state terrorism. In investigating the murder of several judges, Rogas, the honest

8   The word *giallo* [yellow] has been used as a generic term for mystery stories since the publisher Mondadori began to publish detective fiction with yellow covers in 1929; see Mary P. Wood, 'Italian Film Noir', in *European Film Noir*, ed. Andrew Spicer (Manchester: Manchester University Press, 2007), 236.

detective, discovers that the preferred simple explanation that these are the actions of a disgruntled victim of the law conceals a much more complex reality. The murders are being used as the opportunity to blame left-wing political extremists in order to justify political repression of the left, and other anti-democratic activities of the government. Rosi shows the investigative process repetitively. The official cars which Rogas sees on his first visit to the President of the High Court, Judge Riches, enable him to make the connection between the heads of the armed services and the judiciary. Their alliances are personified in the party sequence at the opulent home of the shipping magnate, Pattos, attended by members of the intelligentsia and government, captains of industry, the judiciary and military. The Interior Minister explains to Rogas that, whatever the nominal political persuasion of the government, leaders of factions of left or right share the same class origin. The provocative nature of the assassination of Rogas and Amar, the leader of the Revolutionary Party, and the visual connotations of the statues of Roman politicians forming the background to their fateful rendezvous in the 'National Gallery', reinforce Rosi's insight into the permanence of the Italian political classes. The serial murders indicate what is at stake for them, nothing less than the continuation of a complete political system in which the powerful utilize the entire resources of the state in their own interests.

The character of Judge Riches is depicted in *Cadaveri eccellenti* in static poses while he delivers a key monologue (derived from Sciascia's book) on the ruthlessness of the law, only becoming animated when he demonstrates the principle of decimation, whereby the lower classes are arbitrarily punished for crimes committed by the upper classes.[9] In Riches' febrile delineation of the unethical exercise of power, it is made clear that left-wing protest at social and political inequality generates the fear which is at the root of right-wing terrorism. Max von Sydow's performance as Riches metaphorizes the stasis of a life of privilege and the violent reaction to the destabilizing effects of social protest. However, Rosi's use of ironic distance between official versions of events and those uncovered by Rogas stops short of any ultimate identification of responsibility. Who killed Riches whilst he listened to tapes of Rogas and Amar's meeting is unclear. Although Silvio Gaggi suggests that complete certainty is not a possibility in postmodern paranoia narratives, the oscillation between order and

---

9   Lino Miccichè, *Filmologia e filologia: studi sul cinema italiano* (Venice: Marsilio, 2002), 154–57.

disorder provides new perceptions of complex situations.[10] Rosi visualizes the faces of the powerful and their habitat. Actors, costume and performance styles stress their arrogance and self-importance, their class 'look'. Enormous lamps, book-lined studies, huge rooms, objets d'art, architectural splendour connote a wealthy lifestyle and hint at the financial means needed to sustain it.

Italian terrorism narratives contain many set pieces of showy and spectacular *mise-en-scène*. Classical, neoclassical and modernist architecture and institutional spaces are framed and shot to stress regularity and order. The excesses and decorative aspects of baroque and gothic buildings provide a contrasting, complex spatial paradigm.[11] Internal conflicts and contradictions are externalized in this tension between order and disorder. Omar Calabrese explains this conflict of visual styles as a neo-baroque undermining of the grand meta-narratives.[12] The baroque is not confined to a particular period; it rejects order and stability, and deliberately seeks ambiguity and turbulence. Gothic excess also has this function, as have ultra-violence, spectacular visuals, obsessive repetition and seriality.

Serial crimes disturb the impression of normality preferred by the establishment. Italy is exceptionally rich architecturally so that the range of architectural paradigms chosen as expressive of social or institutional practices or values is particularly significant. Serial violent crimes or repetition of architectural forms and spaces are therefore not meaningless fragments of fractured meaning typical of postmodern narratives. As Angela Ndalianis suggests, 'the serial structure integral to the neo-baroque is an open form that complicates the closure of classical systems'.[13] Seriality functions to attempt to reconstruct order within contexts of labyrinthine complexity.

These are flexible paradigms. Francesco Rosi often uses modernist spaces to connote an open, modernizing principle threatened by the actions of traditional, secret power elites. In *Il caso Mattei* (*The Mattei Affair*, 1972), cool blue tones and modernist architectural spaces are associated with the figure of Enrico Mattei, head of the state hydrocarbon agency, ENI, whose plane crash in mysterious

10   Silvo Gaggi, 'Navigating Chaos', in *New Punk Cinema*, ed. N. Rombes (Edinburgh: Edinburgh University Press, 2005), 118.
11   Mary P. Wood, 'Francesco Rosi: Heightened Realism', in *Projections 8*, ed. J. Boorman and W. Donohue (London: Faber and Faber, 1998), 285.
12   Omar Calabrese, *Neo-Baroque: A Sign of the Times*, trans. by C. Lambert (Princeton: Princeton University Press, 1992), 25.
13   Angela Ndalianis, *Neo-Baroque Aesthetics and Contemporary Entertainment* (Cambridge: MIT Press, 2004), 33.

circumstances is being investigated by the film. Representatives of factions used by Mattei in pursuit of his objective of putting Italian power sources under state control (and who may have had an interest in his death) are associated with the visually complex, cluttered and decorative interiors of the powerful. The identification of his opponents as possibly the French secret service, Italian politicians who would prefer to take corrupt advantage of Italy's natural gas resources, the mafia (threatened by Mattei's interest in bringing employment to Sicily) and American oil interests makes the link between state terrorism and the imperatives of advanced capitalism.

Italian noir's main focus is what Angela Dalle Vacche (following Eve Kosofsky Sedgwick) calls the 'homosocial world' of the male exercise of power and narrative disruption is necessary to gain access to it.[14] This is true of *Indagine su un cittadino al di sopra di ogni sospetto* (*Investigation of a citizen above suspicion*, 1970), even if Elio Petri's study of the mentality of the functionaries who are essential to the activities of state terrorism focuses on the sexual perversities of a pair of lovers. The figure of Augusta, the mistress of the chief of the political section of the Police, known only as 'Il dottore' (a typical Italian honorific), is the disruptive element which facilitates penetration of this closed, male society, the police heterotopia. From the opening sequences we know that 'Il dottore' has murdered her during their lovemaking on the day of his promotion to the post of head of the Political Police. 'Il dottore' is the representative individual who introduces the viewer to the social, institutional and political organization of a state, or para-state organization, and the main thrust of the narrative is to show how men like Il dottore exercise power, how their physical presence and movements coerce their subordinates into accepting the hierarchy and ideologies of the group. However, the narrative flow is broken at frequent intervals by flashbacks to the perverse erotic games played by the couple, so that her pretending to be a schoolgirl or a female terrorist under interrogation acts as a brake on acceptance of iconic male stereotypes of leadership, rationality, and wisdom. Augusta's games show male power as performance, allegorizing the mechanisms of the exercise of legal and illegal power, her dangerous eroticism signalling fears that those outside the male heterotopia will escape control. The manner in which the heterotopias of police, the judiciary, local government, and the financial world coerce the population

14 Angela Dalle Vacche, *The Body in the Mirror: Shapes of History in Italian Cinema* (Princeton: Princeton University Press, 1992), 15. Eve Kosofsky Sedgwick, *Between Men: English Literature and Male Homosocial Desire* (New York: Columbia University Press, 1985).

into accepting their presence and operations as 'natural', whilst masking the brutality of their coercive actions, explains lower-class complicity in the process, particularly through visual representations of the figure of the panopticon. In *Cadaveri eccellenti* and *Indagine su un cittadino al di sopra di ogni sospetto* the panopticon takes the form of the political police laboratory, from which the population is under constant electronic surveillance.

Mario Monicelli's *Vogliamo i colonnelli* (*We Want the Colonels*, 1973) also refers to real events in contemporary Italian history, but is unusual in treating the right-wing coup d'état in comic mode. The characteristics and ethos of the various strands of the armed services are pilloried through representative characters who display the obtuse *esprit de corps* of the infantry, the special boat squadron and other military branches. As with all good comedies, their blinkered outlook and incompetence create an ironic distance for the audience to perceive them as hopelessly out of touch with current opinion and unlikely to succeed in destabilizing the democratic process. Towards the end of the film, however, it becomes clear that there are other, less laughable political elements waiting in the wings for the failure of the coup d'état, and the opportunity to crack down on normal democratic rights of association. Critical reactions indicated Monicelli's success in raising issues around right-wing *golpismo* (the desire to establish authoritarian government through a military coup), which Curti suggests is still a worrying scenario thirty-five years later.[15]

In some respects, *Vogliamo i colonnelli* demonstrates that filmmakers had difficulty not only in conceptualizing the perpetrators of right-wing terrorism, but in achieving production and distribution deals for films on this subject. Antonio Mazza was typical in criticizing the lack of subtlety in the grotesque characterizations of the conspirators whilst acknowledging that the film might make the audience think.[16] At the same time, the film's distributor, the state body Italnoleggio, lacked the resources for an in-depth distribution, something which contributed to the film's only moderate success in first-run cinemas.[17] Nonetheless, articles appear regularly in the trade press of the period commenting on the public's response to examples of the *cinema d'impegno* in the different exhibition sectors. The overall impression

---

15   Roberto Curti, *Italia odia: il cinema poliziesco italiano* (Turin: Lindau, 2006), 148.
16   Antonio Mazza, '*Vogliamo i colonnelli*', *Rivista del Cinematografo*, 5 (1973), 214.
17   Stefano Della Casa, *Mario Monicelli* (Florence: Il Castoro/La Nuova Italia, 1986), 61.

gained from these articles is of surprise (that the public appeared to like serious cinema) and perplexity (as to how to treat it).[18] It is not surprising that recognizable genre templates were used by filmmakers wanting to reach a wider audience for their ideas.

Genre Elaborations

Halfway between politically-engaged cinema and the low-budget cop films which were box-office successes lies the second category of 'quality' versions of the *poliziottesco*. Their targets are the rich, who regard themselves as above the law, and the shady and shadowy organizations that function in parallel to the legitimate organs of the state which they often finance. Although they represent the intelligent end of the *poliziottesco* strand, their visual organization is less complex than the high-budget films, although their plots display the same serial references to historical terrorist violence. Their plots are very clear in attaching blame for anti-democratic acts, even if the ultimate paymasters remain shadowy, powerful figures. Thus, in *La polizia ringrazia* (*The Law Enforcers*, Stefano Vanzina, 1972), the honest detective's investigation reveals in the final reel that the murders of sundry criminals and delinquents are the work of a right-wing vigilante gang. The detective makes the mistake of confronting the ringleader – the former Chief of Police – at a club for ex-policemen with authoritarian sympathies. The final explanations before the honest detective is murdered, and his deputy shown to be a member of the vigilantes, make explicit the anti-democratic views of the detective's former boss and many of his colleagues, present and past. The corruption of the servants of the state and the elimination of social undesirables are both necessary to remove threats to the power of the vigilante squad's financial backers.

The political mindset of these shadowy, anti-democratic elements is made overt in several films. In Massimo Tarantini's *Poliziotti violenti* (*Crimebusters*, 1976), the former paratrooper Major Paolo Altieri (Henry Silva) becomes aware of corruption in his own service and is transferred out of the way to Rome. He uncovers a secret vigilante gang financed by an ultra-rich conservative businessman. He witnesses a terrorist attack in which the perpetrators are armed with assault rifles only newly assigned to the legitimate armed forces and his curiosity makes him, and his girlfriend, a target of terrorism.

18   Alessandro Ferraù, 'Il pubblico è sovrano', *Giornale dello Spettacolo*, 7 (1971), 11.

Plot elements make the point that right-wing terrorism is a tool of the super-rich, reinforced by dialogue where the businessman expounds the educative effect of 'disorder' in orienting public opinion towards faith in a strong state. One of the bleakest 1970s cop films is Sergio Martino's *La polizia accusa: il servizio segreto uccide* (Chopper Squad, 1975). Whilst investigating a series of apparent suicides of men in important positions, the honest cop, Giorgio Solmi (Luc Merenda), realizes that they have been murdered, and discovers the existence of a covert subdivision of the secret service – a reference to contemporary news revelations. Similarly, action sequences, such as the helicopter raid on the hidden training camp, make reference to actual events, whilst using the style of American cop TV shows in the ultra-violence, fast editing and pace. This film is marked by unusually revealing *mise-en-scène* in the sequence where Solmi brings one of the ringleaders, Captain Sperlì (Tomas Milian), to be tried in Rome. The buildings visible from the helicopter's windows are the correlative of the dialogue, in which Sperlì insists that equality is a myth, that some men are better than others and so should lead those weaker, denies the importance of the individual and the concept of democracy. Roman ruins are at the centre of repeated frames, then we see the distinctive shape of the Vittorio Emanuele monument and the Palazzo Venezia from which Mussolini harangued Roman crowds. These aerial long shots make the link between the coercive organization of the Roman Empire, which Mussolini specifically evoked as the antecedent and authority for his own fascist party, and the anti-democratic activities of a cabal of super-rich and right-wing men.

Greater tensions between the realist and the noir style occur in the third category of films whose objects of investigation are social problems, such as drugs, prostitution, strikes, student revolt, anti-social behaviour. Their police investigators are predominantly lone avengers, answering violence with violence and operating on the frontiers of legality. Genre templates of action-film heroes clash with the narrative necessities of the detective genre. The spectator of the action thriller is not usually in possession of greater knowledge than the hero. The political investigation, however, requires distance from the object of the enquiry to create a space for audience comprehension of the meaning of events, hence the use of narrative repetition and seriality. The ultra-violence and convoluted narratives of cop films are also highly revealing, certainly of popular tastes for American films and TV cop shows in their fast-paced action, but also of anxieties about threats to self, family and community posed by street violence and terrorism.

Social problem films in the third category flourished through a succession of popular sub-genres, such as those with city names, and titles featuring the words 'police', 'justice', 'violent', 'investigation' in various combinations, and starring Maurizio Merli or Luc Merenda as the detectives, or – in Tomas Milian's case – villains. These cop films are dark in their engagement with the frontiers of acceptable behaviour and the very number of film versions of cops breaking the law to punish transgression suggests that they perform the function of fragments of a seriality which attempts to reconstruct a new order out of the chaos of contemporary life. As well as the corrupt upper classes, their targets are often the proletariat, depicted in grotesque terms as amoral, selfish and violent, and needing a strong, lone avenger to take them in hand, punish them and restore order. Whilst the histrionic performance style of Tomas Milian lent itself to the embodiment of threats to civil society, the cohort of actors playing detectives were described as *granitico* [granite-like], hard men with athletic bodies and a very limited range of facial expressions. Their hardness is the correlative of their strong sense of civic rectitude. The violence and grotesque elements are motivated in the narrative because they justify the actions of the vengeful cop who discovers the perpetrators of vile crimes and punishes them. In *Roma a mano armata* (*Brutal Justice*, Umberto Lenzi, 1976), Milian plays a hunchbacked psychotic killer armed with a machine gun. Around him cohere a variety of social plagues – under-age delinquents involved in smash and grab, a gang rape, a drug overdose victim and a hold-up in a post office. Milian is amoral, unshaven and untidy. Pitted against him is Maurizio Merli's Inspector Tanzi, thickset, mustachioed and blond, whose unorthodox and violent methods are depicted as necessary to defeat Milian's monster and to restore order. Milian reprises this role in film after film. Because many of the titles of cop films have subordinate clauses such as 'the police are powerless', 'the police cannot shoot', there is a suggestion that the forces of order need greater powers. Films with violent cop protagonists were frequently accused of endorsing a right-wing, conservative ideology but, as Christian Uva and Michele Picchi suggest, the backdrop to these popular films always makes reference to the *anni di piombo* and the atmosphere of anxiety and dread of the 1970s and 1980s.[19] Moreover,

19   Christian Uva and Michele Picchi, *Destra e sinistra nel cinema italiano: film e immaginario politico dagli anni '60 al nuovo millennio* (Rome: Edizioni Interculturali, 2006), 64. See also Lino Miccichè, *Cinema italiano degli anni '70* (Venice: Marsilio, 1980), 131–33.

their incoherence and contradictions find expression in excessive violence and the grotesque, both elements of the neo-baroque, destabilizing received ideas. The turbulence introduced into the narrative worlds of *Roma a mano armata* or Lenzi's *Il cinico, l'infame e il violento* (*The Cynic, the Rat and the Fist*, 1977) enables the activity of the wealthy and corrupt to be likened to gangsterism, and therefore robbed of its mythic cloak.

Whilst less cinematically complex than the politically committed films described above, low-budget genre films are also interesting for their spatial expression of anti-social and anti-democratic behaviour. Locations at the periphery of cities occur frequently. According to Deleuze, filmmakers access a 'third moment' which explains a historical juncture by including insignificant spaces (the 'any-space-whatever' of urban waste-grounds and decay, of the liminal, untidy spaces of the edges of cities).[20] In the case of cop films, anxieties about threats to social stability posed by those outside the legitimate worlds of work and home and worries about the effects on traditional Italian society of rampant materialism find expression in these violent and grotesque outsider figures. The 'haptic' sense of lived space described here indicates or maps the geographic spaces available to the characters.[21] Differentiated from normal society, they invite easy recognition as threats to established order. These cop revenge films could be said to be looking in the wrong place at the wrong time, so to speak. They shift attention away from a social class which manages politics and the economic system in its own interests, whose members enjoy conspicuous consumption themselves, whilst encouraging consumerism as a way of compensating the masses for their lack of political power. Social polarization allegorizes the strategy of tension and the climate of uncertainty about the truth behind events.

The Return to Terrorist Themes

In the early 1990s, and again in the early twenty-first century, films have returned to terrorist themes. The spate of films which revisit the 1970s use the same spatial paradigms as 1970s films to indicate oppositions, but with a subtle difference. They are concerned not so

20   Gilles Deleuze, *Cinema 1: The Movement Image*, trans. by H. Tomlinson and R. Galeta (London: The Athlone Press, 1992), 212 [*L'Image-mouvement* (Paris: Editions de Minuit, 1983)].
21   Giuliana Bruno, *Atlas of Emotion: Journeys in Art, Architecture and Film* (New York: Verso, 2002), 6.

much to promote a left-wing version of events, although they usually do, as to indicate that the problem which is being investigated (corruption or criminality) is to be assigned to traditional forms of masculinity linked to unfettered capitalism, both of which underpin maintenance of the power of a conservative governing class. The moral authority of the investigator figures of recent Italian cinema derives from the fact that their competence in the spheres of both reason and emotion enables them to represent the national as well as the local community. Vittorio Sindoni's *Una fredda mattina di maggio (A Cold May Morning*, 1990) follows the above pattern, whilst reprising the 1970s political class scenario. Set in 1976 in order to access the atmosphere of those years, but based on the later murder of journalist Walter Tobagi, the film shows Ruggero (Sergio Castellitto) campaigning in his union branch for moderation and training opportunities, and in a warm family environment. The representation of the terrorists who assassinate him when he identifies their plans is interesting because, although they display the trappings of the extreme left (Palestinian scarves, pamphlets and shabby-chic clothing), they betray their upper-class aspirations to dominance. The would-be terrorists are upper-middle class students living in surroundings of ostentatious wealth. Their activities and dialogues become increasingly couched in business-school language as their leader, Falk, seeks to establish his own faction and power base. There is no suggestion of an ideological agenda behind their ultra-violent and amoral terrorist murders. Instead the excessive violence, standing as it does in opposition to the democratic process exemplified by Ruggero's activities, disrupts any temptation to absorb the would-be terrorists' world view. The spectacular wide-angle architectural shots of Turin are also excessive, drawing attention to complex realities behind terrorist violence.

Romanzo criminale (*Crime Story*, Michele Placido, 2005), adapted from Giancarlo De Cataldo's successful book, owes more to the lower end of 1970s cop films than to political films, in spite of its high budget.[22] Based on the activities of a Roman gang which rapidly distinguished itself by violence and financial success in the 1970s and 1980s, the film is concerned to embed itself in the context of Italy, with references to terrorist events, massacres and the strategy of tension. Black-and-white actuality footage of demonstrations, and iconic newsreel footage of Prime Minister Aldo Moro in his kidnap cell under the flag of the Brigate Rosse and of the discovery of his body in the back of a car, are juxtaposed to diegetic events which promote

22   Giancarlo De Cataldo, *Romanzo criminale* (Turin: Einaudi, 2002).

an active, retrospective reading of their significance. The character who acts as one of the links between the gang and the police is told to stop his investigation into where Moro is being held, evoking the later revelations of the DC's and America's policy of indifference to Moro's fate by those right-wing factions which rejected any alliance with the left. The 'unreproducible reality' of the digitally generated representation of the Bologna station bombing (in which the gang is implicated) generates considerable emotional force, whilst its very virtuosity draws attention to itself.[23] The Bologna bomb outrage sequences signal the move to the unravelling of the gang's internal relationships, and to their exploitation by powerful, illegal forces on the political right and, from this point on, noir elements increase. Significantly, as the character Freddo talks about his gang's loss of operational control to shadowy paymasters, the car he is being driven in passes the Vittorio Emanuele monument, economically suggesting that these paymasters have a fascist agenda.

The conventions of Italian noir are present in the *chiaroscuro* lighting contrasts, the yellow tones, violence and visual excess, but the link to specific social or political targets is offset by the pervasive atmosphere of criminal cool, the beauty of clothes and objects, and conspicuous consumption. The gang's acquisition of expensive suits and antiques and ostentatiously luxurious villas are connotations of an upper-class lifestyle whilst ruthless violence and criminality make the link to the established template of a wealthy elite using violence to cling on to power. Once again, right-wing terrorism is associated with a conservative upper class, prepared to stop at nothing to retain its position. No-one escapes the corruption: the cop, Detective Scialoja, receives praise for his dogged ten-year pursuit of the gang, but is attracted by the sexual decadence of the beautiful whore Patrizia and by the wealth and designer-clad lifestyle of her lover, the gangster

---

23 Michela Greco, *Il digitale nel cinema italiano: estetica, produzione, linguaggio* (Turin: Lindau, 2002), 1. Gian Luca Rizzo of the Proxima Company has insisted that Italian digital special effects always aim to be invisible as constructions (quoted in Greco, 95). The meaning of the Proxima team's recreation of the Bologna explosion and its aftermath in *Romanzo criminale* lies in its virtuosity, based on its illusionistic recall of contemporary accounts and photographs and the computer generated images of the spectacular explosion of pieces of building and people. The virtuosity insists on the emotional importance of the event, whilst reinforcing the enigma, the 'space of ambiguity' about those responsible. See Ndalianis, 152.

Dandi. *Romanzo criminale* does not escape what Francesco Rosi has called the 'risk of the aestheticization of terror'.[24]

Conclusion

Italian filmmakers have difficulty constructing a concrete closure to the majority of these films depicting investigations into the right-wing power networks responsible for violent events. Explanations of the final level of responsibility for terrorist violence visualize shadowy, or absent, figures, their lack signalling a profound level of unfinished business in conceptualizing a healthy political process. Films which reenact or investigate state or right-wing terrorism have a variety of tropes to draw on, the venality of the Italian political class being represented by the ostentatious luxury of buildings, and by the use of socially coercive interior and exterior space, in which only exceptional protagonists are able to refuse a position of inferiority or acceptance of the status quo. The range of terrorism narratives represents an important political and cultural antidote to accepting the explanations (or lack thereof) of those in power. These narratives are far from simple endorsements of conservative or right-wing values. Rather, an acceptance of the social order is tempered by utopian desires for a just society which more truly represents the diversity of the Italian population. Fears about how power is exercised gain force from the seriality of violent events, anxieties clustering around evocations of fascistic ideals, corrupt practices and misuse of power. Representations of the murder of honest and principled characters (such as detectives, policemen, journalists) or horrific terrorist acts (the murder of Aldo Moro, the Bologna station bombing) are cultural and political crisis points. Negotiated readings break down before the horror and affront to democratic sensibilities. This recourse to affect and emotion allows the presence of oppositional notions of social and political order to surface and discursive struggles over meaning to dominate the conclusions of films set in the violent 1970s and 1980s.

The shiny allure and the spurious glamour of conspicuous consumption and materialism of more recent films set in the 1970s tend to deflect attention from the real problems of contemporary Italy, whilst the conventions of noir insistently point to their existence.

24   Paolo D'Agostini, 'L'incontro: maestri della regia. Francesco Rosi', *La Repubblica Domenica*, 18 February 2007, 54.

2. 'In pieno fumetto': Bertolucci, Terrorism and the *commedia all'italiana*

Alan O'Leary

An Opaque Reality

On the occasion of the release of *Tre fratelli* (*Three Brothers*, 1981), director Francesco Rosi remarked on the sense of confusion experienced by the intellectual attempting to clarify conditions in contemporary Italian society. Rosi recognized the differences from his previous work in the approach taken in *Tre fratelli*, a film which deals with terrorism as part of a wider portrait of Italy and of the Italian family:

> The general social and political situation in Italy is much less clear today than when I made my first films. Twenty years ago, when I made *Salvatore Giuliano* and *Hands Over The City*, my aim was to participate in public life by making films which dealt with collective problems. Reality was clearer and simpler then and I could tell stories about the collectivity, about society, by using only facts. The situation is more complex now, and one needs to rely more on characters, their interrelationships and their reactions to social events in order to make an analysis.[1]

Rosi's assertion that contemporary reality was elusive and accessible only obliquely, and that the 'facts' were of no help in the understanding of contemporary conditions, is symptomatic of a wider feeling of impotence and sense of crisis in the role of the

---

1   Gary Crowdus, 'Personalizing Political Issues: An Interview with Francesco Rosi', *Cineaste*, 12: 2 (1982), 42.

intellectual as commentator during the *anni di piombo*.[2] Gian Piero Brunetta points out that the consequent aversion of the direct gaze from the contemporary world of the *anni di piombo* was characteristic not only of Rosi but also of the other great Italian cineastes:

> I primi ad abdicare alla rappresentazione del presente sono gli autori più affermati, che, per la prima volta, dopo quasi un quarto di secolo, dichiarano conclusa l'esperienza mimetica e realistica e iniziano a praticare i sentieri dell'allegoria, della metafora dell'immaginario, della ricostruzione del passato
>
> [The most respected auteurs are the first to abandon the representation of the present and, for the first time in almost a quarter of a century, they declare the mimetic and realist project to be closed; they take to walking the path of allegory, to utilizing metaphors of the imaginary, to reconstructing the past].[3]

It was not, then, the *cinema d'autore* [auteur cinema] or the *cinema d'impegno* [politically committed cinema] that provided the first cinematic responses to the phenomenon of terrorism and its social consequences in 1970s Italy. The first such cinematic responses were, instead, provided by the genres of the *poliziottesco* [Italian cop film] and the *commedia all'italiana* [comedy Italian style]. For an account of the role of the *poliziottesco* in the representation of terrorism, see Mary P. Wood's chapter in the present volume;[4] the *commedia all'italiana* offers a response to terrorism in films including *Mordi e fuggi* (*Dirty Weekend*, Dino Risi, 1973), *Caro Michele* (*Dear Michael*, Mario Monicelli, 1976), *Un borghese piccolo piccolo* (*An Average Man*, Mario Monicelli, 1977), episodes of *I nuovi mostri* (*Viva Italia*, Mario Monicelli, Dino Risi, Ettore Scola, 1977) and *Caro papà* (*Dear Papa*, Dino Risi, 1979).[5]

---

2   For an account of the 'late' response of auteurist cinema to terrorism, see Enrico Carocci, 'Il terrorismo e la "perdita del centro": cineasti italiani di fronte alla catastrofe', in *Schermi di piombo: il terrorismo nel cinema italiano*, ed. Christian Uva (Soveria Mannelli: Rubbettino, 2007), 115–32. For the broader context of intellectual 'reticence' before the violence of the 1970s, see Jennifer Burns, 'A Leaden Silence? Writers' Responses to the *anni di piombo*', in *Speaking out and Silencing: Culture, Society and Politics in Italy in the 1970s*, ed. Anna Cento Bull and Adalgisa Giorgio (Oxford: Legenda, 2006), 81–94.

3   Gian Piero Brunetta, *Storia del cinema italiano*, ii: *Dal 1945 agli anni ottanta* (Rome: Editori Riuniti, 1982), 796.

4   See also Christian Uva, 'Introduzione', 9–94 (especially 11 and 29–34), and Andrea Pergolari, 'La fisionomia del terrorismo nero nel cinema poliziesco italiano degli anni '70', 159–72, both in Uva, *Schermi di piombo*.

5   Although *Un borghese piccolo piccolo* is not strictly a film about terrorism, but rather about violence and its consequences, it portrays a bureaucrat played by Alberto Sordi who becomes a vigilante in order to avenge the death of his son

Scholarly consideration of this fact has been limited; indeed, the films of the *commedia all'italiana* do not appear in the chapter 'Schermi del terrorismo' in Fantoni Minnella's book on Italian political cinema.[6] Contemporary reviewers tended to dismiss the films as being excessively in thrall to genre models, as in the following extract from a review by G. Guazzini of *Caro papà*, the story of a successful entrepreneur whose son is attached to a terrorist group:

> Come il regista affronti il problema del terrorismo è presto detto scorrendo la fabula del film: se un ingegnere che si batte per la fortuna delle multinazionali e per la 'stabilizzazione dell'ordine mondiale', tradisce una moglie, sofferente a ogni cambio di stagione di mania suicida, con un'amante oggetto, nella miglior tradizione delle commedie all'italiana, non può che essere punito con l'aver covato la classica 'serpe in seno', rappresentata da un figlio in crisi esistenziale che essendo stato per troppo tempo monetizzato per le carenze affettive sofferte, perde il senso del valore del denaro e diviene bieco terrorista, tanto da accettare di condurre un'operazione di azzoppamento del genitore. [...] Come si può intuire siamo in pieno fumetto.[7]

> [The manner in which the director confronts the problem of terrorism is quickly revealed by a summary of the film. A successful engineer who prostitutes himself for the profit of multinational companies and for the 'stabilization of the world order', who is unfaithful to a wife regularly prey to suicidal impulses, who has an eye-catching mistress in the best tradition of the *commedia all'italiana*: inevitably, such a man must be punished. How? By having nursed the classic 'viper in the bosom', here represented by a son in the throes of existential crisis. Having for too long been placated with cash in the absence of parental affection, the son loses all sense of the value of money and becomes a resentful terrorist, finally agreeing to arrange an attack intended to cripple his father. [...] As will be obvious, we are deep in comic strip territory.]

at the hands of a group which may be terrorist but is never identified as such. Still, commentators have tended to discuss the film in relation to terrorism. Peter Bondanella, for instance, unambiguously refers to the son's killer as a 'terrorist', in *Italian Cinema*, 3rd ed. (New York: Continuum, 2004), 327.

6 Maurizio Fantoni Minella, *Non riconciliati: politica e società nel cinema italiano dal neorealismo a oggi* (Turin: UTET, 2004), 114–32. The neglect is, briefly, remedied in Uva, 26–7 and 41, although Uva's book contains no dedicated chapter on the *commedia all'italiana*.

7 G. Guazzini, 'Caro papà', *Cinema Nuovo*, 28: 261 (1979), 53.

It is clear that this final remark is meant as the strongest criticism: an indication of the film's lack of serious engagement with the tragic circumstances it dares to portray. Yet it is equally clear that the judgement can only be a criticism if genre considerations are dismissed, and genre filmmaking (and comedy) *per se* is judged an inappropriate vehicle for the analysis of the terrorist problem.

It may appear paradoxical, given the critical disdain of the genre, that Bernardo Bertolucci should adopt the mode of the *commedia all'italiana* for his 'terrorist' film, *La tragedia di un uomo ridicolo* (*The Tragedy of a Ridiculous Man*, 1981). Yet Bertolucci's film is a tribute to the capacity of Italian film comedy to respond promptly to the circumstances of the *anni di piombo*, and to its capacity to capture the atmosphere of those years.[8] This article will question the commonplace opposition of genre and auteur, represented here by the *commedia all'italiana* and Bernardo Bertolucci respectively, while retaining the opposition as a heuristic to investigate the punctual capacity of the *commedia all'italiana* to apprehend and analyse the conditions of the *anni di piombo*. This capacity will be demonstrated to reside in the *commedia all'italiana* inasmuch as it is a comedy of Italian manners, a genre which satirizes the mores and hypocrisies of the period, often through the portrayal of the family. In the early 1980s, this representation of terrorism as family affair is reprised both in the *cinema d'impegno* (Rosi's *Tre fratelli*; Gianni Amelio's *Colpire al cuore* (*Blow to the Heart*), 1982) and in Bertolucci's auteurist production, *La tragedia di un uomo ridicolo* (1981), a film presented in this article as a late example of a *commedia all'italiana* which had supposedly been another victim of terrorism in the 1970s.

The structure of this essay is as follows: I begin by arguing that the traditional account of *La tragedia di un uomo ridicolo* in terms of Bertolucci's own psychology is incomplete and misleading, and I contextualize the film instead as part of the *commedia all'italiana* tradition. The question of why the comic mode was felt by Bertolucci to be appropriate for the representation of the social effects of terrorism in Italy is used to format my enquiry into the capacities of the *commedia all'italiana* to apprehend early the presence of terrorism. I describe the *commedia all'italiana* as a comedy of manners which

---

8 *La tragedia di un uomo ridicolo* may contain no bombs or shootings, but it is nonetheless the case that, as Lesley Caldwell writes, the film uses 'terrorism as part of [its] examination of contemporary Italy and the place of the family, symbolic and actual, in its culture', 'Is the personal political? Fathers and Sons in Bertolucci's *Tragedia di un uomo ridicolo* and Amelio's *Colpire al cuore'*, in *Speaking Out and Silencing*, ed. Cento Bull and Giorgio, 73.

adopts a stance of 'critical proximity' towards its objects of satire. One aspect of this proximity is the use of familiar male actor-stars for whom the viewer is likely to feel an indulgent fondness, and with whom he (or she?) will be encouraged to identify. The ageing of these stars is, however, one of the aspects that implies the exhaustion of the genre. My conclusion is that it was this very exhaustion which ironically granted the *commedia all'italiana*, in its late appearance in *La tragedia di un uomo ridicolo*, the capacity to characterize the position of the Italian intellectual wrong-footed and perplexed before the fact of terrorism.

Bertolucci's Tragedy of Manners

Bertolucci's adoption of the comic mode for his 'terrorist' film, *La tragedia di un uomo ridicolo* (1981), is a tribute to the capacity of Italian film comedy to respond promptly to the atmosphere and circumstances of the *anni di piombo*.

The film begins as Primo Spaggiari, a well-fed Emilian producer of *salumi* and cheese, observes from the roof of his factory a mysterious altercation that may be the kidnap of his son (neither Primo nor the spectator sees the son's face). He watches the incident through a pair of binoculars just received as a birthday gift from the very son he now seems to witness being abducted – the son whom Primo will later come to suspect of having staged his own kidnap, and who, it becomes clear, has dubious political associations. (Primo himself, believing his son to be dead, hopes to use the ransom money he and his wife have raised in order to save his ailing business.) The binoculars used by Primo function as a metaphor, firstly, for the difficulty of seeing and of understanding what is seen, and secondly for the mediation of the cinematic mechanism itself, and thus for the cinema's difficulty of comprehension in this period. At the film's close, the son reappears as mysteriously as he had disappeared, and the final words of the film, spoken in voice-over by Primo, explicitly challenge the viewer to make sense of what has been witnessed: 'Il compito di scoprire la verità sull'enigma di un figlio rapito morto e risuscitato lo lascio a voi' [The task of discovering the truth of the mystery of a son kidnapped, killed and resurrected I leave to you]. But the project of engaging the spectator in the work of interpretation is intended by Bertolucci less as a task he expects the viewer to perform than as an ironic acknowledgement of his own inability to decipher the circumstances of the times:

The film represents an ambiguousness I feel to be typical of Italian society – and life in other countries, too [...] There are no certainties left. No one knows any longer what the truth is – concerning the Kennedy assassinations or the British spy scandals or the murder of Aldo Moro in Italy. [...] In the Moro case, and the Mattei case, one in fact knows nothing at all about their actual death.[9] [...] Today ambiguity is part of our everyday diet. There's no longer any certainty, including certainty about events. (16)

The complexity of the times becomes in Bertolucci's film an ambiguity that can be expressed but not elucidated. *La tragedia di un uomo ridicolo* transposes this ambiguity from the political to a familial context; as Bertolucci has said, 'the audience and Primo must think his son is dead. Only Barbara [Primo's wife] believes he's alive. Adelfo [a priest friend of the missing son] has heard that he died in a confessional. But this confusion reflects political matters in Italy' (Ciment, 16). If *La tragedia di un uomo ridicolo* takes its cue from the mysterious nature of public events and the disquieting heap of Italy's illustrious corpses, it nonetheless translates these concerns into a familial comedy of manners.

The comedy of *La tragedia di un uomo ridicolo* has rarely been taken seriously. Those critics who registered the slapstick element of the film tended to see it as a lapse in tone: 'trovano posto imbarazzanti episodi comici' [space is allowed to embarrassing comic episodes].[10] And, while certain critics have described the film in its relation to the tradition of the *commedia all'italiana*,[11] most critics have preferred to see the film in the auteurist, even strictly biographical terms standard in Bertolucci criticism. Brunetta writes of Bertolucci's work: 'I film sono così strettamente intrecciati con la vita del regista che, giustamente, un critico francese ha proposto di servirsi, nell'analisi, di una "biografia testuale" come chiave di decodificazione' (664–65) [The films are so closely bound up with the life of the director that one French critic has with good reason proposed to make use of a 'textual biography' as a hermeneutic key]. Brooke Jacobson perceives, in *Tragedia*,

9   Michel Ciment, 'Bernardo Bertolucci Discussing *Tragedy of a Ridiculous Man*', *Film and Filming*, 328 (1982), 12.

10   Piero Sola, '*La Tragedia di un Uomo Ridicolo*', *Rivista del Cinematografo*, 54: 12 (1981), 679.

11   See Fabrizio Deriu, '*La tragedia di un uomo ridicolo* di B. Bertolucci: Il complesso di Crono', in *Schermi opachi: il cinema italiano degli anni '80*, ed. Lino Miccichè (Venice: Marsilio, 1998), 273–82, and Guido Fink, '*La tragedia di un uomo ridicolo*', in *In viaggio con Bernardo: il cinema di Bernardo Bertolucci*, ed. Roberto Campari and Maurizio Schiaretti (Venice: Marsilio, 1994), 102–11.

'repeated incidents of comic discord in an otherwise serious drama
[...] these fragmentary comic instances or absurdities defy reading in
terms of normal plot structure, but they may be seen contrapuntally
to form a subtext which has the quality of a dream'.[12] For Jacobson, *La
tragedia di un uomo ridicolo* is a 'dreamwork masquerading as thriller'
(59), decipherable as a narrative of Bertolucci's coming to terms with
his Oedipal conflicts. The presence of a father/the Father (Primo) at
the centre of the story is read by Jacobson as the auteur's deliberate
inhabiting of the father-space, an act which suggests that Bertolucci
'has made a quantum leap in reconciling his own ambivalence toward
the father' (62).

Other critics less in thrall to the auterist paradigm of the singular
originating (un)conscious have preferred to perceive the mixing of
dramatic and comic modes in *La tragedia di un uomo ridicolo* as an
index of the 'post-modern spirit of the film'.[13] Such a position may
betray an ignorance of Italian film tradition as well as insensitivity
to the means by which comedy on the micro level (the gags and
slapstick) signals that a film text is to be read in a comic key despite
the presence of dramatic events.[14] The notion that the juxtaposition
of the tragic and the ridiculous in Italian cinema is something new
and distinctly post-modern is, in any case, mistaken. The ironic mode
of genre contamination indicated in the title of Bertolucci's film is
typical of the *commedia all'italiana* – a mode that dates back at least to
the late 1950s.

What is peculiar in the widespread reluctance of the critics to
treat *La tragedia di un uomo ridicolo* in terms of the tradition of the
commedia all'italiana is that the cues provided in the film could not
be more explicit. Beyond the mixing of tones indicated by the title
– a mixture of tragic and grotesque typical of Italian film comedy
from the economic boom onwards – there is the fact of the film's
leading man, Ugo Tognazzi, a 'mostro sacro' [cherished household
name] of the *commedia all'italiana* whose presence seems to have
been blatant enough to have blinded most critics to its significance.
As Deriu writes: 'Bertolucci propone la rappresentazione [...] di
un ennesimo personaggio da commedia, in bilico tra frustrazione e
fallimento, mosso da un istinto di "sopravvivenza a ogni costo" che

12   Brooke Jacobson, *'The Tragedy of a Ridiculous Man'*, Film Quarterly, 37: 3
(1984), 58.
13   Yosefa Loshitzky, *The Radical Faces of Godard and Bertolucci* (Detroit: Wayne
University Press, 1995), 85.
14   See Gerald Mast's discussion of 'comic climate' in *The Comic Mind: Comedy
and the Movies* (New York: Random House, 1976), 9–13.

lo spinge a sfruttare il rapimento del figlio' (277–78) [Bertolucci offers the representation of yet another comic personage, caught between frustration and failure, driven by an instinct to survive 'whatever the cost' that impels him to profit from the kidnap of his son].

I describe, below, the key function of the *divi* [stars] in the *commedia all'italiana*. Ugo Tognazzi is among them, as Deriu points out, and he fulfilled the role in the genre of 'interprete di umori, ambizioni e meschinità della profonda provincia settentrionale' [interpreter of the humours, ambitions and mediocrity of the provincial deep north], rather than the Rome represented by Alberto Sordi or Nino Manfredi.[15] The actor-star persona established from film to film denoted a taste for good living that sometimes pitched into a grotesque key of gluttony and erotomania. The aptness of such a profile for the portrayal of Primo Spaggiari in *La tragedia di un uomo ridicolo* is obvious, and the film is an integral and organic part of the actor's as well as the director's œuvre.[16]

Father, Dear

In order to illustrate further what is shared by Bertolucci's film and the *commedia all'italiana*, it is useful to list the points of comparison between *La tragedia di un uomo ridicolo* and *Caro papà*, a film which predates it by two years. Both films concentrate on the father, and the narrative is almost totally restricted to his viewpoint; both fathers claim to have been members of the wartime Resistance, and so represent the move from idealism to materialism in post-war Italy; the sons of both men are enigmatic figures with ambivalent feelings (to say the least) towards their progenitors; both businessmen have frustrated sexual encounters with their sons' girlfriends, who function as metonymic tokens of exchange between the older and younger men; both protagonists are played by familiar actors (Tognazzi and Vittorio Gassman) best known for their work in the *commedia all'italiana*; and the ambiguous endings of both films refuse the relief

---

15 Leonardo De Franceschi, 'L'attore negli anni della crisi', in *Storia del cinema italiano*, xiii: *1977–1985*, ed. Vito Zagarrio (Venice: Marsilio, 2005), 306.

16 De Franceschi (306) speaks of the 'progressivo emergere di accenti patetico-tragici' [gradual emergence of tragic and pathetic tones] in Tognazzi's performances, and the 'approfondimento di un personale discorso sulla vecchiaia' [the development of a personal discourse on ageing] as the 1970s progress, both of which can be said to culminate in *La tragedia di un uomo ridicolo*.

of closure in a way typical of the commedia tradition.[17] In *Caro papà* and *La tragedia di un uomo ridicolo*, the equilibrium of the social order is only superficially righted and is implied to continue awry beyond the credits of the comedy. To close the list without exhausting it, both films represent the social consequences of terrorism in terms which, to paraphrase Dalle Vacche, translate the interrogation of the present into Oedipal myth.[18]

Several writers have considered *La tragedia di un uomo ridicolo* in relation to *Caro papà* and other films (especially *Colpire al cuore*) on the basis of the use in each of the Oedipal configuration.[19] The use of such a configuration in a film about terrorism might have been a way to generalize the conflicts depicted, an attempt to identify an archetype behind a violence that otherwise seemed so historically rooted. We should consider, however, that the enquiry into the relationship of father and son, in an Oedipal key or otherwise, is a longstanding feature of Italian cinema – one thinks of the invocation of the archetype in Pasolini's version of the Oedipus story (*Edipo re [Oedipus Rex]*, 1967; I return to Pasolini below) and of *Ladri di biciclette* (*Bicycle Thieves*, Vittorio De Sica, 1948). As in the latter film, the fathers in *Caro papà* and *La tragedia di un uomo ridicolo* have but one son – not an implausible number of male offspring, but the frequency with which it reappears suggest that we are in the presence, in these films, of a

---

17   Enrico Giacovelli, *La Commedia all'Italiana*, 2nd ed. (Roma: Gremese Editore, 1995), 43. The pseudo-saccharine ending of *Caro papà* has been the object of misunderstanding. Paolo Pillitteri describes the revelation of the son's belated loyalty as a 'hypocritical' move on the part of the filmmakers (*Cinema come Politica: una commedia all'italiana* (Milano: Franco Angeli, 1992), 148); while for Giacovelli, the ending 'concede qualcosa al pathos tradizionale, spinge alla riconciliazione il figlio pentito e il genitore in carrozzella: una timida speranza per gli anni ottanta' [concedes something to traditional pathos and suggests the reconciliation of the repentant son and the father in his wheelchair: a faint hope for the 1980s] (92). One might argue instead that the tearful reconciliation of crippled father and wayward son is so blatant a sop to easy sentiment that the viewer is moved to doubt its sincerity and refuse the closure (or catharsis) it pretends to allow. This reading would be consistent with my argument, below, that the viewer of the *commedia all'italiana* is always actively engaged, coopted by the rhetoric of the film to complete the satirical work begun by the filmmakers.
18   Angela Dalle Vacche, *The Body in the Mirror: Shapes of History in Italian Cinema* (Princeton: Princeton University Press, 1992), 15.
19   See Caldwell, 'Is the personal political?', and Rachele Tardi, 'Representations of Italian Left Political Violence in Film, Literature and Theatre (1973–2005)' (unpublished doctoral thesis, University of London, University College, 2005).

symbolic topology.[20] Might this be patriarchy as such? Dalle Vacche seems to confirm this:

> The latent homoeroticism of the Oedipal myth seems to apply to Italian cinema, which employs 'homosocial' narratives to represent fathers and sons in history and public life, while pushing mothers towards biology and the private sphere. [...] In this scheme, the woman is also an agent of biological continuity enabling genealogies between fathers and sons, thus reinforcing the heterosexual façade of male bonding and historical legacies. (15)

Certainly, the fact that the key faces of the *commedia all'italiana* were all male suggests that the genre was used to negotiate masculinity in Italian society;[21] however, the frequent presence, in this genre as in Italian cinema as a whole, of father-son configurations suggests we are dealing with a negotiation of that form of social organization in which the father is the head of the family and descent and relationship are reckoned through the male line. This form of organization, patriarchy, is figured by Freud in Oedipal terms, and the task of the son is to displace the father as the holder of authority and power. Understood in this way, the presence of the Oedipal theme in *Caro papà* and *La tragedia di un uomo ridicolo* suggests a reading of Italian terrorism as another means of 'killing the father'. What is clear is that the use of the Oedipal mode, whether understood in purely mythical or in Freudian terms, was a means of figuring conflict rather than concord at the centre of the nation, and an index of a society decidedly out of joint.

It might be objected that, despite the many similarities between the two films, we should maintain the distinction between a work like *Caro papà*, which emerges from a genre and one like *La tragedia di un uomo ridicolo* which makes use of generic features in a deliberate, strategic and allusive way. *La tragedia di un uomo ridicolo* is, on such an account, a meta-cinematic exercise engaged in for reasons of present and artistic necessity. However, no competently made film is produced in ignorance of film history and, indeed, all the better films of the *commedia all'italiana* might be described as meta-cinematic (and meta-generic) in this respect – the extreme case being Ettore Scola's *C'eravamo tanto amati* [*We All Loved Each Other So Much*] of 1974. In other words, *La tragedia di un uomo ridicolo* is, ambivalently

---

20 As in *Ladri di biciclette*, daughters and wives are seldom seen or soon marginalized by the story in these films.
21 See Maggie Günsberg, *Italian Cinema: Gender and Genre* (Basingstoke: Palgrave, 2005), 60–96.

but emphatically, a *commedia all'italiana* film – it just happens to have been made by a director better known for a different sort of cinema. In any case, the questions to be asked of Bertolucci's aesthetic choices in *La tragedia di un uomo ridicolo* are the following: why was the mode of the *commedia all'italiana* felt to be appropriate for the representation of the ambiguity of the Italian leaden years? Why was the shift in viewpoint, in terms of Bertolucci's œuvre, from the son to the father necessary in the context of this theme? In order to answer these questions, we need to take a detour through the history of the *commedia all'italiana* and take a glance at its pantheon of stars.

Satirical Proximity

The *commedia all'italiana* was first recognized as a distinct phenomenon in Italian cinema in the late 1950s, though when it was first named in 1959 it was under the label of *commedia di costume* [comedy of manners].[22] *Commedia all'italiana*, a phrase which appears in the discourse of critics the following year, and *commedia di costume* continue to be interchangeable if not synonymous terms throughout the 1960s, though the more familiar term, *all'italiana*, is the one which survives into the period of critical disdain of the genre in the early 1970s: 'passa a indicare una fase ormai esaurita del cinema italiano o semplicemente un modello "negativo" di cinema' (Camerini, 180) [it comes to indicate a now exhausted phase of Italian cinema, or simply a 'negative' model of cinema].

It is worth dwelling on the implications of the original label, *commedia di costume*, and what it reveals about the capacity of the genre to deal with contemporary social and political conditions, and so with the phenomenon of terrorism. The concerns of a comedy of manners are likely to be with 'the behaviour and deportment of men and women living under specific social codes'.[23] Originally, the theatrical comedy of manners was preoccupied with the foibles of the upper classes, and later with the nascent bourgeois classes and their servants. The films we are discussing continue the focus on the bourgeoisie, but the *commedia* as a whole also took a more 'democratic' perspective, reflecting the aspirations of a broader

22   Claudio Camerini, 'I critici e la commedia all'italiana: le occasioni perdute', in *Commedia all'italiana: angolazioni controcampi*, ed. Riccardo Napolitano (Rome: Gangemi Editore, 1986), 179–81.

23   J.A. Cuddon, *The Penguin Dictionary of Literary Terms and Literary Theory*, 3rd ed. (Harmondsworth: Penguin, 1991), 170.

social range during the years of precipitate economic growth that attended the genre's birth. Reflecting these aspirations, the *commedia di costume-all'italiana* becomes at once critique and symptom of the circumstances of the 'Boom'. Giacovelli lists some of the conditions that spawned the genre, including the emergence of the new mass media (the *rotocalchi* [glossy gossip magazines], television) and their celebration of the consumerism implied by the increase in production (42–43). This consumerism found its emblems in the new status symbols, especially the car and the lifestyle it supposedly allowed of romantic possibility and seaside leisure trips, omnipresent as *topoi* in the films.[24] The motif of the car is an excellent example of what we might call the ambivalence of the *commedia di costume-all'italiana* towards the objects of its ridicule: the satire of the motorist in films as different as *Il sorpasso* (*The Easy Life*, Dino Risi, 1962) and *I motorizzati* (*The Motorized*, Camillo Mastrocinque, also of 1962) is a paean to automobility even as it denounces the popular idolatry of the automobile.[25] As the example demonstrates, we may speak of the double face of the genre – one of critique, the other of celebration – something proper to the comedy of manners and something expressed in the definition given of the *commedia all'italiana* in the *Dizionario Zingarelli*: 'genere cinematografico [...] animato in parte da intenzioni di critica di costume, in parte da fini esclusivamente commerciali' [a cinema genre driven partly by purposes of social criticism and partly by purely commercial motivations].

The ambivalence of the *commedia di costume-all'italiana* towards the objects of its satire, its 'double face' of moralist and *sfruttatore* [exploiter], means that it has a certain investment in the conditions and mores that it hopes to expose; at the very least, it does not stand 'aloof'. Hence the provenance of much of the material utilized for the plots of the films, material often derived from the popular media the films liked to burlesque: 'la commedia all'italiana si bagna nella storia della quotidianità, compresa la più parcellizzata, e che non di rado a ispirarla sono state le cronache' [the *commedia all'italiana* immerses itself in the history of daily life, including the most trivial aspects, and has not infrequently been inspired by the daily news].[26] It has been common to argue that the ambivalence of the mode, together

---

24 For an account of the relationship of the *commedia all'italiana* to the new consumerism of the economic boom, see Günsberg, 68–84.

25 *Il sorpasso* ends tragically in a crash that kills its ingenuous protagonist; *I motorizzati* is a film of farcical vignettes and stock comic types.

26 Mino Argentieri, 'La commedia e la storia d'Italia', in *Commedia all'italiana*, ed. Napolitano, 95.

with its exploitation of the lurid aspects of contemporary reality, inclines towards cynicism, or towards its ideological variant of *qualunquismo* [literally, 'whatever-ism', i.e., a self-serving disdain for social and political questions]. The *commedia all'italiana* was 'guilty' of ambiguity and so fell foul of the belief that a text which fails to damn its wicked characters explicitly must be guilty of endorsing their behaviour. We may find such a belief naïve or tendentious, but it has the benefit of reminding us how much work is left to do for the spectator of the *commedia all'italiana* – both in terms of that spectator being the ultimate moral arbiter of the actions portrayed and in terms of his or her self-recognition in the object of the satire. One might well argue that the investment or complicity of the *commedia all'italiana* in the objects of its satire is, in fact, an advantage in the elucidation of social conditions. The satirical proximity (as distinct from critical detachment) allows recognition of the complexity of the conditions portrayed.

In contradistinction to the neorealism from which it was indirectly descended, and from the *cinema d'impegno* which was its ostensible opposite, the *commedia di costume-all'italiana* relied on the construction of a 'typical' (male) Italian identified with a set of iconic faces, including Sordi, Tognazzi *et al.* As Brunetta writes:

> Passando attraverso un gruppo di attori (Tognazzi, Sordi, Mastroianni, Manfredi, Gassman) la commedia dà vita e voce a quel tipo di italiano che la storia ha mandato, suo malgrado, in prima linea [...]. Film dopo film si crea una folla, dove il singolo ritratto diventa emblema di una condizione generale, le voci individuali diventano voci collettive. (762)

> [Employing a particular set of actors (Tognazzi, Sordi, Mastroianni, Manfredi, Gassman) the *commedia all'italiana* animates and gives voice to a type of Italian that history has consigned to the front line against his will [...]. Through film after film a crowd emerges: the portrait of one person becomes the emblem of a general condition; individual become collective voices.]

The fondness created for these heroes of the comedy of manners incarnated in the guise of the *divi all'italiana*, might be described as another form of complicity with the object of satire, in this case with the audience itself. Some critics have seen the creation of such a charismatic 'average Italian' as a form of flattery of the spectator whose behaviour should properly be the target of censure (Camerini, 188–89). It could be argued, rather, that the identification with the actor, the sense of fond complicity with a figure as familiar as, say, Alberto Sordi, was the most effective means of involving the audience in the critique of its own behaviour, and of allowing the viewer of a film like *Un borghese piccolo piccolo* no exit from his or her own complicity with the violence (of workplace, home or street) of the period.

A Mode out of Joint

As a comedy of manners, the *commedia di costume-all'italiana* was well placed to apprehend early the social fact of terrorist violence. Dino Risi's *Mordi e fuggi* can use the flip tone of the cynical 1960s comedy to introduce the more tragic outcomes of the following decade. Risi's film takes a stock comic figure, a philandering fop in a sports car, played by Marcello Mastroianni, and has him kidnapped by a group of anarchists fleeing from a bank raid; kidnappers and hostage alike will die before the guns of a trigger-happy police. The fact that violence defined as terrorist was featured in these films was in itself a polemical move: it asserted that such violence was not alien but inherent to Italian society, and characteristic of its 'manners'.

Nonetheless, the comedy of manners could only go so far in describing the conditions of the day and critics agree that it did not survive the 1970s. As Wood writes: 'Apart from competition from television, the main reason given for the decline was the effect of terrorist attacks'.[27] The idea that terrorism killed off the very genre that was the first to confront it is certainly a refrain in the criticism. According to Giacovelli, terrorism is one of those phenomena (along with ecological degradation and the nuclear threat) that makes the cinematic smile in the 1970s increasingly forced (88); while Masolino D'Amico writes that:

> fu l'aspetto della società italiana a cambiare, e in un modo che sembrava suggerire un commento in chiave drammatica piuttosto che comica. Negli anni dopo il '68 si fece sempre più avvertibile un sentore di conflitto in atto, accompagnato dalle avvisaglie di una violenza di tipo affatto nuovo e inquietante.[28]

> [it was the character of Italian society itself that changed, and in such a way that it seemed to require commentary in a dramatic rather than a comic key. In the years following 1968, the sense became ever

27 Mary P. Wood, *Italian Cinema* (Oxford: Berg, 2005), 47.
28 Masolino d'Amico, *La commedia all'italiana: il cinema comico in Italia dal 1945 al 1975*, 2nd edn (Milan: Il Saggiatore, 2008).

stronger that there was a conflict taking place, borne out by evidence of a completely new and alarming form of violence].

One could perhaps make the account of the demise of the *commedia di costume-all'italiana* more precise by considering the genre in terms of what it was equipped to achieve, given the circumstances of its birth and the character it had established over its decade and a half of life. The signal merit of the *commedia all'italiana* was that it could locate terrorist violence as but one aspect of the violence that permeated Italian society; it could portray terrorism, in other words, as yet another grotesque feature of contemporary behaviour, and so refuse the demonization of the terrorists by insisting on the indigenous character of their actions. However, in order to do so, it was obliged to filter terrorism through the experience of its stock male types. In short, the very character-type that enabled the ferocity of the satire in a film like *Un borghese piccolo piccolo* also limited what could be said by the filmmakers in a comic mode: for Alberto Sordi to become a ruthless vigilante was to sound the death-knell of the typical Sordi character as a comic figure (with some reason, Monicelli describes *Un borghese piccolo piccolo* as the gravestone of the *commedia all'italiana*).[29] To put it another way, the comedy of manners could only present the conditions of the *anni di piombo* as symptomatic of the *qualunquismo* or foolishness of its inherited character-types. Only with difficulty, and at mortal danger to themselves, could these types be imagined planting a bomb in a train station.

The Last Laugh

However, that aspect of the genre which implied its demise was to prove useful for the exercise in comedy that was *La tragedia di un uomo ridicolo*, and so it ensured the *commedia all'italiana* a late if last laugh. This aspect might be glossed as 'generational': by the mid-1970s the screenwriters and directors of the 'Golden Age' comedies (those made in the years 1959–64), and the actors so closely identified with them, were fast passing the age when they could pretend to be the protagonists of the period.

The representation of the young in the films of the 1970s was the representation of a generation alien to the actors and producers of the *commedia all'italiana*; as a consequence, in many of the films the young are shown as strange, uncommunicative, even ugly and dangerous. In *Caro papà*, for example, the young are inscrutable,

---

29 Fabrizio Borghini, *Mario Monicelli: cinquantanni di cinema* (Pisa: Edizioni Master, 1985), 120.

hirsute and menacing. Always in groups, they glower, resentful and taciturn, from the corner at a luxurious party, or ridicule a cowed professor in the corridors of 'La Sapienza' (Rome's oldest and largest university). It was a perception of the young notoriously shared by no less a figure than Pier Paolo Pasolini, and the views he expressed in the journalism of his final years are deliberately echoed in a key piece of dialogue from *La tragedia di un uomo ridicolo*. Ugo Tognazzi speaks these lines as Primo Spaggiari:

> I figli che ci circondano sono dei mostri, più pallidi di come eravamo noi. Hanno occhi spenti. Trattano i padri con troppo rispetto oppure con troppo disprezzo. Non sono più capaci di ridere: sghignazzano. O sono cupi. E soprattutto non parlano più. E noi non sappiamo capire dal loro silenzio se chiedono aiuto o se stanno per spararti addosso. Sono dei criminali.[30]

> [The children around us are monsters, paler than we used to be. They have dead eyes. They treat their fathers with too much respect or with too much disdain. They're no longer capable of laughter: they sneer instead. Or act surly. Most of all, they no longer speak. And we don't know if their silence means they're asking for help or that they're about to shoot us. They are criminals.]

The merging of the *commedia* type represented by Tognazzi and the radical intellectual exemplified by Pasolini is droll and bizarre, though both men were in fact exactly the same age (they were born in the same month in 1922, though Pasolini had been murdered in 1975); Primo therefore represents the exhaustion of a whole stratum of postwar Italians, and especially of its intellectuals. We have seen, above, that intellectuals like Rosi and Bertolucci expressed a perplexity and inadequacy before the conditions of the *anni di piombo*. It is this sense of ignorance and powerlessness that we should notice in the quoted dialogue – the sense of ignorance and impotence before a generation – that, in the films, stands in for the evolution of Italian society beyond the comprehension of its former protagonists. The ageing 'father' is therefore to be read figuratively as a forebear in intellectual decline: 'questo padre prende atto di non avere più gli strumenti per comprendere quanto accade intorno a sé e rinuncia a capire' (De Franceschi, 307) [this father realizes that he no longer has the tools to understand what is going on around him and he gives up trying to understand].

---

30   See Pasolini, *Lettere luterane* (Turin: Einaudi, 1976), 7–8, for the expression of similar sentiments.

Of course there is a generational aspect implied also in the adoption, by Bertolucci, of the mode of the *commedia all'italiana* itself, the mode of the 'fathers' before him:[31]

Possiamo allora azzardare l'ipotesi che Bertolucci, ne *La tragedia di un uomo ridicolo*, abbia voluto da un lato fare i conti con la tradizione della commedia cinematografica italiana (territorio da lui non frequentato, ma in qualche modo incombente, come la figura paterna) e, dall'altro, abbia anche voluto 'giocare a fare il padre', sperimentarsi per una volta dall'altra parte del rapporto che dà luogo al conflitto edipico così intensamente esplorato in altri film precedenti e, è lecito credere, nell'avventura dell'analisi. (Deriu, 281)

[We can therefore propose that Bertolucci, in *La tragedia di un uomo ridicolo*, wanted, on the one hand, to settle his accounts with the comic tradition in Italian cinema (a territory he had avoided, but which was in some way oppressive, like the figure of the father). We can also suggest, on the other hand, that he wanted 'to play at being the father': wanted to experience for once what it felt like to be at the other pole of the relationship that generates the Oedipal conflict so intensely explored in previous films and, one may safely assume, during the experience of psychoanalysis.]

The link between the use of the comic mode and the identification with the father needs to be situated in the context of the social and political situation in Italy, as perceived and experienced by intellectuals in the period. In identifying himself with the father, and in adopting the mode of the fathers, Bertolucci is admitting the exhaustion of the agency and certainties of a form of political cinema, and is admitting the disorientation of the intellectual confronted with the perplexing circumstances of the *anni di piombo*.

---

31   I am mimicking here a critical habit of thinking of Italian cinema in the masculine, indeed the Oedipal terms of paternities and anxieties of influence or displacement. In an essay tellingly entitled 'Dopo la morte dei padri' [After the death of the fathers], Vito Zagarrio talks of a triangle of the generations in Italian cinema in the late 1970s, made up of the 'vecchi maestri' [old masters] of the great auteurs and the directors of the *commedia all'italiana* at one corner, the 'nuovi maestri' [new masters] of Bertolucci at another, and the 'esordi eccellenti' [talented newcomers] of Moretti, Giordana and Bertolucci *frère* (Giuseppe) at the third (15–16). On this account, Bernardo Bertolucci is adopting the attitude and means of the 'fathers' by working within the *commedia all'italiana*. Vito Zagarrio, 'Dopo la morte dei padri: dagli anni della crisi agli arbori della rinascita', in Zagarrio, *Storia del cinema italiano*, 3–39. For a critique of the metaphor of fathers and sons in the critical discourse of Italian cinema, see Catherine O'Rawe, '"I padri e i maestri": Genre, Auteurs, and Absences in Italian Film Studies', *Italian Studies*, 63: 2 (2008), 173–94.

Conclusion: A Potent Obsolescence?

I have asked why the mode of the *commedia all'italiana* was felt to be appropriate for Bertolucci's representation of the atmosphere of the *anni di piombo* in *La tragedia di un uomo ridicolo*. The answer lies in the ambivalent attitudes to their subject material which was native to the *commedia* cineastes, and in the consequent ambiguity of the representation of that subject matter in individual films. I have also asked why Bertolucci shifts from a focus on the son to a focus on the father, and why he does so precisely in the context of his narrative of the *anni di piombo*. The answer lies in the fact that the figure of the father, caught in all his tragi-comic and impotent perplexity before the circumstances of his time, reflects the position of the intellectual faced with the unfathomable problem of terrorism.

The *commedia all'italiana* had the capacity to apprehend early the phenomenon of terrorism and the conditions of the *anni di piombo* because it could embed its stock types in the evolving array of the Italian comedy of manners. But the reliance on these stock types, incarnated in the familiar ageing *divi*, also implied the exhaustion of the mode along with its star protagonists. The marginalization of the ageing protagonist from the 'manners' that surrounded him was reflected, at the artistic and market level, in the increasing marginalization of the *commedia all'italiana* itself; conversely, this made it the appropriate mode in which to embody and symbolize the impotence and marginalization of the intellectual in the same period. The paradox that generates *La tragedia di un uomo ridicolo* is that the potency of the *commedia di costume* inhered in its obsolescence; it was precisely for the reasons that the *commedia all'italiana* had exhausted its explanatory power that it retained, for Bertolucci, its capacity to characterize the times.

3. Primetime Terror: Representations of the Armed Struggle in TV Drama

Giancarlo Lombardi

Italy recently celebrated fifty years of television and much was said, on that occasion, about the role played by the medium in the life of an entire population.[1] Initially the focus of a group experience mostly occurring in public places (the TV set entered bars and cinemas long before it crossed the threshold of many Italian homes), television soon became a determining factor in the acquisition of literacy in the most remote areas of the country. The common saying according to which RAI and its omnipresent variety programme host, Mike Bongiorno, unified the country much more than Cavour and Garibaldi ever did, attests to the importance of a medium that provided a country known for its internal divisions and inequalities with a common language and a common cultural repertoire. Programmes such as *Non è mai troppo tardi* (*It's Never Too Late*, 1960) and *Una risposta per voi* (*An Answer for You All*, 1954) were created with a clear didactic purpose: the TV set replaced the teacher's desk and the dinner table became a school desk for the many Italians who had dropped out of school at a very early age. The unprecedented success of Bongiorno's *Lascia o raddoppia* (*Double or Fold*, 1955) spoke about a country in which it was felt that, through hard study, even the most ordinary person could become an overnight sensation.[2]

1 For several months, one of the most popular TV personalities, Pippo Baudo, hosted a weekly show appropriately entitled *50*; the role played by television in Italy was indeed discussed and analysed at length.
2 The importance of *Lascia o raddoppia* is acknowledged by one of Umberto Eco's most famous essays, 'Fenomenologia di Mike Bongiorno', in *Diario minimo* (Milan: Bompiani, 1963), 30–35.

Alongside these programmes, an entire genre began to provide cultural competence while satiating the viewers' thirst for story-telling: the weekly appointment with the mini-series adaptations of literary texts, the earliest form of Italian TV drama, brought together people of all ages through its 'bardic' function.[3] Mostly based on European and American literary masterpieces, these productions domesticated a world that had long seemed distant and unapproachable for many Italians. Figures such as Jane Eyre, Heathcliff, Aeneas and Emma Bovary became familiar even to those Italians who had never been to school, and when *Les Misérables* was broadcast to general acclaim in 1964, Cosetta suddenly became a very popular name among expecting parents.[4] When the format withered away in the early 1980s, replaced by the more affordable imports from the United States, an entire industry appeared to be virtually disbanded. The sign of a time that witnessed a much higher level of literacy, this event was not, however, as definitive and extreme as a glimpse at the weekly television schedule would suggest. Gone were the many literary adaptations 'made in Italy', but in their place, alongside *Dallas, Dynasty*, and *Charlie's Angels*, one could trace the presence of a new product that bore the imprint of the old mini-series. From the ashes of this genre, in fact, a new form of drama had arisen, a product that spoke about its times, no longer traced the historical and cultural roots of the Western world, but chose instead to reflect (or refract, as I will later discuss) the present.

Most studies of Italian TV drama will usually refer to the many instalments of *La piovra* (*The Octopus*, 1984–2001) to signify this shift, and they are indeed correct in identifying this mini-series as the earliest popular successor of the traditional literary format: not only did it beat its American competitors in the Italian market, but it was the sole programme to be exported at a time when the TV schedule relied quite heavily on programmes produced overseas.

3   TV's bardic function was initially conceptualized by John Fiske and John Hartley in *Reading Television* (London: Methuen, 1978) and further applied, within the context of Italian television studies, by Milly Buonanno, founder of the Osservatorio sulla Fiction Italiana (Observatory on Italian Fiction) in several works, most notably *Il bardo sonnacchioso: la fiction italiana, l'Italia nella fiction. Anno Quinto* [trans.] (Turin: ERI/VQPT, 1994); *Indigeni si diventa: locale e globale nella serialità televisiva* [trans.] (Milan: Sansoni, 1999); and *Le formule del racconto televisivo: la sovversione del tempo nelle narrative seriali* [trans.] (Milan: Sansoni, 2002).
4   For a detailed discussion of the history of the *sceneggiato* (a novel adaptation on television, usually in serial form) see Luisella Bolla, *Incantesimi: Alice nel paese della fiction* (Florence: Vallecchi, 2004).

Melodramatic yet politically engaged, *La piovra* lifted the veil on one of the social concerns that most preoccupied the Italian population: organized crime. On a less successful note, a handful of mini-series and two-part dramas tackled the other phenomenon that shared with the mafia many pages of the newspapers of the time, evoking fear and anxiety: terrorism. This essay will attempt to fill a void in Italian TV studies by analysing the representation of terrorism in Italian TV drama. My critical reading will be developed along two different axes and, as a consequence, in two different stages. First, I will discuss the specific treatment of this subject matter in four different dramas, and thereafter I will conclude with an institutional analysis of the politics of scheduling for *Attacco allo stato* (*Attack on the State*, Michele Soavi, 2006), the most recent of these productions.

In a recent essay on the cinema of Italian terrorism, Alan O'Leary claims that one of its functions was to 'reintegrate the alien'.[5] This function is limited to a group of films that appeared after 1995, a period that witnessed a heated debate on the possibility of granting state pardon to terrorists incarcerated for more than a decade.[6] During this period, which saw the production of several important films on the subject, terrorism virtually disappeared from the TV screen, at least as a topic for prime-time drama. The only exception was *La meglio gioventù* (*The Best of Youth*, Marco Tullio Giordana, 2003), which will not be analysed in my essay for three reasons: firstly, it is analysed in detail elsewhere in this volume; secondly, its treatment of terrorism is, I believe, rather cursory and incidental; and finally, although initially destined for television, it was released in cinemas long before its appearance on RAI Uno, and should therefore be considered a film and not, strictly, a mini-series.

O'Leary's taxonomy of cinematic representations of terrorism identifies three stages preceding the one dedicated to the reintegration of the alien: historical proximity to the *anni di piombo* connotes the first two, with the Moro affair acting as separating landmark, whereas the context of *pentitismo* (the phenomenon of terrorists collaborating with justice) characterizes the third, which refers to films produced from the mid-1980s to the mid-1990s. Of the four dramas I will

5   Alan O'Leary, 'Film and the *Anni di Piombo*: Representations of Politically-Motivated Violence in Recent Italian Cinema', in *Culture, Censorship and the State in Twentieth-Century Italy*, ed. Guido Bonsaver and Robert S. C. Gordon (Oxford: Legenda, 2005), 175.
6   For a discussion of state pardon in relationship to Italian cinematic representations of terrorism see Giancarlo Lombardi, 'Unforgiven: Revisiting Political Terrorism in *La seconda volta*', *Italica*, 77:2 (2000), 199–213.

analyse, *Parole e sangue* (*Words and Blood*, Damiano Damiani, 1982) falls squarely in the post-Moro period, while *Nucleo Zero* (*Nucleus Zero*, Carlo Lizzani, 1984) and *Donne armate* (*Women in Arms*, Sergio Corbucci, 1990) engage fairly directly with the question of *pentitismo* and the end of political terrorism. *Attacco allo stato* falls outside O'Leary's categorization, not only because of its recent appearance, but also because of its nature of docudrama, which would ideally place it alongside the very first film on the Moro affair, *Il caso Moro* (*The Moro Case*, Giuseppe Ferrara, 1988), similarly identified by O'Leary as anomalous.

Of (Bad) Pupils and Masters: *Parole e Sangue*

Damiano Damiani has long been associated with the tradition of politically engaged cinema, which he adapted successfully to the small screen in 1984 with the first instalment of *La piovra*. As previously mentioned, his portrayal of a heroic detective who wages war against organized crime generated enormous media attention and unprecedented audience ratings, contrary to what had happened two years earlier, when RAI broadcast *Parole e sangue* for the first time. The story of Rico, an aspiring terrorist who becomes the leader of a dilettante cell which stages the abduction and the eventual murder of a judge, *Parole e sangue* failed to pique the curiosity of the viewers probably because it did not establish a powerful character involved in a battle of good vs. evil, choosing to narrate the events through the eyes of an anti-hero. In contrast, Milly Buonanno ascribes the success of *La piovra* to strong characterization, coupled with an eclectic combination of genres and a balanced portrayal of a phenomenon that she identifies as the great Italian obsession. Just as *La piovra*'s Corrado Cattani is portrayed as a 'personaggio innegabilmente complesso – a tratti sovrumano per temerarietà e invulnerabilità, a tratti umano, troppo umano [...] un cavaliere senza paura, ma non senza macchia'[7] [an undeniably complex character – at times superhuman for his temerity and invulnerability, at times human, all too human [...] a fearless, but not squeaky clean, knight], the protagonist of *Parole e sangue* appears as his exact antithesis: portrayed with the simplicity of most stock characters, the cowardly Rico shows his courage only in words, inciting others to do his dirty work.

7 Milly Buonanno, *Narrami o diva: studi sull'immaginario televisivo* (Naples: Liguori, 1994), 50. For a monographic study of this drama, see Buonanno, *La piovra: la carriera politica di una fiction popolare* (Genoa and Milan: Costa & Nolan, 1996).

Evoked in its very title, the binary opposition of words and blood, signifying a symbolic schism between ideology and action, rests at the core of Damiani's mini-series. Words here not only come to represent Rico's logorrhoeic monologues on the private radio where he works, nor do they refer solely to the many speeches through which he indoctrinates his peasant cellmate and his bourgeois girlfriend, they also bear direct reference to the mendacious attitude through which he recruits the members of his group. Every time Rico reports on his ongoing relations with the leadership of his organization, he is just lying, since the mysterious terrorist organization from which he is seeking recognition refuses to acknowledge the legitimacy of his claim, thus reducing his statements to 'parole, soltanto parole' [words, only words], as one of the most popular songs of the time put it.

Indoctrination and proselytism are key concepts in the slow development of the story-line: *Parole e sangue* opens with Rico issuing a call to arms on the radio, and soon thereafter, upon his incarceration, he is portrayed again preaching political involvement to illiterate, common (i.e., non-political) prisoners. It is the power of his words that converts Antonio, a peasant convicted for a minor crime, and that ultimately drives him to a dramatic prison break. It is also the power of his words that shakes Fausta away from her bourgeois existence, prompting her to leave behind a rich family, steal her husband's gun and become the first person in the group to pull a trigger and convert words into blood. Damiani's portrayal of the *cattivo maestro* [bad teacher], such a cogent theme in the days which had witnessed the indictment of academics such as Toni Negri and Enrico Fenzi, is further complicated by the presence of Judge Marcucci, who was once Rico's professor, and who is kidnapped and killed by his organization in ways that are likely to remind viewers of the Moro affair. Although Aldo Moro was himself a professor, Marcucci's figure bears no direct reference or resemblance to that of the President of the Democrazia Cristiana. It is through the portrayal of Marcucci, however, that the director's didactic intent becomes more evident, turning *Parole e sangue* into something like a moral fable. Although the line separating good and bad teachers may appear to be blurred in light of the fact that Marcucci (the good teacher) had actually counted Rico (the bad teacher) among his most devoted pupils, Damiani portrays, in no uncertain terms, the unexpected consequences that the profound bond between master and pupil might carry. In an extremely conservative turn, Damiani has Marcucci fall prey to his own liberalism when he opens himself and his world to an ungrateful Rico, who is able to play double agent and plot his abduction while pretending to be an affectionate family friend.

What counts most here is once again the power of words, the words symbolically uttered by Marcucci when discussing his current research on terrorism and communication. The author of a book called *Pena di morte? No, grazie!* [*Capital Punishment? No Thanks!*] and thus representative of what Fenzi once ironically called 'un'estrema sinistra *buona* da contrapporre alla *cattiva'* [a *good* extreme left to be opposed to the *bad* one],[8] Marcucci criticizes the language of absolute incommunicability employed by Rico and others of his generation. Although he appears, at one point, to have supported the student revolts, he now claims that the obscurity of their language is as oppressive as that of the establishment they are strenuously attacking. At a time when the most basic words (he mentions 'liberty', 'justice' and 'friendship') have lost their referent as well as their denotative power, the only coincidence of signifier and signified occurs with murder: 'la morte è il caso unico in cui parola e fatto che esprime sono gli stessi' [death is the only instance in which the word and the fact it expresses coincide].

Yet inflicting death, identified by Marcucci as terrorism's symbolic message, eventually undoes the efforts of any terrorist organization because it will always further their estrangement from the masses they are claiming to defend: 'Le vittime del terrorismo, se identificate come nemici delle masse dalle masse, porterebbero al successo di questo messaggio simbolico, ma le masse non reagiscono così, vogliono la vita e non la morte. Se continuano a lungo così, la gente reagirà' [The victims of terrorism, if identified as enemies of the masses by the masses, would lead to the success of this symbolic message, but masses do not react like this, they want life not death. If they go on like this, the population will react]. And it is indeed failed communication that eventually causes Marcucci's execution – the jurist who had loudly proclaimed his opposition to the death penalty falls victim to the young men and women he once empowered through his words and eventually alienated by highlighting their inability to communicate. Preferring dialogue to action, Damiani peppers his cautionary tale with well-argued tirades against the young men and women who have embraced the armed struggle, so that *Parole e sangue* can be seen as a product willingly created to discourage its

8   Enrico Fenzi, *Armi e bagagli: un diario delle Brigate Rosse* (Genoa and Milan: Costa & Nolan, 1998), 214.

viewers from considering such a choice.[9] However, by the time of its appearance, the days of deregulated radio broadcasting and the student revolts had long passed – the early 1980s led the youngest members of the population away from political engagement, and directed them towards the same bourgeois conformism that would act as a powerful disguise for some of the protagonists of Lizzani's *Nucleo zero*.

Terror in Stealth Mode: *Nucleo Zero*

Nucleo zero (1984) is not the first encounter with terrorism for Carlo Lizzani, a prolific director who had already confronted this issue in 1977 in *Kleinhoff Hotel,* an erotic thriller which portrayed the doomed encounter between a married woman and a German revolutionary. Seven years later, Lizzani found inspiration in a novel by Luce D'Eramo published in 1981, a novel he adapted rather loosely, while remaining faithful to its spirit and its characterization. Filmed and broadcast at a time that was witnessing the slow but steady demise of the largest terrorist organizations, *Nucleo zero* tells the story of a small group of terrorists who have managed to remain untouched because of their ability to act in 'stealth' mode.

The opening scene sets up the unique position of its members by portraying the unexpected arrest of a member of a much larger and more visible organization, Ottobre Rosso, under the very eyes of one of the leaders of Nucleo Zero. What is most disturbing, and particularly essential for a critical reading of this two-part drama, is the context in which this arrest takes place: the sequence opens with a bank robbery, and the burglars who take a hostage are soon revealed to be policemen who have staged this crime to apprehend a terrorist who has long lived a double life working as a bank clerk. This initial reversal of roles, which forces viewers to suspend and reformulate their initial judgement of the very first characters portrayed on the screen, is a *mise-en-abîme* of the viewer identification predicated by the entire mini-series, which will afford the audience only one orienting perspective, that of the members of the terrorist organization. By choosing to destabilize viewers' alignment and allegiance from the very first scene, Lizzani ushers us into a world where nothing can be taken at face value, a world we are asked to experience from the most

---

9   The 'verbose' quality of this drama clearly sets it apart from *La piovra*, which capitalized on the basic tenets of action cinema while retaining a good level of social engagement.

uncomfortable position, that of criminals whose values and actions we are not likely to share.[10]

The anonymity afforded to the members of Nucleo Zero is powerfully rendered by their frequent meetings, held in remote underground train carriages shortly before the train reaches the end of the line, once the other passengers have got off. It is in these scenes that viewers meet the large cast of characters that make up the organization: because they are far too many, the audience is likely to feel disoriented, re-experiencing the same feeling of confusion already evoked in the opening sequence. Too many to be tracked down, too similar to every other passenger on the subway, the terrorists may act undisturbed, in the first part of the drama, under our very eyes as well as those of the population that surrounds them. The inserts that portray the underground train rushing in the dark tunnel act as counter-shots to the frames that witness their meetings. Just like the train, which operates in only apparent darkness, since its destination is clearly known to its conductor and its passengers, the Nucleo Zero organization may seem initially to operate randomly, at the mercy of too many thinking heads, but its direction is clear, just as its inevitable ending point (its demise) is waiting at the end of the line. When its members suddenly disperse, jumping off the subway, afraid that they may have been recognized by a policeman, the terrorists are seen rushing along the tunnels of several subway stations like so many frightened mice.

While Damiani elected to portray terrorism through the cautionary tale of a handful of amateurs, Lizzani focuses on a group of professionals, who have chosen the armed struggle, as one of them says in a voiceover, as a profession and as 'un modo di estrarre l'ordine dal caos' [a way of making order out of chaos]. The long ideological discussions introduced in *Parole e sangue* are here presented in hindsight: metaphorically placed on a high velocity underground train that is leading them to self-destruction, they will say 'ne abbiamo fatta di strada da quando ci occupavamo della

---

10 In *Engaging Characters: Fiction, Emotion, and the Cinema* (Oxford: Oxford University Press, 1995), Murray Smith breaks down the monolithic concept of viewer identification as postulated by theorists such as Laura Mulvey and Mary Ann Doane in order to define three sub-categories which shape the way the audience relates to a film. Recognition, alignment, and allegiance are the names given to these three phenomena, recognition referring to 'the spectator's construction of character' (82); alignment describing 'the process by which spectators are placed in relation to characters in terms of access to their actions, and to what they know and feel' (83); and allegiance pertaining to 'the moral evaluation of characters by the spectator'(84).

lotta di classe' [we have come a long way since we were involved in the class struggle]. Instead of striking at the heart of the state, as Rico and his friends did, the protagonists of *Nucleo zero* kidnap an industrialist and engage in a multiple robbery: in both cases, they are seeking exclusively economic remuneration, possibly for self-financing purposes, and ideology is blatantly absent from their actions. Their source of inspiration is not the Tupamaros but the mafia, which has taught them a lesson in the importance of stealth mode: 'bisogna imparare dalla mafia, da tutti i contropoteri che durano da secoli. Il silenzio come risposta al fragore del nazismo di ieri e dello stato imperialista di oggi, e dei suoi nemici impazziti' [we need to learn from the mafia and from all counter-powers that have lasted for centuries. We need to choose silence as our response to the thundering noise of yesterday's Nazism and today's imperialist state and its crazed enemies].

More bourgeois than revolutionaries, the members of *Nucleo zero* revel in an exhibitionism which is however clearly denied by their clandestinity. Although they cherish until the very end the protection afforded by the fact that, to the press and the police, 'Nucleo zero non è mai esistito' [Nucleo zero has never existed], they are often portrayed as actors on a stage: in this light, the voiceovers which frequently accompany their actions could be seen as theatrical asides. We should read the backdrop to their final arrest in similar terms: we are confronted with a countryside setting which is first presented with Arcadian overtones and then transformed into the site of the miscarriage of one of the female terrorists, shortly before the arrival of the police. The unborn child thus becomes the metaphorical expression of a utopian future that cannot be realized, a utopia that was originally meant to be staged on what the leader of the group once called, conjuring up their undeniable exhibitionism, an empty theatre: 'l'esibizionismo, malattia infantile del terrorismo, simulare, fingere, la risorsa più antica dell'uomo, necessaria per sopravvivere, anche in un teatro vuoto, piano piano il pubblico verrà' [exhibitionism – the childish disease of terrorism – simulation and pretension are the oldest human resources, necessary for our survival: even in an empty theatre, little by little the audience will come].

The audience that comes for Nucleo zero, however, is very different from the one they had anticipated, as the drama ends with a brief glance at the public trial where the organization appears one last time on stage. The only member who has not been charged sits on the opposite side of the courtroom: he is the *pentito* who, by collaborating with justice, may accelerate the downfall of his former partners in crime. Like *Parole e sangue*, then, *Nucleo zero* stages a cautionary tale. However, instead of a warning to youth about the dangers of political involvement, Lizzani's alert resembles the alarm issued all over the Western world after the 11 September attacks: his portrayal of an organization which successfully operates in stealth mode, in fact, seems to invite viewers to paranoia, reminding them to take a closer look at their surroundings, those very surroundings where even their neighbour, someone they have known all their life, could indeed be harbouring a dangerous secret.

Women and Terror: *Donne Armate*

In a study on the role of women in Italian television in the early 1980s, Milly Buonanno stated that violence in prime-time drama was almost exclusively a male domain: 'Le donne sono quasi del tutto escluse dall'esercizio attivo dell'aggressività e della violenza fisica e non ne sono neppure le vittime predestinate: press'a poco nel 90% dei casi, la violenza fisica rimane interna al mondo degli uomini, viene esercitata e subita dagli uomini stessi' [Women are almost entirely excluded from the active exercise of aggressiveness and physical violence, and are not even their predestined victims: in more or less 90% of cases, physical violence remains internal to the male universe, it is performed by and on men].[11] The two remaining productions dedicated to terrorism seem to challenge this statement, however, because they both centre on strong portrayals of women terrorists. Let us not forget that, although the limited portrayal of violent women was, as Buonanno states, 'il riflesso di una definizione culturale della donna quale essere estraneo alla violenza' [the reflection of a cultural definition of woman as extraneous to violence], political terrorism had a long tradition of female involvement in Italy and Germany. Terrorist organizations of the extreme left and right were often headed by couples who soon came to acquire iconic overtones *à la* Bonnie and Clyde: Mara Cagol and Renato Curcio were among the founders of the Brigate Rosse, Barbara Balzerani and Mario Moretti headed the military reconstruction of the organization after Cagol's death and Curcio's arrest, Susanna Ronconi and Sergio Segio were two of the leaders of Prima Linea, and at the opposite end of the

---

11   Milly Buonanno, *Cultura di massa e identità femminile: l'immagine della donna in televisione* (Turin: ERI, 1983), 75.

political spectrum Francesca Mambro and Giusva Fioravanti were at the helm of the Nuclei Armati Rivoluzionari.[12]

Donne armate (1990), the final chapter in Sergio Corbucci's long directorial career, represented a notable departure from the body of comedies and spaghetti westerns that constitute the majority of his output. This two-part drama is named after two very different women: an escaped terrorist and the prison officer who unintentionally allows her to flee. Initially portrayed as rivals, the two are soon brought together by the realization that they are both victims of a corrupt official who has facilitated the escape of the terrorist so that she can be killed soon after, while the police officer is intended to be a mere pawn who will forfeit her career for her induced negligence. Although the set-up and the time-frame seem to allow for immediate contextual reference, Nadia and Angela are no Thelma and Louise: Corbucci's hand is much heavier in the depiction of a universe with no grey areas, mostly populated by cardboard characters. Apparent victims of men portrayed as corrupt and calculating sexual predators, the two protagonists survive on the strength of their weapons and these weapons eventually phallicize them, making them threatening and almost as invulnerable as the male protagonists of a spaghetti western.

Corbucci's world is clearly divided along gender lines, and the women either demonstrate great solidarity with one another or they perish for their attempt to cross over to the darker, masculine side. When Nadia and Angela start dancing in a night-club, trying to stave off the sexual overtures of the men around them, the director is paying homage to Bertolucci's *Il conformista* (*The Conformist*, 1970), yet its only intertextual reference can be located in a generic evocation of the treacherous and seductive world of the Secret Service, which ruins the protagonist of Bertolucci's film and threatens the safety of the protagonists of *Donne armate*. Ultimately, what remains of this mini-series is a rather incidental portrayal of terrorism as an event from the past, an event that has shaped a character whose suffering is safely hidden by an aggressive exteriority; because of the predicaments with which she is faced, viewers are meant to sympathize with Nadia, the abrasive terrorist, especially in light of the loyalty she displays in the end, as she interrupts her escape to go back and save Angela. Behind her abrasiveness lie courage, loyalty and great intelligence, demonstrated by her ability to solve the complex plot laid out at her expense. Regardless of these virtues, she still remains a criminal; her

12 The BR commando that conducted Aldo Moro's abduction also contained two other famous couples: Anna Laura Braghetti and Prospero Gallinari, and Adriana Faranda and Valerio Morucci.

final escape cannot be tolerated and she is, inevitably, returned to jail at the close of the drama.

Although, chronologically, *Donne armate* belongs to the visual representations of terrorism informed by the events of *pentitismo*, this is probably the closest an Italian television production has ever come to reintegrating O'Leary's alien, even if such a reintegration is not actual but virtual, since Nadia's physical imprisonment is counteracted by a display of nobility of character. Quite appropriately, the song accompanying the closing credits, sung by Lina Sastri, the actress who plays Nadia, tells the story of a woman who acknowledges the many mistakes she has made, and realizes that her loneliness is a necessary state of her present condition:

> ma che ce penz'affà
> tante 'sta vita me l'aggio giucata accussì [...]
> nun me n'importa si nun me vulite
> addà sta sule pe' pute' cantà

> [why do I keep thinking about it
> I gave my life away like this [...]
> I don't care if you don't want me
> you've got to be alone if you want to sing].

Strengthened by what Buonanno identifies as 'l'asprezza senza ritorno di una vita sprecata nelle scelte di violenza dei "tempi brutti" che raggiunge spesso accenti di verità' [the unfailing sourness of a life wasted on the violence of the 'bad times', often portrayed in realistic fashion], this portrayal of the woman terrorist paves the way for the more nuanced characterizations that were to appear, in the years that follow, on the big screen.[13]

Unsung Heroes: *Attacco allo Stato*

No longer the object of current fears, political terrorism became a phenomenon that, in the 1990s, appeared to invite historicizing reflections; yet the Brigate Rosse resurfaced at the end of that decade, shooting and killing Massimo D'Antona in 1999, and proving that the last decade had indeed been 'uno *stand by* tanto lungo da assomigliare a una pace' [a time-out that lasted so long it actually resembled

---

13   Milly Buonanno, 'Donne Armate', in *Sceneggiare la cronaca: la fiction italiana, l'Italia nella fiction. Anno Terzo*, ed. Milly Buonanno (Turin: VQPT Nuova Eri, 1992), 149.

peace].[14] Indeed, the murder of Massimo D'Antona, followed three years later by that of Marco Biagi, reopened old wounds and generated a new and different reflection on political terrorism in Italy. Following the 11 September attacks, terrorism has assumed new paralysing overtones which have pervaded the discourse of the media. Three years after the Moro affair was revisited on the big screen by Marco Bellocchio and Renzo Martinelli, Michele Soavi directed a docudrama on the return of the Brigate Rosse, refusing to gain the critical distance that waiting a few more years would have afforded him. His portrayal of the return of the BR does not partake of the paranoid attitude towards terrorism that characterizes much American television (24 is the most blatant example of this discourse) because it falls within a different genre of television drama, which has increasingly gained visibility and acclaim in Italy during the past decade: it is a celebratory, almost epic form of docudrama which aims to praise the glorious achievement of a number of unsung heroes. The Holocaust, mafia and terrorism have been the subject, in recent times, of a number of mini-series whose protagonists are not the forces of evil, but the forces of good that have successfully fought against evil. Ideal successors of *La piovra's* Cattani, the protagonists of *Ultimo* (*Ultimate*, Stefano Reali, 1998), *Marcinelle* (*Inferno Below*, Andrea and Antonio Frazzi, 2003), *Perlasca* (*Perlasca: The Courage of a Just Man*, Alberto Negrin, 2002) and *Attacco allo stato*, to name but a few, acquired notoriety through dramatizations that inevitably simplify the complex histories that are their subject.[15]

Derek Paget maintains that the main goals of docudrama are 'to re-tell events from national or international histories, either reviewing or celebrating these events; to re-present the careers of significant national or international figures [...]; to portray issues of concern to national or international communities in order to provoke discussion about them'.[16] Soavi portrays the actions of the new Brigate Rosse in the spirit outlined by Paget: presented as a group of

14   Pino Casamassima, *Donne di piombo: undici vite nella lotta armata* (Milan: Bevivino, 2005), 143.
15   The most successful primetime mini-series produced in Italy during the last ten years, *Ultimo, Perlasca* and *Marcinelle* dramatize real events that occurred during the last century. *Ultimo* tells the story of a heroic *carabiniere* captain who wages war against the mafia, *Perlasca* portrays the life of the man who has come to be remembered as the Italian Schindler, while *Marcinelle* re-tells the events surrounding the death of many Italian mineworkers at Bois De Cauzier in 1956.
16   Derek Paget, 'Codes and Conventions of Dramadoc and Docudrama', in *The Television Studies Reader*, ed. Robert C. Allen and Annette Hill (London and New York: Routledge, 2004), 196.

dangerous but incompetent fanatics, the terrorists are displaced in the diegesis by the special team of detectives who will soon disband them. It is no accident that, at the helm of this team, Soavi places a carabiniere captain portrayed by Raoul Bova, the fierce warrior who fought the mafia in the last instalment of *La piovra* and again in the three instalments of *Ultimo*. Visually narrated in the post-MTV style common to much contemporary Italian crime drama, *Attacco allo stato* hides poor characterization and conventional dramatic development behind sophisticated shot composition, eccentric camera movements and a striking use of cool colours. Viewers are thus indirectly invited to read the murders of D'Antona and Biagi in the light of the eventual apprehension of their perpetrators, and not as dangerous and dramatic symptoms of the reappearance of a social malaise signified by the recurrence of terrorism.

Caught in a universe that recalls *CSI, Law and Order* as well as their Italian counterparts *Distretto di polizia* (*Police District*) and *RIS*,[17] the audience is thus lulled into accepting the extremity of Soavi's telescoping of events, as well as his creation of composite and fictional characters, common elements to docudrama here pushed further so as to fall squarely into appropriate generic conventions. The members of the captain's team are thus reduced to stock characters, and some comic mileage is derived from their being *carabinieri* officers of Southern origins. Equally reductive is the portrayal of the captain's superiors, bureaucrats prone to irrational outbursts of rage. Raoul Bova's character is the sole recipient of a balanced characterization, although Soavi cannot resist the temptation of portraying him as a modern-day lonely warrior when he pictures him repeatedly sitting at the bottom of the swimming pool, lost in deep and solitary contemplation. The terrorists are equally victims of stock characterization: the fictional counterparts of the two most famous members of the commando, Nadia Lioce and Cinzia Banelli, are portrayed in a stark contrast that is meant to signify their opposite personalities and destinies.[18] While Lioce's alter-ego, Lidia, is always alone, connected to the world through the sophisticated technology that will eventually betray her, Banelli's Carla is seen leading a true double life, her duties as teacher and wife openly contrasting with her commitment to the Brigate Rosse. As a consequence, much is made

---

17 R.I.S., the acronym of Reparto Informazioni e Sicurezza [Security and Intelligence Division] refers to the secret service branch of the Italian armed forces.

18 For a contrastive discussion of these two figures, see Casamassima, 131–47.

on a diegetic level of Lidia's decision to try and expel Carla from the group: because this decision will lead to the eventual downfall of the entire group, Soavi telescopes the event, overcharging it with dramatic elements and anticipating it with countless cliff-hangers. When Lidia is carted off to jail, viewers are left with the image of her resisting her captors, the disturbing waving of her Medusa hair to remind them of the extreme danger she once posed; Carla's eventual arrest, occurring much later in the show, is anticipated by a number of extreme close-ups of one of her eyes. Carla's eye is there to remind viewers that the fear it betrays is that of a woman who is not fully committed to the armed struggle – there is another part of her (another eye/I) which will eventually lead her to collaborate with justice so that the child she is bearing will have a better future.

While generally true to the substance of the events, Soavi's presentation is clearly endowed with excessive dramatic elements, and viewers are left no room to empathize with any of the members of the Brigate Rosse, Carla included. All our sympathies are unquestionably addressed to the policemen who cannot even celebrate the success of their investigation (though it might well be argued that Soavi is doing the celebrating for them): in the final sequence of the drama, directly after the capture of the last terrorist, they receive a phone call which summons them to the football stadium, where a derby match between local teams is likely to cause violent confrontations. Behind the easy conclusion that a policeman's job, like that of a housewife, is never done, lies a bleaker, more symbolic reminder that political terrorism, even in its latest and briefest events, is a form of civil war, the civil war that is symbolically re-enacted each time two teams from the same city face each other on the football field.

Ideology and the Politics of Scheduling

A study conducted in 2003 by the Project for Excellence in Journalism revealed that, in the United States, 79 per cent of the population gets its national and international news through television.[19] It is likely that television has also now become the main source of news information for the majority of Italians. Considering that all the mini-series analysed in this article were broadcast in prime-time,

---

19   Project for Excellence in Journalism, *The State of the News Media, 2004: An Annual Report on American Journalism* (Washington, DC: Project for Excellence in Journalism, 2005), www.stateofthemedia.org/2004/ [accessed 5 August 2010].

right after the news, it is not difficult to imagine how the flowing element of television, as theorized by Raymond Williams, would lead viewers to receive their content as heavily reflective of the real world, and not as completely fictional.[20] When television dramatizes terrorism, it does so because it locates in this phenomenon elements of fictionworthiness *and* newsworthiness. If we were to assume the audience to be a passive, unresisting receiver of the ideological discourse couched in TV programming, then we would have to assume that dramas such as *Attacco allo stato* are likely to be received unproblematically as informed and objective transpositions of recent historical events. However, television has long stopped being considered a window on the world, and scholars such as David Morley and Ien Ang have taught us that worldwide audiences are not so naïve, engaging with television and its contents through a process of ideological negotiation and thus placing their position as viewers along a spectrum of possibilities that range from dominant to resistant.[21] Regardless of the viewers' ability to negotiate their relationship to the televisual text, it is imperative to question the discourse within which such a text is inscribed and, at the same time, it is equally important to combine content analysis with a discussion of institutional practices of scheduling.

Attacco allo stato was originally aired on Canale 5 on Monday 22 May and Tuesday 23 May 2006 at 9 pm, shortly after the news (*TG5*) and *Striscia la notizia*,[22] a satirical newscast that counterbalances the overtly Berlusconian ideological slant of Canale 5's news broadcasting. On the eve of its premiere, the programme had already made the news, since much discussion revolved around the reactions of the relatives of the victims of the terrorist attacks portrayed in the mini-series. Olga D'Antona, who had been invited to a VIP screening of the drama held at the University of Rome a week before, lamented the absence of reference to the direct responsibilities of government officials for the death of Marco Biagi. In particular, no reference had been made to the positions taken by the Minister for Justice, nor had there been any visual representation of the consequences suffered by

20 Raymond Williams, *Television: Technology and Cultural Form* (London: Wesleyan University Press, 1974).

21 See David Morley, *The 'Nationwide' Audience* (London: British Film Institute, 1980) and *Interpreting Audiences* (London: Sage, 1993). See also Ien Ang, *Watching Dallas* (London: Methuen, 1985) and *Watching Television* (London: Routledge, 1991).

22 The punning and rhyming title is untranslatable and can mean something like 'Drag the News' or 'The News Creeps/Slithers/Grovels'. One meaning of 'striscia' is 'strip', as in comic strip.

the Interior Minister who had been forced to resign after a man he had refused to protect had been shot by the BR. The drama summarized the condition of the victims and the patent injustice suffered by their relatives in one simple sentence, uttered by the actress portraying Marco Biagi's widow: 'Lo stato ci ha lasciato soli' [The state has abandoned us].

Broadcast immediately after the news, from which it was separated solely by advertisements, *Attacco allo stato* set out to present a version of the story that thus purported to be true, a version that celebrated the intelligence of the forces of counter-terrorism while downplaying the political responsibilities of a government led by the direct owner of the channel which broadcast the mini-series, Silvio Berlusconi. Incidentally, it is worth remembering that *Attacco allo stato* was broadcast at a significant time in the recent political history of the country, sandwiched between Berlusconi's defeat in the April 2006 election and his subsequent defeat at the institutional referendum held two months later.

It is important to combine analysis of content and institutional discourse in a study of the role played by contemporary televisual dramatizations of terrorism. At a time when terrorism has become ever more a source of anxiety worldwide, it is crucial to take a second, more direct look at the way television chooses to represent recent history. No longer a window on the world but a mirror held up by institutions whose presence deeply affects viewers' perceptions of history, television should thus be seen not as a purveyor of information but as a prism that refracts, more than reflects, an ever-changing image of our world. Whether it chooses to portray terrorism through a cautionary tale on the dangers of political militancy (*Parole e sangue*), or as an insidious presence that may lurk around the corner, in the houses of our closest neighbours (*Nucleo zero*), whether it gains distance from its destructive power by representing it incidentally (*Donne armate*) or by placing emphasis on the heroism of the civil servants who defeated it (*Attacco allo stato*), television never fails to colour the events it portrays. Its events are not presented but represented, not reflected but refracted through the prismatic ideology embodied by the institutions that regulate its discourse.

Section 2
Family Motifs and Feminizing Terror

4. Keeping it in the Family:
Politically Motivated Violence in *Tre Fratelli,* *Colpire al Cuore* and *Segreti Segreti*

Max Henninger

Italy in the 1980s: Prefatory Remarks

In 1998, the Italian radical-left journal *DeriveApprodi* published an issue devoted to the theme of exile. The contributions focused especially on the experiences of political militants who fled Italy during the late 1970s and early 1980s. These militants had been charged with crimes ranging from association with an 'armed band' to political homicide, but the fundamental 'crime' of which they were guilty was their membership of the various groups and organizations associated with the Autonomia Operaia movement. Many of those who did not flee the country were incarcerated.[1]

In their article 'Gli anni Ottanta: Le generazioni dell'esilio' [The Eighties: The generations of exile], two younger members of Italy's radical left, Antonio Conti and Andrea Tiddi, reflect on how the exile and incarceration of this generation of political militants affected their own politicization:

Esilio, dunque qualcuno è stato mandato via. Ma cosa avvenne davvero? La storia che noi, come 'giovani antagonisti' degli anni

---

1   On Autonomia Operaia, see Steve Wright, *Storming Heaven: Class Composition and Struggle in Italian Autonomist Marxism* (London: Pluto Press, 2002), 20. For general background on the radical movements that preceded Autonomia Operaia and from which it developed, see Robert Lumley, *States of Emergency: Cultures of Revolt in Italy from 1968 to 1978* (New York and London: Verso, 1990).

Ottanta, possiamo raccontare è una storia che parte da un'assenza, e un'assenza di quelle che pesano, politicamente soprattutto. [...] L'effetto più immediato dell'esilio è stato quello di una frattura generazionale.[2]

[Exile: the term implies that someone was sent away. But what really happened? The story that we, as 'young antagonists' of the 1980s, can narrate is a story that begins with the absence of those who mattered, especially politically. [...] The most immediate effect of exile has been a generational fracture.]

Conti and Tiddi emphasize that understanding the political and cultural climate of 1980s Italy requires one to reflect on the consequences of this 'generational fracture' not just for those who went into exile but also for those younger Italians like themselves who stayed behind and came of age during the years that followed. Disorientation, fear and isolation are some of the phenomena Conti and Tiddi cite as having been absolutely central to their experience of the period:

bisogna pensare l'esilio come metafora/limite della sconfitta di tutto un movimento che, da quel momento, ha trovato anche la propria fine come fenomeno collettivo, ha conosciuto una fine politica nel senso più pieno della parola. Ovverosia l'effetto esilio, l'essere fisicamente tagliati fuori dalla politica, ha funzionato non solo per chi materialmente è stato espulso dalla vita sociale, per chi è andato 'fuori' o finito 'dentro', ma anche per chi è rimasto, perché è rimasto solo, è rifluito dall'essere un soggetto collettivo a una monade individuale, spaurita, rancorosa, e che del rapporto col potere ha conservato solo la paranoia per la polizia. (19)

[we need to think of exile as the limit/metaphor of the defeat of the entire movement which, from that moment, faced its own demise as a collective movement, and came to know a political end in the fullest sense of the term. Whatever the effect of exile, being physically cut off from political engagement had consequences not only for those who were physically expelled from society, whether by going 'outside' or by ending up 'inside', but also for those who remained – because the latter were left isolated, and from being collective subjects became individual, frightened and embittered monads who retained only a paranoia about the police from their experience of engagement with power.]

---

2   Antonio Conti and Andrea Tiddi, 'Gli anni Ottanta: le generazioni dell'esilio', *DeriveApprodi*, 7: 16 (1998), 19.

Two phenomena referenced by Conti and Tiddi are relevant to discussions of contemporary Italian cinema's representations of politically motivated violence: an absence related to the political persecution of the late 1970s, and a generational discontinuity that was in no sense natural but due, rather, to specific historical and political developments (most importantly, the mass arrests of April 1979).[3] No account of the cinematic representations of *lotta armata* [armed struggle] produced in 1980s Italy would be complete without reference to these phenomena. Even the most recent cinematic representations of the period utilize a number of narrative techniques whose emergence can be traced roughly to the period between 1980 and 1985, and which need to be related to the experience Conti and Tiddi describe.

The Family as Ideological Trope

It is now common knowledge that there exists a considerable cinematic corpus narrating the politically motivated violence associated with Italy's radical left and, in particular, with clandestine insurrectionary groups such as Prima Linea and the Brigate Rosse (BR). This new awareness is largely due to the success of Marco Tullio Giordana's 2003 chronicle of post-1968 Italy, *La meglio gioventù* (*The Best of Youth*). One of the most striking features of Giordana's film is his choice to narrate the historical period in question by means of a family saga, a story of two brothers.

Giordana's choice of narrative strategy was by no means original. Family relations and generational conflict are absolutely central to such films as Francesco Rosi's *Tre fratelli* (*Three Brothers*, 1981), Gianni Amelio's *Colpire al cuore* (*Blow to the Heart*, 1982), and Giuseppe Bertolucci's *Segreti segreti* (*Secrets, Secrets*, 1984). All three of these films frame post-1968 Italy's history of political violence in terms of family and generational conflict. The persistence of this narrative

---

3   On 7 April 1979, a magistrate associated with the PCI, Pietro Calogero, issued warrants that led to the arrest of whole areas of the far left or forced activists into exile. It was asserted that Autonomia Operaia and the BR were the same organization, and that figures like Toni Negri, a radical academic, and other 'cattivi maestri' [bad teachers] were the theorists behind terrorist praxis. On the arrests of 1979, see Giorgio Bocca, *Il caso 7 aprile* (Milan: Feltrinelli, 1980) and CARI (Commitee Against Repression in Italy), 'April 7: Repression in Italy' in *Semiotext[e]* 3: 3 (1980), 172–77. This issue of *Semiotext[e]* contains a wide selection of documents relevant to the 1979 arrests.

strategy in films dealing with lotta armata can largely be traced back to the work of Rosi, Amelio and Bertolucci.[4]

That these three directors formulated their narratives of *lotta armata* at a moment when the historical agents represented in those narratives had been silenced – when those agents were 'fuori' [outside] or 'dentro' [inside], as Conti and Tiddi say – is a fact of Italian cinematic history that merits more attention than it has received. The recurrent choice to represent these historical agents as the protagonists of family narratives cannot be attributed to accident or authorial whim.

Notwithstanding the fact that they are often fraught with conflict, the families that feature in the films of Rosi, Amelio and Bertolucci tend to present themselves as somehow complete in themselves. Often, even the character who functions as a signifier of *lotta armata* – the terrorist – is a family member. He or she does not threaten the family from outside, but from within. The relationship between the family and the protagonists of *lotta armata* seems almost always to be one of inclusion. There is, however, much to suggest that what actually occurs in these films is not genuine inclusion but rather a semblance of inclusion founded on exclusion.

The strategies that Rosi, Amelio and Bertolucci employ to narrate Italian history are themselves a politically problematic part of that history. As such, they raise general questions about historical representation and narrative – questions about how historical facts and their ideological interpretation relate to one another within historical narratives, or about how the coherence imposed on history by such narratives can function as a vehicle for moral judgement.

How is the process of state-ordained exclusion that preceded and prepared the ground for these films related to their particular framing of Italian history? To what extent are their strategies for establishing narrative coherence premised on the absence of which Conti and Tiddi speak? And if moral judgement is passed in these films, who is moralizing about whom?

---

4   While the present analysis focuses on Italian cinema, it should be noted that there is a parallel history of the use of such narrative strategies in literary representations of *lotta armata* which can be traced at least to 1973 when Natalia Ginzburg published *Caro Michele* (Milan: Mondadori), a novel in which one young man's radicalization is framed within a complex narrative of generational rupture, alienation and loss as it plays out within a middle-class family. There is no shortage of later novels that portray the history of *lotta armata* in terms of family and generational conflict. See, for instance, Nerino Rossi, *La voce nel pozzo* (Venice: Marsilio, 1990); Vincenzo Consolo, *Lo spasimo di Palermo* (Milan: Mondadori, 1998).

One of the most striking features displayed by the films of Rosi, Amelio and Bertolucci is the sense of an ahistorical temporality they convey. While all three directors gesture occasionally towards specific historical developments (the partisan history of Emilio's father in *Colpire al cuore*; Italy's accelerated post-1945 industrialization and the internal migration of former land-workers to the factories of the north, as exemplified by the character Nicola in *Tre fratelli*), there is an inherently mythical or archaic quality to all three narratives, related to the archetypal character of the experiences they narrate (an encounter between brothers following their mother's death; a son's betrayal of his father; a disobedient daughter's fall from grace and quest for moral atonement).

Not only do all three directors elide a historical event absolutely central to questions of *lotta armata* in 1980s Italy, the repression of the country's radical movements at the end of the 1970s, those historical phenomena that are explicitly referenced – such as the partisan struggle – are also arguably the least adequate for grasping the specificity of *lotta armata* during the 1970s and 1980s. There was certainly a superficial analogy between the partisan struggle and the activities of groups such as the BR (just as there were historical contacts between former partisans and certain members of that organization). But presenting the two as somehow continuous with one another precludes recognition of how, for example, the definitive break with the partisan strategy of rural guerrilla warfare following the death of Giangiacomo Feltrinelli in 1972 was one of the most important choices of those who would go on to become the protagonists of post-1968 *lotta armata*.[5]

Violence in the Home: *Tre Fratelli* and *Colpire al Cuore*

Only one scene in Rosi's *Tre fratelli* represents an instance of politically motivated violence. Most of the film is devoted to discussions that take place between the three brothers on the eve of their mother's funeral. These discussions are often about political issues. At one point, Nicola (a Fiat worker in Turin) argues with his brother Raffaele (a magistrate in Rome) because he feels Raffaele does not distinguish clearly enough between the combative Italian labour movement of the period and clandestine insurrectionary groups that engage in the practice of political homicide or terrorism. Nicola defends the labour

5   On this point, see for example Mario Moretti, Carla Mosca and Rossana Rossanda, *Brigate Rosse: una storia italiana* (Milan: Anabasi, 1994).

struggles of the 1970s with the words: 'Io ho il diritto di esprimere il mio malcontento e di lottare senza per questo dovermi trovare un bollo di assassino stampigliato sulla fronte!' [I have the right to express my discontent and to protest without having the mark of assassin branded on my forehead!]. The wildcat strikes and demonstrations of Italian workers 'sono separati da un abisso dagli atti di terrorismo' [are separated by an abyss from acts of terrorism], Nicola insists, pointing out that he has himself participated in strikes: 'Certo i miei scioperi per cambiare l'ambiente li ho fatti anch'io e qualche fastidio alla ditta l'ho dato, non dico di no' [Sure, I've been on strike too, trying to change how things are organized, and I've been an irritation to the company, I don't deny it]. To suggest that this violence makes him somehow complicit with terrorism is unacceptable to Nicola. 'E allora la violenza della catena di montaggio?' [But what about the violence of the assembly line?], he asks.

I have cited statements that, out of context, may appear ingenuous or articulate to the reader, but in fact, throughout the scene, Nicola makes an excited, impatient and confused impression. Raffaele – who argues that anyone who does not wholeheartedly endorse the political principles of the Italian republic or interferes with the smooth functioning of its institutions is by definition on the side of the terrorists – is characterized as calmer and more reasonable. He is beset by powerful fears, as his nightmare of being assassinated will later reveal, but they seem not to affect his ability to reason logically in conversation. The argument between Nicola and Raffaele is very obviously one between a younger and an older, more experienced brother. It is in fact by pointing out that he is some twenty years older than Nicola – and not by some argument directly relevant to the issue being debated – that Raffaele ends the discussion to his own advantage.

There is another scene in the film that sees Raffaele correcting the erroneous assumptions of the working class. In that scene, he has just spoken to his Roman wife on the telephone. She is profoundly upset by the death threats he receives and voices her concern for his safety. After he has calmed her down in his characteristically patient manner, a group of working-class men calls him to their table at the local inn. The men are discussing whether or not someone who witnesses a political murder and recognizes the assassin should contact the police. The workers want to know what Raffaele thinks of the matter. His position is as clear as in his argument with Nicola. Those who commit murder for political motives deserve unconditional condemnation, he insists. Their behaviour is irrational and abnormal; it threatens the very foundations of Italian society. Political murder is a practice founded on fear, and 'la paura non può essere un sentimento normale su cui si fonda una società. La paura è un'eccezione, la regola deve essere la fiducia, sennò come si può vivere?' [fear cannot be the normal sentiment on which to base a society. Fear is an exception, trust must be the rule; if not how can we live?].

The workers listen attentively to Raffaele. They are clearly impressed by his warning against 'la follia di pensare di poter cambiare tutto e subito' [the folly of thinking you can change everything at once]. Here, as in his discussion with Nicola, Raffaele appears both as the more eloquent speaker and as the more rational thinker. This time, his authority derives less from his age than from his social position. To the workers who have asked him to their table, he is the successful university graduate who has climbed the social ladder to the point of leading a comfortable middle-class life in Rome. Tellingly, the conclusions arrived at in both conversations correspond fairly closely to the positions reiterated by 1970s PCI functionaries in their condemnation of the Italian radical left: not only should workers distance themselves in the clearest possible terms from political violence and denounce those who engage in it, but they should refrain even from independently organized strikes and demonstrations, since these too are ultimately complicit with terrorism.

Against the abrasive and disruptive activities championed by the young hothead Nicola ('esprimere il mio malcontento' – 'lottare' – 'dare fastidio alla ditta') [to express my discontent – to protest – to be an irritation to the company], the more mature Raffaele sets a simple principle of 'living', specifying that this presupposes not just trust, but also stability, continuity and regularity. The heartbeat heard on the soundtrack during the final moments of the assassination scene dreamt by Raffaele (as well as over the opening titles) confirms this association of living with continuity. The viewer's sense that the heartbeat could stop at any moment prepares him or her for the lesson that political radicalism is a force for death, because it is by definition disruptive. The heartbeat that must not be interrupted is ultimately not just Raffaele's, but also that of Italy's endangered social and political order.

The title Gianni Amelio chose for his 1982 film on Italian insurrectionary leftism, *Colpire al cuore*, suggests a similar symbolism, although the narrative strategies employed in that film are in some ways quite different from those of *Tre fratelli*. In *Colpire al cuore*'s coming-of-age story, the most important family relationship is not one between siblings, but one between a father and his son.

It is worth stressing that Amelio uses the generational motif in a way that is fundamentally different from its invocation in the article by Conti and Tiddi. In *Colpire al cuore*, generational conflict has an archaic or mythic character. It is generational conflict in the most obvious and restricted sense – a conflict between a parent and his child. Conti and Tiddi use the category of the generation in a way that is at once more loose and more historical: when they speak of 'l'eclisse di una generazione intera dalla scena politica alla fine degli anni Settanta' (19) [the eclipse of an entire generation from the political scene at the end of the 1970s], they are referring to a set of individuals whose most important common characteristic is not that they have parents or children, nor even that they were born around a certain year (the age differences within this 'generation' of political militants were often considerable), but rather that they participated in a political project that began and ended during a certain historical period.

Colpire al cuore seems at first glance to involve not a valorization of stability, trust and continuity but rather an acceptance of discontinuity and even of betrayal. The rupture or 'blow to the heart' that appears only as a terrifying possibility in Rosi's film actually occurs in *Colpire al cuore*, in the form of the breaking of the filial bond when Emilio reports his father to the police.

Yet the differences between *Tre fratelli* and *Colpire al cuore* should not be exaggerated. The rupture featured in Amelio's film hardly reflects a categorical acceptance of discontinuity and betrayal. Emilio's denunciation of his father is an exceptional betrayal, and its result (the father's arrest) appears as a kind of rectification rather than as a destructive act *tout court*. Emilio can be seen as shouldering the psychological burden of (symbolically) slaying his misguided father so that what was askew in their family can be set right. He effectively creates the conditions for a new conviviality, this one morally and politically well-founded. Seen in this way, his exceptional act presents itself as a confirmation of the rule – that of stable and continuous human relations, both on the microcosmic level of the family and on the macrocosmic one of society.

While it is certainly an act of faithlessness and an instance of discontinuity within one particular family, Emilio's action also guarantees the stability and continuity of the social and political order in general. It does so by contributing to the elimination of terrorism and its numerous baleful effects (which include the alienation of sons from their fathers, Amelio suggests). The film does not valorize disloyalty to the father as such, but much of it is apologetic with regard to Emilio's disloyalty to his own particular father, who has gone astray morally and politically. The film's message is ultimately quite simple: the limits of kinship-based loyalty are reached when another family member departs from the legal order not just in word but also in deed, and when patient discussion is no longer enough to make him turn back. While this message could arguably already be extrapolated from some scenes in *Tre fratelli*, it is formulated explicitly – indeed, with brutal clarity – only in *Colpire al cuore*. The net result of the two narratives is the same: the politically motivated violence of the radical left is presented as a force for death, devoid of all enabling or empowering characteristics; sympathy with that violence is presented as a grave and dangerous aberration; and loyalty to the Italian state wins out over every other consideration.

Female Silence in *Tre Fratelli* and *Colpire al Cuore*

It is worth emphasizing another common feature of these two films. Their principal characters are not just members of the same family (where they function as signifiers of larger tendencies within the Italian society of the 1970 and 1980s), but also almost exclusively male. It seems that for both Rosi and Amelio, women have no proper place in politics. In *Tre fratelli*, the most important forum for political interaction is the family conversation, and the interlocutors (the three brothers) are all men. Raffaele's wife plays an absolutely marginal role. Not only does she never leave Rome (and hence never make an appearance in the place where the conversations take place, the southern Italian home-town of Raffaele and his brothers), but what little we learn about her suggests an existence limited to fretting about her husband's safety. What is more, the event which brings the three brothers together again —after some time, we assume — is nothing less than the death of their mother. In *Tre fratelli*, the marginalization or even permanent silencing of female voices seems to be a precondition for political discourse.

The most prominent female character in *Colpire al cuore*, Giulia, is apparently unable to act without a man by her side. As soon as her boyfriend and co-conspirator Sandro is killed, Emilio's father steps in to protect her. It is the other principal character of the film, Emilio, who subsequently seals Giulia's fate by denouncing both her and his father to the police. His decision to do so is the final result of a conflict between males (between a father and his son). In short, Giulia tends to suffer the actions of male characters rather than act on her own account. The fact that she speaks far less than these male characters marginalizes her even further, since the plot progresses in large part by means of verbal interaction, much as in *Tre fratelli*. In both films, politics is explored by means of discussions, and discussions are presented as the domain of men.

Some scenes in *Colpire al cuore* – such as those in which Emilio follows Giulia to her hiding place or photographs the meetings between her and his father – suggest that the father-son relationship around which the film is structured contains elements of sexual rivalry. Other scenes suggest that Emilio's disenchantment with his father is due to the latter's neglect of the other semi-prominent female character of the film, Emilio's mother, and that Emilio reproaches his father for having allowed family relations to become increasingly loveless. The estrangement of Emilio's parents from one another emerges clearly from the fact that Emilio's mother knows nothing about her husband's political activities. She never becomes fully aware of Emilio's conflictual relationship to his father and is entirely excluded from the developments that drive the plot. Nor does the antagonism between Emilio and his father ever soften Emilio's attitude towards his mother. One scene features Emilio insulting her while she works at her typewriter, headphones placed over her ears. She smiles, unable to hear him, as he addresses her ignorance of the catastrophic – and male-driven – events that are being prepared: 'Sei una povera stupida, non sai niente' [You poor, stupid thing, you know nothing].

If Emilio's symbolic slaying of his father can be read as a disturbing but somehow tragically necessary attempt to set right what has gone wrong both in his family and in Italian society, then the typewriter scene shows that this rectification involves Emilio adopting a ruthlessness similar to his father's moral and political monstrousness. Outwardly or in terms of their behaviour, Emilio and his father are quite alike. The difference between them resides largely in their divergent goals. His father's actions are directed at a political ideal that is never quite spelled out, but which entails moral disintegration for the family and political havoc for the state, while Emilio's aim at a restoration of order on both levels. What is striking about this constellation of conflicting motives is its gendered nature, and the fact that women never actively participate in the conflict, but only passively suffer its results.

Family, State, and Society in *Tre Fratelli* and *Colpire al Cuore*

The pitiful situation of Emilio's mother is ultimately only one more index of his family's dysfunctional condition. If his father – the dangerous political maverick – is ultimately to blame for this condition, what are we to conclude about the relationship between family, state and society implicit in the symbolic economy of Amelio's narrative? Clearly, the crime for which Emilio's father needs to be punished is not just that of rejecting the political principles of the Italian republic, but also that of neglecting his marriage and his family – a crime that begins with him devoting more attention to Giulia than to his wife. Led astray by misguided political ideas, the father betrays the 'natural' community that is the family, stripping the interpersonal relations within that community of whatever feelings of affection and mutual trust may originally have characterized them. Much as in *Tre fratelli*, the implication is that any inclination involving hostility towards the established legal and political order is inherently morbid and destructive – in the sense that it erodes the foundations of harmonious conviviality. The family serves as the prime signifier of such conviviality.

The narratives crafted by Rosi and Amelio both display a tendency to implicitly identify family, state and society, or at least to establish a parallelism between them. In these narratives, a critical or subversive political stance is never only politically dangerous, but always also 'unnatural' and anti-social. That even the most tentative departure from the political order poses a threat to the stability of the family is implicit in the heated arguments between Nicola and Raffaele that occur in *Tre fratelli*, and it becomes explicit in the plot of *Colpire al cuore*.

Crucially, Emilio's denunciation of his father to the police presents itself not as the destruction of intact family relations, but rather as a decision taken where such relations no longer exist. Emilio's family is already a broken and loveless one at the beginning of the film. The question he faces throughout *Colpire al cuore* is that of how to behave towards the one who has allowed his family to decline into a condition of internal strife, alienation, and anomie. Tellingly, the criteria by which he finally manages to answer this question are those of a political morality whose ultimate guarantor is the state – a morality whose central imperative is to obey the law and denounce those who do not.

It would be misleading to say that *Colpire al cuore* sets up a binary opposition between the political principles enshrined in the Italian state and moral (family-based) loyalties. The film suggests, rather, that the family can function properly only where those political principles are respected. Not having respected them is one of the crimes of which Emilio's father is guilty. This fundamental complicity of the family with the state is crucial for understanding the portrayal of *lotta armata* not just in Amelio's film, but also in those of Rosi and Bertolucci.

Mother and Terrorist: *Segreti Segreti*

Women are not always consigned to marginal roles in Italy's cinematic narratives of political violence. Bertolucci's *Segreti segreti* has a female protagonist, Laura. She is the only member of an armed insurrectionary group to feature prominently in the film. In the final scene, she becomes a *pentita*, a collaborator: *Segreti segreti* ends with Laura handing herself over to the police and stating the names and addresses of her associates in the interrogation room.[6] Here, as in *Colpire al cuore*, the narrative achieves closure by means of an act of betrayal and denunciation. And as in *Colpire al cuore*, this act is preceded by the working-out of family conflicts. This time, however, the motif of political militancy is developed in a way that thematizes questions of gender far more explicitly.

Laura's stay at her family's country estate, following the murder scene that opens the film, is so rife with sexual imagery and allusions to Freudian tropes (bloody stockings, guns between splayed legs) that the viewer often wonders whether he or she is watching a film on *lotta armata* or on Laura's problematic relationship to her own womanhood (as it is defined by the other female characters in her film, and especially by Gina, her former nanny). In fact, Laura's identity as a terrorist is inseparable from the conflict that arises, on the one hand, from her inability to play the role of the innocent little girl and, on the other, from her refusal to become a mother. This refusal is presented as an irreverent, even blasphemous choice. Its explicit verbal articulation (during a dialogue between Laura and Gina) immediately provokes the response: 'Non bestemmiare' [don't swear/blaspheme].

The country estate sequence leaves the viewer in no doubt why Laura's choice evokes such horror. The scene that sees Gina turning

---

6   See Ruth Glynn's essay in this collection for a discussion of the relevance of *pentitismo* to *Segreti segreti*.

her back on Laura (after having discovered that the innocent, upper middle-class life style Laura cultivates is a sham) employs a wide range of Freudian tropes. It does so to suggest that Laura is a kind of anti-mother – a phallic, gun-toting dispenser of death. As the film will go on to show, Laura's choice not only means the generational sequence will not be extended into the future (in the form of the son Gina wishes Laura would have); it also leads to violent death for the preceding generation (Laura's mother, who commits suicide after learning that Laura is wanted by the police). *Segreti segreti* is, among other things, the story of a young woman's penis-envy ruining her family through and through.

Like Rosi and Amelio, Bertolucci identifies political militancy with the disintegration of the family and the violent disruption of a continuity that is literally vital, even sacred (the heartbeat in *Tre fratelli*; generational continuity in all three films, and especially in *Segreti segreti*). In *Segreti segreti*, as in *Tre Fratelli* and *Colpire al cuore*, the only safeguards and remedies that exist against these catastrophic consequences of misguided political choices reside in the state, or more precisely in the police.

The moral imperatives implicit in these narratives are as clear as their articulation around the tropes of family and generational conflict is intricate: don't strike if you are a worker (*Tre fratelli*); denounce your fellow-worker if he is guilty of political homicide (*Tre fratelli*); denounce your father if you discover he is collaborating with the political underground (*Colpire al cuore*); choose matrimony and motherhood over politics if you are a woman (*Segreti segreti*); turn yourself over to the police if you are guilty of political homicide (*Segreti segreti*).

The mother/terrorist dichotomy of *Segreti segreti* is strongly reminiscent of the binary oppositions that Fredric Jameson has analysed as the constitutive 'ideologemes' (basic ideological units) of certain nineteenth-century literary narratives. In *The Political Unconscious*, Jameson resorts frequently to the 'semiotic square' developed by A.J. Greimas – a diagram that visually represents a narrative's constitutive dichotomies in a way that allows for extrapolating a larger 'palimpsest of meaning' from a single ideologeme. The semiotic square can be understood as a first approximation of the way in which a narrative crafts an 'imaginary relationship' to 'transpersonal realities such as the social structure'.[7]

Segreti segreti's mother/terrorist dichotomy can be represented in the form of the following semiotic square:

7   Frederic Jameson, *The Political Unconscious: Narrative as a Socially Symbolic Act* (Ithaca, NY: Cornell University Press, 1981), 30.

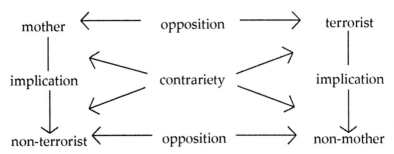

In Bertolucci's film, the figures of the terrorist and the mother are consistently played off against each other. Not only does Laura choose to become a clandestine political militant rather than give birth to a child, but Laura's own mother commits suicide when she learns of this choice. This twist of the plot further underscores the opposition between the two terms. The mother is by definition a non-terrorist – the first term 'implies' the latter, in Jameson's terminology – and her relationship to the terrorist is therefore necessarily one of 'contrariety'. In Bertolucci's film, this necessity is expressed in the experience of profound shock that prompts Laura's mother to end her own life.

Conclusion: Family – State – History

Such semiotic squares could easily be drawn up for all films discussed here. Why is this Greimasian device so well suited to the analysis of narratives articulated around ideologemes of family and generational conflict? One reason appears to lie in the ultimately static character of the square. The square is certainly helpful in elucidating the way a plot unfolds, or the dynamic and diachronic features of a narrative. As has just been seen, it can help explain a twist of the plot such as the suicide of Laura's mother. On closer inspection, however, one finds that what it really helps explain is the peculiar sense of necessity that often accompanies such twists of the plot. The semiotic square helps expose a narrative's underlying presuppositions and it does so by identifying the fixed coordinates and rules that determine what 'must' happen.

If the square works well for the narratives analysed, this is perhaps because those narratives are themselves, in a sense, static. As noted above, one of the most striking features of the narratives of *Tre fratelli*, *Colpire al cuore*, and *Segreti segreti* is that they appear to be set in a time more reminiscent of non-historical genres such as myth or the fairy tale than of conventional historical narration. How is the mythic or non-historical time proper to these narratives related to their tendency to identify family, state and society?

Only a very preliminary answer can be offered here. I want to suggest that, in some ways, the films of Rosi, Amelio and Bertolucci are reminiscent of nineteenth-century assumptions about the family and the state, and about the relationship of both to history. Some aspects of these films strongly recall the classic Hegelian conception of this relationship, even as they revise it in important ways.

In his *Lectures on the Philosophy of History*, Hegel links the possibility of historical narration to the existence of the state, simultaneously establishing a dichotomy between such narration and family history. The latter is for him fundamentally pre-political and ahistorical. According to Hegel, the family is by definition not the domain of historical events, being characterized by a circular or redundant temporality, that of generational continuity understood as an extra-historical fact of nature.[8]

In the films of Rosi, Amelio and Bertolucci, one finds the same three categories (family, state, history) at work, but they are put to a different use. The conceptual constellation that underpins the three narratives both strongly recalls and significantly transforms the Hegelian model. As argued above, the three directors tend to identify family and state, or at least to assume a parallelism between them. This explains why, for example, the political morality of the state is the final arbiter even in family matters (*Colpire al cuore*). What can now be added to this observation is that what is in danger of being rendered invisible in the revised Hegelian model is the category of history.

This would seem to be one of the main reasons not just for the mythic or archaic quality of the three narratives, but also for the fact that the violence of the terrorist tends to appear in them without any proper historical context or serious political motivation. The viewer of the films learns next to nothing about the political considerations that lead certain characters to engage in the practice of political murder, and so the question of what socio-historical developments may have led to such considerations tends not to arise. The two nameless assassins in *Tre fratelli* are a particularly glaring example of the terrorist as a mysterious, even demonic figure, but the viewer of *Colpire al cuore* remains similarly in the dark about the motives of Sandro and Giulia. As for the Laura of *Segreti segreti*, she could just

8   See Georg Wilhelm Friedrich Hegel, *Lectures on the Philosophy of History*, trans. by J. Sibree (London: G. Bell, 1910 [1840]).

as well be a regular killer, for all one learns about her political views and their historical context.

The 'terrorists' of Rosi, Amelio and Bertolucci are less the products of a specific social and political history than threatening strangers whose existence is simply taken for granted, like that of the villain in a fairy tale. Where an attempt is made to provide motivation for their actions, that motivation tends to be purely psychological, rather than properly political (as with Laura). It tends to be more closely related to developments proper to the family than to the specific social and political history of 1970s and 1980s Italy.

In writing his *Lectures*, Hegel seems to have been thinking mainly of the family of clan societies. He was of course not familiar with the nuclear family of 1980s Italy. What is striking is that Rosi, Amelio and Bertolucci treat the nuclear family as if it were as far removed from history as Hegel makes clan societies out to be. What is more – and notwithstanding the peculiar alliances and parallelisms between family and state one encounters in their films – the three directors ultimately follow Hegel not just in removing the family from history, but also in depoliticizing it. There is nothing paradoxical about this, since the state does not appear in their narratives as a properly historical or political phenomenon either: its authority and its ability to shelter and punish are as mysterious as the demonic fury of the terrorist.

It was suggested above that if Rosi, Amelio and Bertolucci can successfully elide much of the history of 1970s Italy, this is for specific historical and political reasons. Their elision can in many ways be interpreted as a symbolic act that complements a material process of state repression on the level of the cultural imaginary, erasing all recollection of those who have been physically expelled from Italian society. The erasure of history that *Tre fratelli*, *Colpire al cuore* and *Segreti segreti* bring about makes the terrorists featured in these films strangely apolitical and ahistorical characters, demonic forces for death that exist somewhere on the fringes of society or are produced within it by moral and psychological perversions which are presented as anything but political. The tropes of family and generational conflict analysed above are a symbolic substitute for this erased history – one that could arguably have been told only by those silenced by the arrests of 1979.

How historiographical deletions are symbolically compensated for, and by whom, is a political issue. While the articulation of ideologemes such as *Segreti segreti*'s mother/terrorist dichotomy certainly serves to depoliticize certain phenomena (such as that of political homicide), these ideologemes are far from being politically neutral themselves. In this sense, one might say Conti and Tiddi are only telling half the story when they describe Italy's transition to the 1980s as a 'fine politica nel senso più pieno della parola' (19) [political end in the fullest sense of the term]. While this characterization is certainly quite accurate with regard to the radical movements of the 1970s, Italy's early cinema of *lotta armata* shows that the historical moment it dealt with also marked the emergence – or perhaps the restoration – of a politics very different from that championed by the radical left.

5. To Strike at the Heart of Family and State: Gianni Amelio's *Colpire al Cuore*

Ellen Nerenberg

Beyond the political aims that the Aldo Moro kidnapping and detention were intended to accomplish, Moro's symbolic utility to the Red Brigades as the victim of political violence should not be under-estimated.[1] Indeed, the choice of Moro instead of a member of the judiciary, which had until that point served as the preferred group to target, is highly significant. As the former Prime Minister of the Republic (1963–68; 1974–76), Moro could be said to have had a paternal role in government. As President of the Democrazia Cristiana, his position as regards the party could also be seen as located at the apex of its vertical hierarchy, and not without patriarchal valences. In collaboration with the then head of the Partito Comunista Italiano, Enrico Berlinguer, Moro engineered (or, continuing in the vein of paternal metaphors, fathered) the 'historic compromise', the very coalition he was on his way to publicly ordain on 16 March 1978 when he was ambushed in Via Fani. In fact, as Robin Wagner-Pacifici observes, in the 'social drama' of the Aldo Moro affair, the breach that Moro's kidnapping prised open was partially due to his paternal figuration. Moro's symbolic fatherhood was plainly expressed, in fact, in the headline in the 17 March 1978 edition of the newspaper *La Repubblica* that described the reaction of Milan's DC headquarters

---

1 See Robin Wagner-Pacifici's germinal study of the Moro affair, *The Moro Morality Play: Terrorism as Social Drama* (Chicago: University of Chicago Press, 1986). Wagner-Pacifici capitalizes on the events' symbolic valences and, following Kenneth Burke, does not focus on the symbolism of atomized events so much as 'on the symbols themselves as they mov[e] into and out of *systems* of symbols' (emphasis in original, 15).

to Moro's kidnapping: 'It is as if they had kidnapped our Father' (Wagner-Pacifici, 76).

The relay of father, family, state and terrorism as portrayed in Gianni Amelio's 1982 feature film, *Colpire al cuore* (*Blow to the Heart*), is the subject of this essay. Specifically, Amelio's film provides the opportunity to explore the issue of generational difference, often cast as naked Oedipal tensions between father and son and a recognizable characteristic of Italian films treating the subject of terrorism in the first half of the 1980s.[2] Generational conflict manifests itself in Amelio's film on three separate levels: thematic, formal and extra-cinematic, the three areas of principal focus in these pages.[3] Rather than reenact the scenario of the terrorist as the offspring of 'cattivi maestri' [bad teachers], Amelio's film significantly inverts the conventional Oedipal configuration.[4] While such an inversion may reproduce a binary that hinges on the same axis, the way in which the problem of generational tensions goes beyond simple thematics to inform issues of formal and extra-cinematic significance as well sets *Colpire al cuore* apart from the cohort of other films exploring Italian terrorism. The concept 'extra-cinematic' will be divided in this essay into two areas for consideration: extra-cinematic discourse (which addresses largely industry concerns) and extra-cinematic context, which will mean the social and historical context in which the film is situated.

My focus in these pages is on inter- rather than intra-generational tension, which distinguishes this essay from others in this collection that also explore the deployment of the family as a trope in the cinematic representation of terrorism in Italy. The 'frattura generazionale' [generational fracture] described by 1980s militant activists Andrea Tiddi and Antonio Conti suggests generational fault-lines that are

2   In addition to Amelio's feature-length treatment, both Francesco Rosi's *Tre fratelli* (1981) and Giuseppe Bertolucci's *Segreti, segreti* (1984) are predicated on family configurations. See Max Henninger's essay in this collection for a cogent critique of the role of the family as the instrument of historical revision.

3   See Alan O'Leary, 'Film and the *Anni di Piombo*: Representations of Politically-Motivated Violence in Recent Italian Cinema', in *Culture, Censorship and the State in Twentieth-Century Italy*, ed. Robert Gordon and Guido Bonsaver (Oxford: Legenda, 2004), 168–78.

4   On the notion of 'cattivi maestri' in the film see *Gianni Amelio: le regole e il gioco*, ed. Emanuela Martini (Turin: Lindau, 1999), 47. Lesley Caldwell addresses the father-son dynamic in Amelio's film but in the context of the development of feminist psychoanalytic critiques of the family in the 1970s ('Is the Political Personal? Fathers and Sons in Bertolucci's *Tragedia di un uomo ridicolo* and Amelio's *Colpire al cuore*', in *Speaking Out and Silencing: Culture, Society, and Politics in Italy in the 1970s*, ed. Anna Cento Bull and Adalgisa Giorgio (Oxford: Legenda, 2006), 69–80). Neither is a focus in these pages.

horizontal in configuration.[5] The generational discontinuity deriving from this fracture occurs along the horizontal axis of sibling relations rather than the vertical axis conceived of in a more genealogical sense of parent to child transmission.

The inside/outside dichotomy ('dentro'/'fuori') which Max Henninger probes in his essay in this collection captures what Marco Baliani describes in *Corpo di Stato*, his dramatic monologue on the Moro affair, as a constitutive characteristic of young Italians involved in the *movimento* (the left-wing protest movement) during the 1970s. What is significant about Baliani's dramatic narrative is the memory of how members of his generation strained against the inside/outside division. Remembering the Roman Spring of 1978, Baliani begins with his feeling of euphoria at the news of Moro's abduction and traces the arc of his growing disquiet during the subsequent fifty-four days of the kidnap. Like others of his generation, Baliani sought exit from the inside/outside binary, a desire for sublation expressed in the phrase 'né con le Brigate Rosse, né con lo Stato' [neither with the BR nor with the state].[6] I will return to tensions stretching between horizontal and vertical axes as they relate to manifestations of inter-generational conflict in *Colpire al cuore* which, alongside *Maledetti vi amerò* (*To Love the Damned*, Marco Tullio Giordana, 1980) and *La tragedia di un uomo ridicolo* (*The Tragedy of a Ridiculous Man*, Bernardo Bertolucci, 1981), marks a relatively early effort following the Moro affair to represent Italian terrorism within the codes and contexts of Italian feature films.

Colpire al cuore centres on the relationship between Dario (Jean-Louis Trintignant), a professor of literature at Milan's Università Cattolica, and his fifteen-year-old son, Emilio (Fausto Rossi). The companionable relationship between father and son with which Amelio begins gives way to antagonism as Emilio grows ever more aware of Dario's involvement with an unnamed terrorist organization. During a weekend visit to his grandmother's villa in Bergamo, Emilio meets a former student of Dario's, Sandro (Vanni Corbellini), and his partner, Giulia (Laura Morante). Already an avid amateur photographer, Emilio photographs his father with Giulia and Sandro. Back in Milan a short while later, Emilio sees Sandro's lifeless body lying in the street, following a violent skirmish between terrorists and *carabinieri*. Guided by his own conservative impulses,

5 Antonio Conti and Andrea Tiddi, 'Gli anni ottanta: le generazioni dell'esilio', *DeriveApprodi*, 12: 16 (1998), 19.
6 Marco Baliani, *Corpo di stato: il delitto Moro* (Milan: Rizzoli, 2003), 57.

Emilio reports what he knows to the authorities and both father and son are questioned. A few days later, after a chance sighting of Giulia on the street, Emilio follows her to an apartment in a squalid housing complex on the city's edge. Shadowing his father, he photographs Dario's meeting with Giulia at the Brera Pinacoteca and leaves the photographic proof where he is sure Dario will find it. When Dario meets Emilio in Bergamo, the clash between father and son reaches its dramatic climax, a scene I shall discuss fully below. Returning to Milan, Dario drives to Giulia's apartment to ensure her immediate departure. With Emilio looking on, they are apprehended by agents of law enforcement.

As this brief plot summary reveals, *Colpire al cuore* is predicated thematically on the tensions between father and son. In fact, although terrorism offers itself as the protagonist of the film it is, at the same time, curiously absent. 'Colpire al cuore dello stato' [to strike at the heart of the state] was the eminently familiar BR slogan, and in both his title and film, Amelio either excises or represses the presence of the state. As David Bruni has observed, 'È il caso del terrorismo, che (a partire dal titolo) sembrerebbe dover essere il vero protagonista del film, e che è invece presente solo come un fattore drammatico decisivo nel processo di progressiva *degenerazione* e isterilimento dei rapporti interpersonali' [Terrorism would, beginning with the title, appear to be the protagonist of the film, but it is instead only a decisive dramatic factor in the progressive *degeneration* and sterility of interpersonal relationships].[7] Explicit references in the film to terrorism are few and explicit references to the BR limited to one instance. In addition to the title, Emilio comments on the 'bavero anti-proiettile' [bullet-proof bib] worn by Giulia and Sandro's son (a remote reference at best). The only explicit reference to the BR, that is, the only time the organization's name is pronounced, comes in the tinny, distant voice of the TV newscaster describing the scene of Sandro's death which Emilio has just witnessed in Milan's Piazza dell'Arcivescovado. Indeed, the only 'red' in the film's unified visual field pertains to Emilio in the shape of his red sweater and scarf, which he wears continually.[8]

Generational tension surges to the fore at the film's dramatic climax and so prominent is this theme that some critics find

---

7 David Bruni, '*Colpire al cuore* di G. Amelio: lo sguardo discreto', in *Schermi opachi: il cinema italiano degli anni '80*, ed. Lino Micciché (Venice: Marsilio, 1998), 244, emphasis added.

8 See also Marie Orton, '"Terrorism" in Italian Film: Striking the One to Educate the Hundred', *Romance Languages Annual*, 11 (2000), 309.

terrorism, despite the film's title, to be 'quasi un pretesto [....] per prendere di petto il rapporto padre-figlio in uno spazio drammatico spoglio, essenziale' (Bruni, 244) [almost a pretext to confront head-on the father-son relationship in a stripped-down and essential dramatic space]. Various revisions of the project, from the screenplay to the final, filmed version, increasingly narrow the players and their interactions, until the point where all of Emilio's affective energy is channelled in the direction of his father and his adolescent erotic energy is cathected onto Giulia.

The tension between Dario and Emilio finds its most dramatic expression in two 'stripped down and essential' spaces that the film renders quite literal: at night in the central piazza in Città alta [upper city] in Bergamo and, shortly afterward, in a deserted Via Vittorio Emanuele, the main artery of Bergamo's Città bassa [lower city], in the light of early morning. Although I will return to these parallel scenes, for the moment I wish simply to recall an exchange of dialogue that exemplifies the generational tension I have been describing. 'Che cosa ti aspetti da me', Dario asks, 'Vorresti un padre che ti dicesse dov'è il bene e dov'è il male? [...] Padri perfetti non ci sono più.' [What do you expect from me? Do you want a father who can tell you where good and evil are? Perfect fathers don't exist any more.]. 'Figli perfetti ancor meno' [Nor do perfect children], his son responds.

Still other significant manifestations of generational antagonism are present in the film, and the weekend visit to the Bergamo villa yields several of the film's most significant scenes in this regard. The first takes place in the room housing the vestiges of Dario's life before marriage, family and career. Out of the flotsam and jetsam crowding the room (and the frame), Sandro draws from the bookshelf a photograph album and in it serendipitously finds the photograph (dated 11 June 1944) of an adolescent Dario carrying his Soviet-issue Sten machine gun. Although later in the film Amelio will rely on photography's silent powers of surveillance, in this relatively early scene he reinforces what he makes visible with dialogue, a light – yet didactic – synchronization of sight and sound.

Since Emilio already knows about his father's activist past, albeit only hazily, a partial function of the scene is to introduce Sandro as a presence encroaching upon the father-son symbiosis: not only has Sandro intruded upon a Sunday family outing, he also tacitly claims to understand Dario better than Emilio. Even if, as Morando Morandini has suggested perhaps too optimistically,[9] Emilio sees

9 'Rapporti critici', in *Gianni Amelio*, ed. Gianni Volpi, (Turin: Scriptorium, 1995), 31.

Sandro as a 'big brother' and grieves his death, this would not exclude the rivalrous feelings Emilio clearly displays towards him. Surely the sibling problem for Emilio is not Sandro so much as Dario, who would clearly prefer the role of big brother to father. If the sweatshirt Sandro is wearing at his death acts as the metonym linking him to Emilio, the machine gun lying between Sandro's corpse and the fallen carabiniere officer in the Piazza dell'Arcivescovado connects him to Dario. More than establish Sandro's claim on Dario, however, the scene in the Bergamo villa also creates the link between the partisans who took up arms at the end of the Second World War and the unnamed, latter-day revolutionaries who are everywhere evoked but virtually nowhere specifically mentioned.

The bookshelf, figuratively, speaks volumes about Dario's history and the photograph album is not the only evidence of his development that it yields. In addition to the photographic evidence of Dario's youthful activism, as well as the elementary school primer Emilio invites him to examine, Sandro discovers a copy of José Ortega y Gasset's 1929 *La rebelión de las masas* [*The Revolution of the Masses*]. Unlike the wartime photograph of Dario, which requires explanation, Amelio lets the book speak for itself. The Ortega volume emphasizes the linkage of generational identity to social revolution and helps bring into proximity the two Darios, the adolescent partisan and the professor of literature, who perhaps has not left entirely behind him an interest in politics and civic life. This balancing act, ambivalent though it may be, aligns Dario's character even more closely with that of Toni Negri, professor of political science at the University of Padua found guilty of 'armed insurrection against the powers of the state', and who served two prison sentences, the first from 1979 to 1983 and the second, once he had returned from France, dated 1997–2003.

Dario's interest in Ortega, a public intellectual and professor (the chief exponent in Spain of nineteenth-century German philosophy) who held public office and joined in extra-parliamentary attempts to undermine the government (first that of Primo de Rivera and then of King Alfonso XIII), is not surprising, for radical and progressive thinkers across the globe were, in the 1960s, interested in Ortega's work and that of others of his generation of Spanish intellectuals. The scene between Sandro and Emilio visualizes Dario's history as a cluttered repository, a jumble that makes it impossible to determine how current Dario's interest in Ortega y Gasset might be. In other words, the 1960s ferment of foment may not have lasted until 1982, the film's historical frame, and what remains is a deliberately vague and ambivalent delineation of Dario in the film's present.

Perhaps Dario has outgrown the sentiment of rebellion and Ortega y Gasset. For example, when shown teaching, Dario is simply declaiming Gérard de Nerval's novella *Sylvie* (1853) *ex cathedra*, hardly fulminating against hegemony. When Dario mentions his recent election to the directorship of the university faculty, he seems, if nothing else, to have left Ortega truly on the shelf and, in joining the other 'baroni', also to have joined a different social and professional generation.[10] Although the narrative will ultimately prove the contrary, Emilio's view of Dario as a middle-aged father whose radical tendencies are limited and contained (in photographs enclosed in albums, on shelves within rooms within houses) is the prevailing one.

In addition to the explicit presence of Ortega, the focus on music and photography during the sequences composing the outing to Bergamo also comments on the idea of generation and degeneration, as Bruni outlines. While Dario, his guests and his mother enjoy the afternoon on the verandah, Emilio opts for the indoors, maintaining his distance from the group, and the way Amelio frames his figure within the window frame imposes symmetry, balance and control. This arrangement is also the literal manifestation of the inside/outside binary referred to above. The camera's classically composed frame presents Emilio at the window, where he takes several photographs of his father and the young couple. When Dario's mother exhorts him to sing the popular song, 'Rondine al nido' [Homing Swallows], Dario complies with good humour. Shortly afterward, Emilio puts a recording on the phonograph of Beniamino Gigli singing the same song. More than a preference for a professional over an amateur or for the 'original' over a copy removed by one generation of reproduction, this scene captures Emilio's desire to control both sight and sound, bending each to his will.

Technology gives Emilio mastery: the camera gives him control over what he sees, the phonograph over what he hears. Both apparatuses preserve an image, one visual the other acoustic. Yet even though there is preference for the original, Emilio is not interested in the greater authenticity of Gigli's recording of 'Rondine al nido' so much as in purging the trace of his father: he can eclipse the vision of his father by turning away or he can delimit it photographically. Concerning Dario's audible trace, Emilio can and does drown him out. The preference for the recording (which Gigli would have made before 1940, and which had become a staple of his radio performances

10   'Baroni' [barons] is an ironic term used to refer to figures of power in Italian universities.

in the 1930s) underscores the theme of generational inversion and locates Emilio, properly turned out with a tie for a Sunday visit to his grandmother's house, squarely in his grandfather's generation: rather than usurp Dario's position, Emilio has bypassed him entirely.

The inter-generational tension throughout *Colpire al cuore* subtends crucial formal properties, a topic that has received far less scholarly attention than the Oedipal thematic re-enacted by father and son. Emilio's mastery over Dario in the Bergamo sequences – not only in the frames of the Sunday outing but those of the second, climactic visit to the city as well – is as visual as it is thematic and symbolic; consequently, I now turn to an examination of the film's strategies for visually formalizing the theme of generational clash and conflict.

The last scene in the Bergamo sequences features a slow and deliberate tracking shot which moves parallel to the villa, where Emilio commands a stable, static position at its most central location (or 'heart'). Emilio's immobility is contrasted to the slow prowl of the camera as well as the action of the other characters: Dario and Sandro have also been on the move, their conversation inaudible but doubtless made up of 'secrets', and Giulia follows a slight distance behind them. The camera comes to a halt to reveal the tableau of psychological tensions the sequences at the villa have been working to establish. Hailed by Gigli's sublime voice, the characters have turned so that their gaze, along with the viewer's, is drawn upward to the source. This deep-focus shot includes all the principals, placing them in their relative positions of power. Dario and Sandro occupy the bottom third of the frame, Giulia the middle third, and Emilio high above them all. Moreover, this spatialization also portrays the characters' psychological inter-relationships. Dario and Sandro occupy one plane in the immediate foreground. Between them and Emilio figures Giulia, who visually links the lower, foregrounded part of the frame with its highest part and deepest point of focus. Here we find Emilio, like some *éminence grise*, whose position is superior in every sense.

If Bergamo helps Emilio achieve visual and thematic ascendancy in the inter-generational struggle with Dario, Milan helps whittle him down to size and the shuttling back and forth between Milan and Bergamo underscores the growing strain between father and son. The Milanese cityscape (and the characters' movement through it) also emblematizes a generational divide, sometimes played out as Gothic and contemporary but a divide that points to other binaries that are also visualized in the film: an alternation between urban/

suburban and, significantly, the competition for visual dominance along the vertical and horizontal axes.

The Oedipal tension founded on the struggle for ascendancy and superiority, if attained, does not always prevail, as the scene following the shoot-out at the Piazza dell'Arcivescovado illustrates. This armed strike against the forces of order has occurred at the heart of the city (if not the state) and, unlike the scene of the villa, it shows an Emilio not only cut down to size but actually dwarfed by his surroundings. The divide between the centre of the old, medieval city and its sprawling periphery informs another urban split in the film in the form of Bergamo, itself a city split in two (*città bassa* and *alta*). Although Amelio learned of the availability in Bergamo of a villa that could serve as Dario's childhood home only shortly before that segment was to begin shooting, Bergamo's cityscape nevertheless performs some of the binaries I have been describing.[11] Amelio acknowledges that the Milanese cityscape visually refers to 'l'aria pesante del periodo' (Martini, 145) [the period's feeling of heaviness] but also to its place as the 'moral capital' of the early 1980s, and from this duality a remarkable ambivalence emerges in the film's representation of terrorism.

The scene in the Piazza dell'Arcivescovado is essential for the way it conflates the genesis and effects of left- and right-wing terrorism in the 1969–82 period. Adjacent to the Duomo, the Arcivescovado is readily recognizable, yet it is set against the backdrop of a Milan which, Amelio hoped, could be presented at once (and contradictorily) as identifiable and indeterminate. Although, as stated above, Amelio wished to invoke some precise connotations by setting *Colpire al cuore* in Milan, at the same time he also sought to defamiliarize the cityscape. As he said, 'Nel film, ti accorgi di straforo che a sinistra del fotogramma c'è il Duomo, una volta, di giorno, quando passa Giulia, o che un'altra volta siamo in Piazza Fontana' (Martini, 146) [In the movie you are only dimly aware of Milan's Duomo in the frame, once during the day, when Giulia passes by it, or that in another scene we are in Piazza Fontana].

John Foot observes an opposite effect, however. The use of the Brera courtyard for the central scene of Emilio's surveillance places Amelio among directors seeking to make their films visually Milanese through the deployment of such icons as the Duomo, the Pirelli

---

11   *Regia di Gianni Amelio*, ed. Mario Sesti (Naples: Edizioni Scientifiche Italiane, 1992), 117.

Tower, or the navigli (the canal area of the city).[12] Amelio's intention to defamiliarize the Milanese cityscape could be said to fall short of the mark precisely for the associations the Arcivescovado conjures: one of the Duomo's dependent buildings, it lies just a few hundred metres from Piazza Fontana, the site of the 1969 bombing attributed to right-wing terrorists. This reference is not lost on an informed viewer and calls into question the relationship between the aftermath of violence that Emilio witnesses (left-wing in origin) and the events that took place in Piazza Fontana some fourteen years earlier.

While slippage toward an inchoate representation of armed political violence in this period earns Amelio no points with those seeking greater clarity on the genesis of terrorist activities in the *anni di piombo* (and in fact leaves the film's representation of terrorism open to criticism along these lines), it nevertheless plays a key role in the visual presentation of Emilio. At the conclusion of the sequence in which Emilio recognizes Sandro's corpse and complicity, the long shot shows Emilio disappearing into the vanishing point, flanked almost casually by the Arcivescovado. In brief, the city swallows him whole. As Emilio moves out of sight at the end of the scene displaying the aftermath of the shoot-out, so he also moves against the (emotional and psychological) current of those who, rushing toward the scene of the crime, might wonder whether this is yet another *strage* [massacre] to afflict the area. Amelio's point is not to distinguish between the origins of terrorist violence in either precise locale; rather, the tumult of the scene – the rush of onlookers and ambulances in the immediate aftermath of the shoot-out – underscores just how similar in aspect are the consequences of armed political violence. Emilio's disappearance here corresponds to the similarly composed shot with which *Colpire al cuore* ends when Emilio, dwarfed by the architecture that surrounds him, once more moves away from the camera and against the (emotional and psychological) current in which others are immersed.

The architecture of Milan, whether Gothic or pseudo/neo-rationalist, tends toward the miniaturization of the human form, a character's visual dominance notwithstanding. Despite this levelling tendency, Amelio reinscribes the hierarchical aspect of the tension between generations (and between strongly held political beliefs) by opposing father and son along the vertical and horizontal axes of the frame. Amelio exploits the vertical axis to underscore the inversion of

---

12   John Foot, *Milan since the Miracle: City, Culture, Identity* (Oxford: Berg, 2001), 76.

the father-son relationship and emphasize the psychological distance between Dario and Emilio that increases as the film progresses.

The film's establishing sequence displays father and son harmoniously occupying the same horizontal space. Their close proximity in the centre of the frame matches visually their friendly banter, though it is clear that Emilio displays less *bonhomie* than his father. Proximity and shared space recede however, in the scenes that follow to emphasize a more vertical relationship, spatially as well as figuratively. The Bergamo sequence already established Emilio's superiority over Dario, at least in visual terms. Emilio's dominance of the vertical axis makes up a motif in the film, most notable in the scenes set in Bergamo and in the university lecture hall.

The first shot of the episode in the lecture hall reveals Dario in profile, seated at a table on the dais. He is crammed into the left of the frame, miniaturized by the over-sized chair he sits in, the wide expanse of the gleaming tabletop throwing the composition of the shot off-kilter: there is no room for Dario and even inanimate objects attain greater visual status. When Emilio enters, over Dario's voice intoning Nerval, his body, shot from the front, centres the frame. These oppositions – large and small, central and peripheral, static and mobile, father and son, dominant and dominated – are thrown into keen relief by the high-angle point-of-view shot from the top of the lecture hall. Dario sits at the base of the steep, amphitheatre-like room; if the chair at the podium dwarfed him, Emilio's point of view makes him even smaller. The use of the rationalist architectural appointments in the lecture hall as well as the university corridors Emilio and Dario will soon pass through – so swiftly evocative of aesthetic codes of the 1930s – recalls Bertolucci's *Il conformista* (*The Conformist*,1970), for which Trintignant, who played Marcello Clerici in that film, was best known in Italy.

Il conformista is a valuable cultural and cinematic referent for Amelio, who has said that for the character of Emilio he wanted 'the son of the conformist' (Volpi, 119). Briefly, Bertolucci's 1970 film of Alberto Moravia's 1951 novel *Il conformista* tells the story of Marcello Clerici (Trintignant), a young man in fascist Italy who, wishing to 'atone' for a murder he believes he committed as a child, offers himself as an informer to the branch of the security apparatus responsible for the repression of anti-fascism. Clerici's assignment is to spy and inform on the anti-fascist activities of his former professor, now teaching in Paris. The recitation of Nerval in *Colpire al cuore* reminds the viewer that Trintignant is, in fact, a French actor, *the* French actor of Bertolucci's film. As the son of the conformist, Emilio, like Trintignant's Clerici, also becomes an informer on the clandestine activities of a resistant group; consequently, Emilio, too, is associated with the fascist inclinations of his fictional antecedent.

The jockeying for a dominant position along the visual vertical axis finds correspondence in the film's rearrangement of action and locale. The round trip from Milan to Bergamo occurs twice in *Colpire al cuore*, at its beginning and conclusion. These visual (or visualized) rearrangements of horizontal and vertical positions are consistent with Emilio's fondness for anagrams, as made evident in the opening of the film. With companionable silences between them, Emilio and Dario engage in simple anagramming in a pastoral setting near (we are to assume) Bergamo.

Anagramming emphasizes the limits of recombination and, perhaps, of the kind of social and political revolution the film's terrorists seem intent upon. Anagrams call for the dismantling of component parts (letters in a word) in the service of the creation of a new signifier. The rule of proper anagramming, however, is that the new signifier must be created from the already existing set of letters. This structure, it could be argued, is the source of the game's beauty. To be sure, concern for structure and place is consonant with Emilio's wooden character. The shuffling of letters in anagramming may transform an existing relation into something new, even something surprising, but the transformation, like subject positions in an Oedipal configuration, are clearly limited. The relocation of action from Milan to Bergamo mirrors these limits: whatever momentary transformation may take place in their positions *vis-à-vis* each other, Dario and Emilio only ever occupy the same circumscribed positions. This corresponds to Max Henninger's commentary, in this collection, on the ways in which A. J. Greimas's 'semiotic square' may be useful in examining the structure of family in Giuseppe Bertolucci's *Segreti segreti* (*Secrets, Secrets*, 1984). The absence of exit from circumscribed positions within the social structure that Henninger identifies at work in *Segreti segreti* finds consonance with the reading of *Colpire al cuore* proposed here.

While Bergamo may not have been Amelio's first choice of location for the exterior sequences not situated in Milan, its topography nevertheless contributes to the thematic representation of the struggle for visual dominance. The film's dramatic climax, for example, unfolds in three sequences placed in three quite distinct locales within Bergamo: Città alta, Città bassa, and the waiting-room of the funicular that marks their union. Dario finds Emilio in the same funicular waiting-room where, in a scene already described, Emilio's detour from routine had worried his parents. The waiting-room marks conjunction on several levels that are not simply topographical. For example, the funicular is where Emilio first sees Giulia, the shared object of interest and mediating presence between father and son, and where Emilio first observes her unnoticed. This scene activates his voyeuristic inclination (he really is the 'son of the conformist' after all), which urges him to trail Giulia furtively through the streets of Milan and, ultimately, at the Brera, where he photographs her with Dario, the very photograph his father scornfully tosses at him in the funicular waiting-room, disparaging his son's inflated notions of paternal piety and civic duty.

Emilio and Dario's union is drawing to its close and, not surprisingly, they leave behind them the place of convergence, and begin to move toward the collapse of their relationship polarized vertically by Città alta and bassa. The camera tracks behind the characters as they make their way through the empty streets of Città alta, where, in the central piazza, Dario finally confronts Emilio with the risks associated with doing one's 'duty'. Dario insists that, 'Non è la verità che si vede dal buco della serratura [....] dal buco della serratura sembriamo tutti ladri, tutti assassini' [You can't see the truth through the keyhole.... through the keyhole we are all thieves, all murderers]. Reference to the keyhole naturally serves to reinforce the critique of voyeurism at work in the film, but it also recalls, perhaps too obviously, notions of a Freudian primal scene, which Freud described in his case study of Sergei Pankejeff, 'The Wolf Man', in his 1918 essay 'From the History of an Infantile Neurosis' and which has its place, too, in the psycho-sexual relation between father and child.[13] Once more one may briefly and profitably compare *Colpire al cuore* to *Il conformista*. Bertolucci visually insists on Marcello's voyeuristic impulses, linking them to sexual deviancy which in turn is associated with political deviancy (i.e., fascism). At this point, extra-cinematic discourse collapses into extra-cinematic context. For although Amelio wanted Emilio to be seen as the 'son of the conformist', a part memorably played by Trintignant, the Dario of *Colpire al cuore* is *not* that father: he is not Marcello Clerici, the conformist himself.

---

13   Sigmund Freud, 'From the History of an Infantile Neurosis', in *The Standard Edition of the Complete Psychological Works of Sigmund Freud*, ed. James Strachey in collaboration with Anna Freud assisted by Alix Strachey and Alan Tyson; trans. by James Strachey, 24 vols (London: Hogarth Press and the Institute of Psycho-analysis, 1953–1974), xvii (1955), 1–122 ['Aus der Geschichte einer infantilen Neuroes', in *Sammlung kleiner Schriften zur Neurosenlehre*, 5 vols (Leipzig and Vienna: Deuticke, 1906–22), iv (1918)].

It is in the heart of Città alta, too, that Emilio rejects the theory of terrorism's 'cattivi maestri', telling his father that, in fact, not only had Dario taught Emilio nothing, but that his brightest pupil was now 'il più idiota' [the most idiotic] of Emilio's instructors. The cut that follows reveals it all: no longer Città alta but Città bassa, no longer the darkness of night but early morning light, no longer the Dario of his Sten-toting, Ortega-reading period (all stuff of the villa on the hill, all literally behind him in the background), but a 'barone', no longer a father less interested in hierarchical notions of child-rearing, but the man willing to embrace fully his role as *pater familias*, if only it will win him back his son.[14]

However, the most significant change that Città bassa marks is that the possibility of father-son rapprochement has disappeared. The son Dario clasps against the background of the neoclassical *propilea* – a shot made memorable by the film's publicity material – is like a cadaver whose spirit has taken flight leaving behind only its abject carcass.[15] However inert Emilio may seem in his father's embrace, he is already resolute in his decision to accept that the keyhole has indeed revealed thieves and murderers and that, as a responsible citizen, he should contact the proper authorities. In fact, Amelio renders the keyhole and the partial vision it affords quite literal in the film's last scenes, where the camera offers Emilio's point of view of the arrival of the police at Giulia's home.

The images of the police distorted by the *jalousie* glass at the social housing block where Giulia lives represent Emilio's flawed vision (not to mention judgment) as well as the representation of terrorism in *Colpire al cuore* in its extra-cinematic context. As Olivier Assayas has observed, '*Colpire al cuore* è un film su quel preciso momento in cui il bambino diventa uomo nel senso che diventa capace di *vedere*, capace di comprendere e di giudicare' (Sesti, 35) [*Colpire al cuore* is a film about the precise moment in which a child becomes an adult capable of *seeing*, capable of understanding and judging].

Perhaps the hazy references in the film, shot in the Spring of 1982, to unnamed terrorist organizations may be seen in the perspective of the increasing public awareness of terrorism of other stripes in Italy. Officially, the Italian state had passed a series of laws between 1975 and 1981 that 'extended police powers of search and seizure,

---

14   Indeed, along with Ortega y Gasset, Dario has also left behind in the villa on the hill the man who so willingly changes nappies, a task he graciously and carefully discharges in the first Bergamo sequence.
15   See Caldwell, 77, for a different, though consonant, reading of this scene.

increased the time that defendants could be held before trial, and enlarged immunity for police use of force' (Orton, 308). If the state had enacted special laws to juridically manage the anomie created by a broad spectrum of actors, it faced a different challenge on the socio-cultural front, where such efficacious remedies as special laws were less available. A chain that includes links forged by the seismic rumblings of P2 and Gladio, the December 1981 BR kidnapping of US Brigadier General Dozier in Verona, and the deaths of bankers Michele Sindona and Roberto Calvi connects the *anni di piombo* to the year Amelio's film was released.[16] However muted the references to terrorism may seem, *Colpire al cuore* nevertheless hit its mark, judging from the treatment of Amelio following this film. As he observed, 'dopo *Colpire al cuore* è stato duro. Porte chiuse, sbarrate' [It was hard after *Colpire al cuore*. Closed, barred doors]. It was only with *I ragazzi di via Panisperna* [*The Boys from Via Panisperna*], a 1988 RAI production, that he felt 'in qualche modo [...] riconciliato con il fare cinema' (Martini, 136) [in some way [...] reconciled with film-making].

The intergenerational tension present in *Colpire al cuore* indicates also the extra-cinematic discourse with which the film enters into dialogue in 1982. All of Amelio's films, as David Bruni (246) has observed, exhibit some generational conflict, though not necessarily in the guise of the father and son pairing of *Colpire al cuore*. The tension helps us understand the representation of terrorism, to be sure, but also the state of the Italian film industry circa 1982, the decade of 'fatherless' directors as Lino Micciché has observed.[17] The crisis state that the Italian film industry entered into in the beginning of the 1980s bears all the hallmarks of a generational crisis, with the upstart offspring medium – television – placing material obstacles in the path toward production. In fact, since so many critics refer to the 'youth' of the 1980s, those new 'fatherless' directors, some attention to a generational divide makes sense. Micciché, harking back to the vanguard hope of 1968, christens the new generation of filmmakers

---

16   See Sergio Flamigni, *Trame atlantiche: storia della loggia massonica segreta P2* (Rome: Kaos, 2005); Paul Ginsborg, *A History of Contemporary Italy 1943–88* (Harmondsworth: Penguin, 1990), 423; Paul Ginsborg, *Italy and its Discontents: Family, Civil Society, State 1980–2001* (New York: Palgrave, 2003), esp. 142–48; and Giancarlo Lombardi, 'Terrorism, Truth, and the Secret Service: Questions of Accountability in the Cinema of the *stragi di stato*', *Annali d'Italianistica*, 19 (2001), 285–302.

17   Lino Micciché, 'Gli eredi del nulla: per una critica del giovane cinema italiano', in *Una generazione in cinema: esordi ed esordienti italiani 1975–1988*, ed. F. Montini (Venice: Marsilio, 1988), 251–58.

in Italy 'gli eredi di nulla' [the heirs of nothing]. Similarly, Alessandra Levantesi notes that

[la] generazione del 1968, che easuritasi l'inebriante e breve stagione dell'Utopia, non aveva voluto o saputo assumersi quello che dovrebbe essere il compito di ogni generazione: costituirsi un anello di congiunzione fra passato e futuro, trascorrendo (metaforicamente e non) dal ruolo di figli a quello di padri e madri.[18]

[The generation of 1968, once the brief and intoxicating moment of Utopia had passed, did not want or learn to take on the role that ought to be the task of every generation: that of constituting a chain conjoining the past and the future, passing (figuratively and otherwise) from the role of children to that of parents.]

The formal, thematic, and extra-cinematic choices used to signify generational struggle in Amelio's film serve to decontextualize terrorism in Italy in 1982, the year *Colpire al cuore* was made. This decontextualization begins with the unmooring accomplished by the film's title: 'Colpire al cuore' is but half of the notorious BR slogan 'Colpire al cuore dello stato' [to strike at the heart *of the state*], which described the organization's aim in kidnapping magistrates and government officials, evidently carried out to leverage detained comrades-in-arms. The disappearance of the state from Amelio's project enables a reading of the various levels on which antecedents (biological, socio-political, and aesthetic) are at once acknowledged and dispatched. The excision of the state from the title is akin to the operation of anagramming described above; it is a simple recombination of elements that, even if suppressed or cut away, are still present. No matter the socio-historical decontextualization, and despite the film's open ending, its message was nevertheless disquietingly clear: Italian terrorism is at once naked and veiled, felt as near as the heart, viewed as distant as the state.

---

18 Alessandra Levantesi, 'Memorie di un recensore militante: Il cinema italiano', in *Schermi opachi*, 90.

6. Terrorism, a Female Malady[1]

Ruth Glynn

Writing in 1992 about novels of the 1970s and early 1980s which depict political violence and terrorism, Beverly Allen notes a consistent 'gendering of "terrorism" as male. Practically without fail', she writes, 'novelistic representations of Italian political violence show it as appropriate to masculinity but not to femininity and show its perpetrators are male'.[2] Allen goes on to argue that the gendering of terrorism as male ensures the gendering of the victim as female, specifically, with reference to an age-old literary construction, 'the victimized "Italia", the silent, victimized woman' (167) of the Italian nation itself. She concludes by asserting that 'where novels gender "terrorism" as male and its victims as female [...] they offer reassurance to the dominant class' (171). The unarticulated implication of Allen's convincingly argued position is that a gendering of terrorism as female would offer no such reassurance but rather constitute a greater threat to the dominant class and to what Allen sees as Italy's feminized and victimized silent majority. The premise underlying her argument is consonant with that of a number of studies on cultural representations of female perpetrators which posit female-gendered violence as particularly traumatic and threatening, or as what Sergio

1   I wish to thank the Arts and Humanities Research Council for granting me a Research Leave Award to complete this chapter and other articles forming part of my project on women, terror and trauma in Italian culture.
2   Beverly Allen, 'Terrorism Tales: Gender and the Fictions of Italian National Identity', *Italica*, 69: 2 (Summer 1992), 166. Allen's consistent use of scare quotes when referring to 'terrorism' signals that the designation is not her own but rather that of the texts she is analysing. Her aim is not to challenge such labelling but to explore the representation of acts defined as terrorism in the texts under investigation.

Lenci, himself the survivor of a terrorist attack, articulates as a double wound, when he claims that 'la donna ti ferisce due volte rispetto all'uomo' [woman wounds you twice in comparison to man].[3]

Yet, within only a couple of years of the publication of the latest of the novels about which Allen writes, the Italian public was presented with a cinematic corpus which, albeit for a brief moment, effects a feminization of terrorism that provides a challenge to the claims implicit in Allen's analysis. This corpus comprises Carlo Lizzani's *Nucleo zero* (*Nucleus Zero*, 1984), Giuseppe Bertolucci's *Segreti segreti* (*Secrets, Secrets*, 1984) and Marco Bellocchio's *Diavolo in corpo* (*Devil in the Flesh*, 1986). All three films feminize the threat of terrorism to some degree and, in the case of the first two, focus to a significant extent on the figure of the female terrorist. In her recent work on cinematic representations of the violent woman, Hilary Neroni asserts that 'the violent woman appears at moments of ideological crisis' and that 'such an ideological crisis occurs when strictly defined gender roles [...] break down'.[4] While Neroni clearly privileges gender issues as the prime motivator of ideological crisis, however, I would conversely suggest that *any* ideological or cultural crisis *may* manifest itself as an anxiety over gender issues. In the specific case of Italian film of the mid-1980s, I would contend that the ideological crisis triggering the emergence of the figure of the female terrorist was rooted as much in the specific strategies employed to contain the threat of terrorism in those years as in a perceived alignment between Italy's recent experience of feminism and women's active participation in political violence.

Thus the feminization of the terrorist threat in Italian cinema must be examined in the context of Italy's attempts to eradicate political violence in the 1980s, a period in which terrorism was not just a phenomenon of the very recent past (as popular memory might suggest, by equating the *anni di piombo* exclusively with the 1970s) but an ongoing reality from which Italy was only tentatively beginning to emerge. Throughout the decade, political violence continued to make headlines in the Italian media. These headlines had two different formats. The first comprised sporadic reports of grave acts of violence – bombings, kidnappings and assassinations – reminding the public that terrorism still posed some level of threat to Italian

3   Sergio Lenci, *Colpo alla nuca* (Rome: Editori Riuniti, 1980), 130.
4   Hilary Neroni, *The Violent Woman: Femininity, Narrative and Violence in Contemporary American Cinema* (Albany: SUNY University Press, 2005), 18.

civil society.[5] The second consisted of more regular reports relating to the containment of the threat of left-wing violence in particular: news of the mass arrests and subsequent court trials that took place throughout the decade. Instrumental to the containment of terrorism was the legal-cultural innovation of *pentitismo*, a formal mechanism affording significant reductions in sentencing for prisoners who collaborated with the authorities by naming their fellow militants.[6] While, on the one hand, this innovation would prove extremely powerful in bringing to an end the widespread use of political violence by militant groups, on the other hand, the information to which the public was exposed in the mid-1980s confirmed the alarming magnitude of the threat posed by political violence at its peak and, for the first time, shed light on the full extent and the nature of women's involvement in acts of terrorism.[7]

In light of these considerations, I would suggest that the films of the 1980s are best read not as post-traumatic narratives or narratives of 'post-terrorism' but rather as narratives of ongoing collective and cultural trauma.[8] Just as *pentitismo* functions to contain the threat of political violence and civil unrest, limiting its potential for damage to state and society, so too trauma – of its very nature – is a psychical reaction that works to repress, contain or limit the threat of violence and its potential damage to the psyche.[9] Trauma narratives function

---

5 According to political scientist Giorgio Galli the impact of the continuing violence does not lead Italian public opinion to immediately appreciate that the mass arrests following the Dozier kidnapping in 1982 spell the end of the armed struggle as a significant political strategy, *Piombo rosso: la storia completa della lotta armata in Italia dal 1970 a oggi* (Milan: Baldini, Castoldi, Dalai, 2004), 203. Although he refers specifically to the Brigate Rosse alone, Galli's observation may be taken as symptomatic of the wider public fears still surrounding terrorist organizations of all political hues in the 1980s.

6 Although state collaboration was practised by individual terrorists at least as early as 1980, it was in 1982 that the introduction of the so-called 'Cossiga Law' formalized the procedure through which information leading to arrests could be exchanged for a reduction in sentence.

7 Women's participation in political violence increased as the 1970s wore on, so that women were most prominent in leadership positions in the late 1970s and early 1980s. The mass arrests of 1982 offer an interesting snapshot of the membership of one particular BR formation at that time: of the 147 people questioned 107 were men and forty women (Galli, 205–06).

8 On the idea of a cinema of 'post-terrorism', see Fabrizio Natalini, 'Diavolo in corpo', in *Marco Bellocchio: il cinema e i film*, ed. Adriano Aprà (Venice: Marsilio, 2005), 185–89.

9 Elizabeth Wheeler's description of how the two main components of post-traumatic stress disorder function as containment is particularly instructive: 'Although vivid and overwhelming, flashback is a form of emotional containment,

as containment narratives, narratives that struggle to contain a threat which may be unacknowledged yet is discernible in its very absence or unacknowledged state. As Leigh Gilmore reminds us, 'no trauma narrative is easy to tell' so that 'trauma emerges in narrative as much through what cannot be said of it as through what can'.[10] Similarly, Lacan stipulates that we know that an event is traumatic not because we uncover a direct experience of the trauma but rather 'on the basis of the traumatic consequence it ha[s] on the actual behaviour of the subject'.[11] It is only through this kind of indirect route – through the recognition of hysterical symptoms, for instance – that we can encounter a repressed trauma, whether individual or collective.

This essay examines the films of the mid-1980s as symptomatic and hysterical reactions to the collective and cultural trauma inflicted by Italy's experience of terrorism. My analysis is limited to those texts in which the female protagonist overtly dominates the cinematic exploration of terrorism and its effects: Giuseppe Bertolucci's *Segreti segreti* and Marco Bellocchio's *Diavolo in corpo*.[12] Here, I examine the similar strategies employed by the two films to contain or repress the terrorist threat, regardless of whether that threat is embodied by the female perpetrator or the female victim: while *Segreti segreti* feminizes the threat of terrorism by addressing the figure of the female terrorist, in *Diavolo in corpo* the threat of terrorism is projected onto the figure of a female victim or survivor who, significantly, is never identified or explicitly presented as such. The comparison of the two films leads us towards an understanding of the ways in which the feminine may be invoked in an attempt to contain the threat of terrorism; of the relationship between narratives about political violence and social order; and of the respective anxieties aroused by perpetrators and

in which past trauma lives in the psyche as an encapsulated island, quarantined away from the rest of memory, while psychic numbing is by nature a form of emotional containment, whether through avoidance of feeling, amnesia or the inability to feel'. Elizabeth A. Wheeler, *Uncontained: Urban Fiction in Postwar America* (New Brunswick: Rutgers University Press, 2001), 11.

10   Leigh Gilmore, *The Limits of Autobiography: Trauma and Testimony* (Ithaca: Cornell University Press, 2001), 46.

11   Jacques Lacan, 'The Nucleus of Repression', *The Seminar of Jacques Lacan*, i: *Freud's Papers on Technique 1953–1954* (Cambridge: Cambridge University Press, 1988), 189 ['Le noyau du refoulement', in *Le Séminaire de Jacques Lacan*, i: *Les Écrits techniques de Freud 1953–1954* (Paris: Seuil, 1975), 211–223].

12   While *Nucleo zero* also engages in an interesting way with the figure of the female terrorist, Lizzani's film does not, on the whole, equate terrorism with woman in the way that *Segreti segreti* and *Diavolo in corpo* clearly do.

victim-survivors in the context of pentitismo and efforts to leave terrorism behind in the Italy of the 1980s.

Segreti Segreti and the Threat of the Female Terrorist

One of the earliest cinematic representations of the figure of the female terrorist, Giuseppe Bertolucci's *Segreti segreti*, is set in a world composed almost entirely of women, all of whom harbour secret desires or knowledge. This world is constructed upon a series of mother-daughter relationships which are connected by an act of terrorism – the murder of a judge in Venice – carried out by Laura, a well-to-do member of the Brigate Rosse. Following the murder, Laura takes refuge in her childhood home in Northern Italy, where her nanny Gina, a mother-figure of sorts, tacitly intuits Laura's guilt. Laura then departs for her own house in Rome, where her mother, Marta, acts also as a surrogate mother to Laura's best friend, Renata, herself the mother of a teenage daughter. The action shifts to the earthquake-devastated Southern region of Irpinia, where the funeral of Laura's dead comrade takes place in the presence of his mother, stepmother and stepsister. Back in Rome, Laura's mother commits suicide after learning of her daughter's guilt and Laura herself is arrested and questioned by a female judge who has just been informed by her little girl of her husband's infidelity.

The plot revolves around the central figure of Laura and the impact of her violent actions. If it is true that 'the trauma of the violent woman manifests itself in the defence mechanisms that films must utilize in order to depict this figure' (Neroni, 39), then it is also true that Italian culture more widely has frequently sought to contain the threat of the female perpetrator by de-feminizing her, an interpretive act which serves to preserve the socially accepted equation of masculinity and violence, femininity and victimhood.[13] *Segreti segreti* eschews this dominant norm, however, favouring instead an established cinematic motif for the containment of female violence that presents precisely the opposite portrait of the violent woman: the figure of the *femme fatale*, whose very excess of femininity is symptomatic of her status as a hysterical construction.

13   A model for the defeminizing of the perpetrator in Italian culture might be Torquato Tasso's Renaissance epic, *Gerusalemme liberata* (1581). Here, Clorinda's femininity is erased in those scenes associated with her castrating violence, only to be restored and reinscribed in the moment of her victimhood when she is fatally pierced by Tancredi's phallic sword.

In the film's opening scene, Laura carries out the cold-blooded shooting of a judge after her comrade Pietro, who had been assigned to carry out the murder, loses his nerve and accidentally shoots himself instead of the target. The calm and controlled manner in which Laura takes charge of the situation and dispenses violence with apparent indifference, killing not only the judge but also Pietro, would seem to corroborate Allen's implicit construction of female violence as particularly threatening. It would also seem to illustrate H.H.A. Cooper's rather more explicit and hysterical expression of the idea that 'the single-minded, fanatically inhuman hostility or contempt for the victim's humanity [...] is typical of the pitiless attitude many women terrorists are capable of assuming. It is one that men find curiously hard to match'.[14] This initial scene, set in the dark and labyrinthine backstreets of Venice, also goes some way towards establishing a film noir aesthetic and constructing the protagonist as a *femme fatale*, in the terms posited by Neroni:

> The *femme fatale* hardly ever commits actual physical violence [...].
> Instead, she almost always uses a gun. [...] This sleek, cold, phallic
> weapon is the perfect accessory to the *femme fatale*: it both matches her
> highly stylized representation, and her insensitive demeanour. [...]
> This weapon also allows the *femme fatale* to continue looking beautiful
> when committing violence [...] it leaves much of femininity intact.
> (25–26)

Throughout the film, Laura's dress and demeanour are such that her femininity remains largely unquestioned. However, it is only in the scene in which she visits her friend Renata, who has been hospitalized after a suicide attempt, that the portrayal of Laura becomes highly stylized and explicitly constructed in the mode of the *femme fatale*. The iconography is overtly sexual, as Laura's red dress dominates the screen and the camera follows her movements around the room. Yet it is some way into their conversation that Renata – who is portrayed not only as mentally unstable but also as a highly sensual figure of excess (she explains that it is her excessive self-love that has led her

---

14   H.H.A. Cooper, 'Woman as Terrorist', in *Criminology of Deviant Women*, ed. Freda Adler and Rita James Simon (Boston: Houghton Mifflin, 1979), 152. My employment of the term 'hysterical' here, as elsewhere in the article, is consciously at odds with the psychoanalytic tradition that ascribes hysteria to women whose behaviour transgresses societal norms. In applying the term to male reactions to women's transgression, I seek both to suggest that such reactions are extreme, groundless and irrational and to imply that they share with the psychoanalytic discourse of hysteria a symptomatic desire to control the behaviour of women.

to start playing games with her life) – suddenly becomes conscious of Laura's very striking red dress and dark glasses. Renata's suggestion that Laura's attire is atypical of her usual appearance recalls Mary Ann Doane's analysis of the *femme fatale*, rooted in Joan Riviere's theorization of femininity as masquerade. As Riviere constructs it, womanliness is a mask which women engaged in traditionally male activities may adopt in order to 'avert anxiety and retribution feared from men'.[15] Doane is interested in the way in which such a theorization of femininity as a process of masquerade and veiling can serve to 'ally women with deception, secretiveness, a kind of anti-knowledge or, on the other hand, situate them as privileged conduits to – a necessarily complex and even devious – truth'.[16] Following Doane, Laura's adoption of the mask of femininity may be seen as a disguise employed to conceal her appropriation of masculinity in BR militancy and the deployment of a gun. The threat that such an appropriation of masculinity poses is reinforced by her wearing of dark glasses which signifies, in cinematic terms, 'an active looking' and a usurping of the gaze which 'poses a threat to an entire system of representation' (27). But the dark glasses also function as a kind of veil, exemplifying 'the disparity between seeming and being, the deception, instability and unpredictability associated with the woman' (46). Although Laura's glasses shield her eyes, preventing Renata from reading therein the guilty secret she harbours, they also call attention to the very fact that her womanly appearance is a disguise.

Laura is constructed as a *femme fatale* only in order to be deconstructed as such. Doane's assertion that 'womanliness is a mask which can be worn or removed' (25) is exemplified in Laura's feminine disguise being systematically undone through the removal first of her glasses and then of her dress. The loss of the glasses alone, in a clear allusion to the Hollywood convention of representing the *femme fatale*, is enough to undo Laura's appropriation of masculinity, for Renata's insistence that she remove the glasses precisely so that she can see her properly re-inscribes Laura's femininity through an insistence upon what Laura Mulvey would call her 'to-be-looked-at-ness'.[17] Renata's subsequent removal of Laura's dress so that she

15   Joan Riviere, 'Womanliness as Masquerade' (1929), in *Formations of Fantasy*, ed. Victor Burgin, James Donald and Cora Kaplan (London: Methuen, 1986), 35.
16   Mary Ann Doane, *Femmes Fatales: Feminism, Film Theory, Psychoanalysis* (New York and London: Routledge, 1991), 3.
17   Laura Mulvey, 'Visual Pleasure and Narrative Cinema', *Screen*, 16: 3 (Autumn 1975), 12.

can try it on herself completes the undoing of the masquerade: Laura is literally 'exposed', wearing only her slip, the foundation for her disguise, when Renata's nurse enters the room unexpectedly. As Laura hastily re-clothes herself in Renata's dressing gown, she begins the process of identity realignment that culminates in an equation, or identification, between 'madwoman' and 'terrorist'. The scene closes with Renata as femme fatale dictating camera framing and movement; clothed in Laura's dress and glasses, sitting in the chair Laura had sat in at the start of the scene, she talks of her own self-directed violence ('se voglio mi ammazzo' [if I want, I'll kill myself]), while Laura assumes the role of patient, clad in Renata's white hospital garb and lying in her bed.

The identification created here between madwoman and terrorist is a device through which the threat of terrorism is simultaneously presented and contained within *Segreti segreti*. The equating of Laura as terrorist with Renata as madwoman (an association later reinforced when Pietro, the murdered terrorist, is described by his step-mother as the 'figlio di una matta' [son of a madwoman]), means that terrorism is embedded in a discourse of female psychopathology. The implicit equation between Laura's psychopathological terrorist activities and Renata's self-harming is a comparison overtly made by Bertolucci when he refers to what he sees as 'una quota di autolesionismo che il terrorista porta con sé, un gesto autodistruttivo' [a quota of self-harm that marks the terrorist, a self-destructive gesture].[18] While on the one hand the notion of self-harm questions the strict division between perpetrator and victim presented in the opening scene, the pathological discourse in which terrorism is embedded in *Segreti segreti* combines with the limitation of female violence to the figure of the *femme fatale* to distance Laura as female terrorist from the average or 'normal' woman.[19] In this way, a clear restriction is placed on the violence itself in order for the traditional idea of the feminine to be preserved.

18 Giuseppe Bertolucci, 'Intervista', *Segreti segreti* DVD (Rome: Istituto Luce, 2004).
19 It is notable that representations of women terrorists in Italian film offer atypical cinematic constructions of both women and terrorists. Laura's lack of interest in maternity and her lack of involvement in a romantic relationship are characteristic of the cinematic female terrorist, but a deviation from the norm of cinematic representations of women. Similarly, the emphasis on psychopathology differentiates the cinematic portrait of the female terrorist from that of her male counterpart; even when psychoanalysis *is* applied to male-centred portraits of terrorism, the tendency is to offer an Oedipal construction of generational struggle, as discussed by Ellen Nerenberg in this volume in relation to Gianni Amelio's *Colpire al cuore* (1983), rather than a pathological diagnosis.

The second way in which the threat of violence is presented but contained in *Segreti segreti* is the construction of the environment in which terrorism takes place as one composed almost entirely of women. The rarity of such a phenomenon in Italian film recalls film noir's tendency to offer examples of abnormal settings or behaviour that defy patterns established for social interaction, so that 'the defining contours of this group of films are the product of what is abnormal and dissonant'.[20] Such men as are presented in *Segreti segreti* are either tragically inept – this is the case of Pietro, who shoots himself in the foot – or else risible caricatures (e.g., Marta's new lover who is urinating against a tree when Laura sets eyes on him). The excision of positive representations of men and masculinity from the text effects a kind of symbolic textual castration which is consonant with the threat of castration that Doane sees embodied in the figure of the *femme fatale*, a figure she identifies as 'an articulation of fears surrounding the loss of stability and centrality of the self, the "I", the ego' (2). In such a context, Doane adds, 'the phallus becomes important only insofar as it might be absent, it might disappear. It assumes meaning only in relation to castration' (45). While on the one hand the excision of strong male characters from the text suggests that women's appropriation of violence is bound up with an emasculation of men, it also serves to minimize the threat of terrorism by locating it in a world far removed from a recognizable representation of Italian social and political reality. Ultimately, the excision of men and the political world with which they are traditionally associated results in a denial of the political rationale of Laura's violent actions, and ensures that terrorism itself is framed in terms of what Elaine Showalter might call 'a female malady'.[21]

20 Sylvia Harvey, 'Woman's Place: The Absent Family of Film Noir', in *Women in Film Noir*, ed. E. Ann Kaplan, rev. edn (London: British Film Institute, 1998), 35.
21 Elaine Showalter, *The Female Malady: Women, Madness, and English Culture, 1830–1980* (New York: Pantheon, 1985). Showalter's exploration of the application of psychopathological discourses to women's behaviour is particularly revealing when considered in the light of the comparative constructions of Laura's and Pietro's implicit motivations for participating in terrorism in *Segreti segreti*. Working-class Pietro's participation is constructed as a rational response to deprivation: his involvement is contextualized in relation to the devastation and neglect of Irpinia, so that his militant and anti-state activities may be understood as a form of socio-political critique. As no such motivation is evident in Laura's wealthy background, her participation in terrorism is constructed as being situated entirely in the realm of the private, demanding a psychological rather than a political explanation.

As a female malady, the threat of terrorism can and must be contained within the institutions of the state. The conventions of film noir are such that 'the *femme fatale* ultimately loses physical movement, influence over camera movement, and is often actually or symbolically imprisoned by composition as control over her is exerted and expressed visually'.[22] In accordance with those conventions, Laura is framed in increasingly enclosed spaces until such time as the narrative culminates in her physical containment and the restoration of both masculinity and social order, represented by the policemen who arrest Laura and deliver her to the investigating magistrate. Although the magistrate is female, the delivery of Laura to the law effects a restoration of social order which ensures that 'the ideological operation of the myth [of the *femme fatale*] is thus achieved by first demonstrating her power and its frightening results, then destroying it' (Place, 56). Whereas Laura's first encounter with a judge, in the film's opening scene, had cast her in the role of cold-blooded killer, her next encounter with the law at the film's close portrays her imprisoned in the role of sobbing and submissive *pentita*.

The decisive conclusion of *Segreti segreti* signals that the myth of the *femme fatale* functions here not only as a male fantasy articulating and exorcizing a fear of the violent woman, but also as a wider cultural fantasy articulating and exorcizing a fear of terrorism. Once before the investigating magistrate, Laura capitulates in a highly improbable manner; she willingly collaborates with the institutions and representatives of the state by volunteering, without any encouragement, the names of her companions in militancy. Although the magistrate's ambivalent reaction does reveal a certain anxiety about the status and nature of the unsolicited confession, the film's closing images (which frame Laura behind bars and in an ever more constricted space, as the camera retreats to the sound of her voice slowly fading out) partake in a contemporary cultural projection of *pentitismo* as a panacea for terrorism. Far from offering a particularly threatening or traumatic image of female-gendered terrorism, then, *Segreti segreti* concludes with a vision of terrorism as a compliant woman reduced to tears, silenced and detained by the state. Despite the film's gendering of terrorism as female, its *denouement* cannot fail to offer reassurance to Italy's dominant class and silent majority. Yet its very 'will to contain', discernible in its overly neat conclusion and its exaggerated insistence on the power of *pentitismo* to eradicate terrorism, simultaneously signals that Italian culture is

---

22   Janey Place, 'Women in Film Noir', in Kaplan, *Women in Film Noir*, 56.

still desperately seeking to exorcize the fears, and work though the trauma, of the *anni di piombo*.

Diavolo in Corpo and the Threat of the Female Victim

Equally symptomatic of a desire to exorcize the terrorist threat from the national unconscious is the negative response that greeted the release of Marco Bellocchio's *Diavolo in corpo* two years later. Fabrizio Natalini suggests that the film's lack of popularity with the Italian cinema-going public is due to a disinclination on the part of Italian audiences to deal with the subject-matter of terrorism, a reaction that may be interpreted as a form of psychological repression:

> nel 1986, in Italia praticamente nessuno aveva la voglia (o la capacità) di parlare degli 'anni di piombo'. [...] La grande rimozione avvenuta su quel periodo della storia patria [...] fa temere che il pubblico delle sale non sia ancora preparato a interrogarsi sugli aspetti politici del nostro passato, preferendogli storie più intime e private. (188)

> [in 1986, in Italy, almost nobody had the desire (or the capacity) to talk about the *anni di piombo*. [...] The repression brought to bear on that period of national history [...] is such that the cinema-going public is not yet ready to confront the political aspects of our past, preferring instead more intimate and private stories.]

At first glance, however, Bellocchio's film offers no more threatening a vision of terrorism than does *Segreti segreti*. Rather, it provides precisely the kind of intimate story Natalini suggests the public might prefer to a political exploration of the recent past, and is far better known for its explicit sexual content than as a commentary on Italy's experience of terrorism. Set in Rome, the plot centres on the relationship between Giulia Dozza, an apparently fragile and emotionally unstable young woman, engaged to an imprisoned terrorist-turned-*pentito*, and Andrea Raimondi, the schoolboy son of Giulia's psychotherapist. Bellocchio's film shares with *Segreti segreti* a desire to assert *pentitismo* as a panacea for left-wing terrorism. Although *Diavolo in corpo's* courtroom scenes raise concerns about the dubious motivations surrounding the confessions of 'i cosiddetti *pentiti* che hanno moltissimo interesse a formulare le accuse' ['the so-called *pentiti* who have a considerable interest in making accusations'], those concerns are only ever partially audible and, as if in collusion with the audience's desire to repress the reality of terrorism, are swiftly drowned out on both diegetic and extradiegetic levels. Moreover,

the imminent release of Giulia's fiancé, the repentant and subdued
Giacomo Pulcini, presents no threat at all to civil society at large: his
self-penned ode to mediocrity with its tribute to the prospect of a quiet
life, marriage and children in a post-terrorist future combines with
his sexual passivity to neutralize any potential threat that Giacomo
as terrorist might embody. Like *Segreti segreti*, then, *Diavolo in corpo*
presents *pentitismo* as a supreme form of containment and appears to
offer reassurance that the threat of terrorism is safely located in the
past.

However, despite abounding with images and institutions of
containment, Bellocchio's film ultimately fails to contain the terrorist
threat it presents and this, I would contend, is the cause of the
audience unease noted by Natalini. As in *Segreti segreti*, it is through
the figure of the female protagonist, constructed as both *femme fatale*
and madwoman, that the threat of terrorism continues to operate.
Diavolo in corpo's construction of Giulia as *femme fatale* is governed
less by her capacity for violence, as is the case of Laura in *Segreti
segreti*, than by her overt and unbridled sexuality, a key characteristic
of the *femme fatale*. In view of the power she exerts over both Andrea
and his father, a rather unsympathetic character, Giulia may be seen
to possess an ability to seduce and control almost any man who
crosses her path. Moreover, she is consistently portrayed as sexually
'aggressive': it is she who usually initiates sex with Andrea and also
with Giacomo, who finds her masturbation of him too forceful. As
Neroni asserts, the sexual characteristics of the *femme fatale* are 'both a
manifestation of society's fantasy of the underside of femininity [...]
and also something more elusive (and thus undeniably threatening
to society)' (Neroni, 22). That the threat embodied by Giulia as
sexually aggressive *femme fatale* is psychological, rather than physical,
is suggested in a surreal scene in which Andrea's father recalls (or
possibly fantasizes – this remains unclear) a naked Giulia chasing
him around his office as he fearfully rejects her advances. His personal
loss of dignity is compounded by his loss of control of the clinician-
patient relationship and by the failure of the scientific discipline he
practises to control the behaviour of the sexually aggressive woman
who is the object of his therapy. The castration anxiety underlying
both this episode and the portrait of Giulia as *femme fatale* throughout
the film more generally resurfaces most explicitly in the scene in
which Giulia watches over a sleeping Andrea and, scissors in hand,
raises the sheet covering his body, gazes down at him and says:
'io te lo posso tagliare, faccio presto... è facile' [I can cut it, I'll be

quick… it's easy], before proceeding to snip what the audience, after a moment's hesitation, must surmise is his pubic hair.

Unacknowledged Oedipal tensions surely underlie the psychoanalyst's highly emotive response to his son's relationship with Giulia, but the specifically psychopathological nature of his warnings that Giulia is 'completamente pazza' [completely mad], that 'le donne ti portano in manicomio' [women drive you to the madhouse] and that 'i pazzi sono pericolosissimi, ti si appiccicano addosso' [the mad are very dangerous, they stick to you] provides an extreme and entirely hysterical alignment of femininity, madness and contagion. The fears that underlie these declarations lend weight both to Naomi Segal's reading of the *femme fatale* as a phenomenon rooted in male self-exculpation and to Jane Ussher's observation that 'the discursive practices which create the concept of madness mark it as fearful, as individual, as invariably feminine, as sickness; and they function as a form of social regulation'.[23] In addition to articulating a personal evaluation of the danger posed by Giulia, Professor Raimondi's words also provide overt expression of the construction of Giulia as hysteric or madwoman implicit throughout the narrative. Indeed, the very opening scene, providing a moment of empathy and identification between Giulia and an agitated and apparently crazed young African woman assailed by demons, serves to align Giulia with the figure of the madwoman from the very outset and to frame her within a discourse of alterity, marginality, irrationality and madness.[24] That initial portrait of Giulia develops throughout the narrative, so that the recurrent depictions of her wild and sudden bursts of emotion, oscillating between extremes of gaiety, anger, sadness and vacuity in

---

23   Naomi Segal, *Narcissus and Echo: Women in the French 'récit'* (Manchester: Manchester University Press, 1988), 34–5; Jane Ussher, *Women's Madness: Misogyny or Mental Illness?* (New York: Harvester, Wheatsheaf, 1991), 12. Doane, too, identifies a pathological construction in the composition of the *femme fatale*: 'the *femme fatale* is an ambivalent figure because she is not the subject of power but its *carrier* (the connotations of disease are appropriate here)' (2).

24   The Woman-as-other construction that is presented here extends not only to the *femme fatale* and madwoman but also, as alluded to in the film's title, to the figure of the witch. As Simone Arcagni has observed, woman for Bellocchio is 'fuori dalla Norma, folle e strega. Giulia è il primo di questi personaggi che incarnano un ideale antico di donna che collima con quella della strega' [beyond the norm, lunatic and witch-like. Giulia is the first of those characters who incarnate an ancient ideal of woman which corresponds with that of the witch]. 'Diavolo in corpo', in *Le forme della ribellione: il cinema di Marco Bellocchio*, ed. Luisa Ceretto and Giancarlo Zappoli (Turin: Lindau, 2004), 120.

an apparently inexplicable manner, serve to prepare the ground and lend support to Professor Raimondi's 'diagnosis' of madness.

However, where *Diavolo in corpo* departs from *Segreti segreti* is in the application of the twin motifs of the *femme fatale* and the madwoman to a female protagonist who is not the perpetrator but rather the victim of terrorism. Never overtly presented as such, Giulia may be one of the many victim-survivors whose family members have been killed in the *anni di piombo*, as is intimated in a brief scene in which she visits a commemorative plaque in honour of a 'Colonello Mario Dozza [...] vittima del terrorismo' [Colonel Mario Dozza [...] victim of terrorism]. Yet no further exploration or elucidation of this scene is offered; no investigation of the connection between the death of the man we assume to be her father and her psychological state or behaviour, no exploration of how her father's death might relate to her relationship with her fiancé (possibly her father's killer), or his decision to become a *pentito*. In short, no attempt at all is made to address Giulia's status as a victim of terrorism. Rather, while alluding to Giulia's victimized status, the narrative works simultaneously to veil over and invalidate her suffering by equating her with the *femme fatale* and enveloping her in a discourse of madness. These narrative strategies serve to distance her from the rest of society and to divert attention from the wider societal problems from which her personal suffering arises.

In order to understand what underlies the drive to invalidate Giulia's suffering and to dismiss her as a doubly dangerous woman, both *femme fatale* and mad, it is instructive to turn to theoretical constructions of the threat played by the victim or survivor in a traumatized society. In his study of Holocaust survivors, Leo Eitinger observed that 'war and victims are something the community wants to forget; a veil of oblivion is drawn over everything painful and unpleasant. [...] As time passes the victim of the disaster will only be a disturbing reminder of unpleasant experiences'.[25] Expanding on Eitinger's work, Judith Herman theorizes that, contrary to expectation, the victim may pose an even greater socio-psychological threat in a traumatized society than the perpetrator. As Herman explains, while the voice of the perpetrator may be silenced, that of the victim (who makes demands of the listener) cannot. She writes: 'the victim asks the bystander to share the burden of pain. The victim

---

25   Leo Eitinger, 'The Concentration Camp Syndrome and its Late Sequelae', in *Survivors, Victims and Perpetrators: Essays on the Nazi Holocaust*, ed. Joel E. Dimsdale (London: Taylor and Francis, 1980), 159.

demands action, engagement, and remembering'.[26] Moreover, 'when the victim is already devalued (a woman, a child), she may find that the most traumatic events of her life take place outside the realm of socially validated reality. Her experience becomes unspeakable', so that 'the study of psychological trauma must constantly contend with this tendency to discredit the victim or to render her invisible' (8).

Following Herman, I would suggest that it is precisely that tendency to discredit the victim or render her invisible that underlies *Diavolo in corpo*'s failure to fully recognize and address Giulia's victimized status. For a public eager to repress the memory of recent violence and reassure itself that the threat of terrorism has been eradicated, neutralized or contained by the culture of *pentitismo*, the victim – who cannot be silenced or banished like the perpetrator – continues to raise the spectre of violence and threatens to disturb the process of psychological repression at work in the wider community. Thus, the fragility of the female victim, far from offering reassurance to the dominant social order as Allen had conjectured, becomes in *Diavolo in corpo* both the focus and the articulation of societal anxieties too painful to address. Indeed, both the overburdened and disorganized nature of *Diavolo in corpo*'s plot and the failure to identify Giulia's victimized status may be read as symptomatic of that wider process; as resulting, that is, from an inability on the part of the film's creative team to address consistently the still open wounds of the *anni di piombo*.

Consequently, where *Segreti segreti* closes with the containment and confession of the terrorist, extracting her from a discourse of psychopathology (the realm of the feminine, the enigmatic, the secret) in favour of one of crime and punishment, no such discursive repositioning is possible in *Diavolo in corpo*. However, the film closes with an image of the 'leaking capsule of trauma' (Wheeler, 12), literally presented in the tears that fall from Giulia's eyes as she listens to Andrea renouncing all forms of political ideology before reciting and commenting on the final tragic passage of Sophocles' *Antigone*. While Andrea represents the hope of a younger generation uninterested in political ideology and sensitive to its tragic consequences, Giulia's cathartic tears provide some limited promise of release from the emotional containment of trauma.

26   Judith Herman, *Trauma and Recovery: From Domestic Abuse to Political Terror*, rev. edn (London: Pandora, 2001), 8.

Conclusion

Perhaps it is only by contrasting cultural representations such as *Segreti segreti* and *Diavolo in corpo* that we can begin to understand the relative anxieties clustering around the figures of the perpetrator and the victim in the post-*pentitismo* climate of the mid-1980s. The feminization of terrorism employed in both films and the application of the twin motifs of the *femme fatale* and the madwoman to terrorist and victim alike provides a very revealing blurring of the boundaries between perpetrator and victim which must be explained in the light of a collective desire to close the book on the *anni di piombo*.[27] For while the containment culture of *pentitismo* was welcomed by the Italian public as the harbinger of a new post-terrorist era and pressed into action as a panacea for terrorism, it was poorly equipped to deal with the ongoing threat embodied by the victim, still 'at large' in Italian society. This is eloquently attested to by the similarities in stylistic conventions and the differences in the narrative edifice between Bertolucci's and Bellocchio's films. Here, contrary to Beverly Allen's expectations and assumptions, the feminizing of the terrorist in *Segreti segreti* ultimately offers reassurance to its Italian audience, but that of the victim in *Diavolo in corpo* displays instead the greater psychological threat that the victim may pose in a traumatized society.

---

27 Significantly, it is in the context of the *pentitismo* debates in the mid-1980s that the various organizations dedicated to advancing the rights and interests of the relatives of victims of terrorism agglomerate in a bid to ensure that the needs and sensitivities of victims and survivors are adequately represented within those debates.

Section 3
Screening Moro

7. Screening the Moro Case

Rachele Tardi

This essay examines three Italian feature films dealing with the abduction of Aldo Moro by the Brigate Rosse (BR) in 1978. All three rewrite the Moro case in significant ways, by filtering it through particular genres (classical tragedy, political thriller, fantasy) and by excluding from effective representation the political motives of the BR. Even when the films allude to the covert political actions of the state, they tend to inflect the representation of Moro's jailers towards their personal situation or towards Moro's personal tragedy.

The films are, in order of their cinema release dates, *Il caso Moro* (*The Moro Case*, Giuseppe Ferrara, 1986), *Piazza delle cinque lune* (*Piazza of the Five Moons*, Renzo Martinelli, 2003) and *Buongiorno, notte* (*Good Morning, Night*, Marco Bellocchio, 2003). They are discussed here in reverse chronological order, starting with *Buongiorno, notte*, to which the greater part of this essay is devoted. In a prelude to the discussion, I argue that Leonardo Sciascia's book, *L'affaire Moro* (1978) [*The Moro Affair*], provided a template for Bellocchio's film, as it did for many other texts dealing with the Moro case. In the conclusion to the essay I invoke the notion of erasure of historical memory to reflect on what is absent from all these filmic representations and why.

The Shadow of Sciascia

Although the explicit source text for *Buongiorno, notte* was the 1998 memoir, *Il prigioniero* [*The Prisoner*], written by former *brigatista* Anna Laura Braghetti in collaboration with journalist Paola Tavella, Bellocchio's film is also shadowed by the implicit presence of Sciascia's

L'affaire Moro.[1] Originally published in 1978, shortly after the abduction and killing of Moro, Sciascia's text has remained fundamental for subsequent accounts and representations of the case.[2] Through its analysis of Moro's letters it presents a view both of the fifty-four days of his imprisonment and of the actions of the state. It also alludes to a possible involvement of the secret services in the abduction of Moro and in the police's failure to find him, allusions which become full-blown conspiracy theory in *Il caso Moro* and *Piazza delle cinque lune*. Giuseppe Traina, among others, has noted the strongly political nature of Sciascia's text, which 'si risolve soprattutto nel denunciare inflessibilmente, nelle sue ambiguità e nei suoi oppurtunismi, il comportamento del cosiddetto "partito della fermezza", che rifiutò qualunque trattativa con i terroristi e ogni tentativo di salvare Moro' [above all comes to denounce in no uncertain terms the ambiguous and opportunistic behaviour of the so-called 'hard-line party', which refused to undertake any negotiation with the terrorists and failed to make any effort to save Moro].[3]

Three main motifs of *L'affaire Moro* recur, singly or together, in many later representations of the Moro case. They are the narrative of a 'sciogliersi dalla forma' [dissolution of form],[4] the positing of a paradoxical or problematic relationship between truth and literature, and the use of metaphors of light. The first of these motifs is introduced by Sciascia with an allusion to Luigi Pirandello: 'Moro comincia, pirandellianamente, a sciogliersi dalla forma, poiché tragicamente è entrato nella vita. Da personaggio ad 'uomo solo', da 'uomo solo' a creatura: i passaggi che Pirandello assegna all'unica possibile salvezza' (72–73) [Moro begins, in a Pirandellian manner, to dissolve from form once he has dramatically entered into life. The transitions from stage character to 'solitary man' and from 'solitary man' to creature are those which, according to Pirandello, lead to the only salvation possible]. The implicit reference here is to the opposition

---

1 Anna Laura Braghetti and Paola Tavella, *Il prigioniero* (Milan: Feltrinelli, 2003; orig. Milan: Mondadori, 1998); Leonardo Sciascia, *L'affaire Moro* (Palermo: Sellerio, 1978).

2 See, for instance, Marco Baliani, *Corpo di stato: il delitto Moro: una generazione divisa* (Milan: Rizzoli, 2003), 83; Giancarlo De Cataldo, *Romanzo criminale* (Turin: Einaudi, 2004), 124–25. *Aldo Moro: una tragedia italiana* (Teatro Eliseo: Rome, 2007), the play by Corrado Augias and Vladimiro Polchi, is based on Moro's letters and uses Sciascia's reflections to annotate them.

3 Giuseppe Traina, *Leonardo Sciascia* (Milan: Bruno Mondadori, 1999), 45.

4 Sciascia, *L'affaire Moro*, 72. Translations from this text are modified from the translation by Sacha Rabinovitch, *The Moro Affair* (London: Granta Books, 2002).

in Pirandello's work between 'form' and 'life', that is to say between the more or less fixed and rigid form or mask which each person (or literary character) assumes and presents to others, as well as (often) to himself or herself, and the multifaceted 'life' teeming within that same person. When the form is dissolved, a personal existential crisis is triggered.[5] In the case of Moro, the 'dissolution of form' recalls the fall of Sophocles' heroes. In both instances the protagonist becomes a creature alone in the face of an inescapable fate, not recognized by those around him, who prefer to consider him 'no longer himself', mad even.

The second motif in Sciascia's book, taken up by many subsequent texts, is the paradoxical relationship it establishes between truth and literature:

> L'impressione che tutto l'*affaire* Moro accada, per così dire, in letteratura, viene principalmente da quella specie di fuga dei fatti, da quell'astrarsi dei fatti – nel momento stesso in cui accadono e ancora di più contemplandoli poi nel loro insieme – in una dimensione di conseguenzialità immaginativa o fantastica indefettibile e da cui ridonda una costante, tenace ambiguità. Tanta perfezione può essere dell'immaginazione, della fantasia; non della realtà. (*L'affaire Moro*, 28)

> [The impression that everything which occurred in the Moro affair did so, as it were, *in literature*, derives mainly from the elusiveness of the facts, a sort of withdrawal of the facts – when they occurred and even more so when seen together in retrospect – into a dimension of unfailing imaginative or fanciful consequentiality, from which a constant stubborn ambiguity overflows. Only in fantasy, in dreams is such perfection achieved. Not in real life.]

This partially ironic comment on the imaginative 'perfection' of the Moro affair is complemented by Sciascia's remarks on the literary properties of his own text. Asked about this in an interview, he stated that it is: 'letteratura e spero che sia buona letteratura, di quella che fa sentire la verità'[6] [literature and hopefully good literature, the kind

---

5   For this line of interpretation of Pirandello see Adriano Tilgher, *Studi sul teatro contemporaneo* (Rome: Libreria di Scienze e Lettere, 1923), and the two essays by Sciascia, *Pirandello e il pirandellismo* (Caltanissetta: Sciascia, 1953) and *Pirandello e la Sicilia* (Caltanissetta: Sciascia, 1961).

6   This and the following statements are taken from an interview given by Sciascia to Stefano Malatesta, 'Io vi accuso!', *Panorama*, 26 September 1978, and quoted in Anne Mullen, *Inquisition and Inquiry: Sciascia's Inchiesta* (Market Harborough: Troubadour, 2000), 54.

that enables the truth to be heard]. He also stressed how the text, written in the heat of the moment, just a few months after the event, oscillates in style 'tra la ricostruzione documentaria, l'analisi testuale e "l'alto" giallo letterario' (Mullen, 54) [between documentary reconstruction, textual analysis, and the 'high' literary detective story], a mixture of elements that to some extent anticipates, again, *Il caso Moro* and *Piazza delle cinque lune*.

The third motif that suggests that Sciascia's text is a template is the presence of frequent metaphors of light, present especially, as I will demonstrate, in *Buongiorno, notte*. *L'affaire Moro* begins with a description of a walk and the sight of fireflies, evoking Pier Paolo Pasolini's definition of Italy, from the early 1960s onwards, as a country from which the fireflies had disappeared.[7] The latter had been, for Pasolini, a symbol of the piety and hope of the old Italy in the period before the economic miracle and the definitive establishment of the new system of power. Furthermore, in more than one passage, Sciascia emphasizes that the abduction and killing of Moro was characterized by moments in which clarity, the sort of clarity that dazzles, is rejected and replaced by an 'invisibilità dell'evidenza' (*L'affaire Moro*, 41) [the invisibility of the obvious]. Accordingly, he recalls the location of the BR's 'people's prison', where Moro was held captive in suburban Rome, so accessible and yet so untraceable.

Buongiorno, Notte: The Woman, the Prisoner and the Armed Group

In *Buongiorno, notte*, Marco Bellocchio specifically wanted to examine a woman in relation to the Moro case, one who had chosen a path of violence. His film gives prominence to the internal perspective of the BR's hideout and 'people's prison' and to the subjectivity of Chiara (Maya Sansa), the only woman of the group, from whose perspective we view Moro. Contrasted with Chiara's perspective are those of the other *brigatisti* – Mariano (Luigi Lo Cascio), Primo (Giovanni Calcagno) and Ernesto (Pier Giorgio Bellocchio) – and the external perspective of the media and public opinion. Bellocchio develops the gradual but never radical separation between Chiara and the others, a subjective isolation that allows her to identify her own situation with that of Moro (Roberto Herlitzka). The other *brigatisti* are represented as a group whose internal dynamics and whose differences from opposing groups (notably, the state) are carefully described. This

7   Pier Paolo Pasolini, '1 febbraio 1975: l'articolo delle lucciole', in *Scritti corsari* (Milan: Garzanti, 1975), 166–67; Sciascia, *L'affaire Moro*, 11–14.

representation raises issues about the group's generational difference from Moro as well as its relation in terms of gender to Chiara. The director, in fact, claimed to have represented Moro as 'un padre rispetto a dei giovani, a dei figli degeneri'[8] [a father in comparison with the young, the degenerate children], and to have wanted to express the contradictions of the choice of armed resistance through a female character in a masculine world.

Although she is one of Moro's jailers, Chiara embodies, with Moro, the human pivot around which the film revolves. Moro, whose whole body is rarely presented on screen, is a magnanimous character, with elements of the Sophoclean hero. Like the latter he is a solitary man unable to communicate, not because of lack of will or personal limitations but because, for those around him, 'love of family', and 'dedication to the common good' are words that no longer make sense.[9] There is, however, a key difference between Moro and the heroes of Sophoclean tragedy or of classical tragedy more generally. The latter are the source of their own actions, they are free to make decisions, to choose how to act in response to the fate that has been dealt to them, and they may choose well or badly. Moro is a captive and has no such freedom of choice in relation to his fate. Bellocchio's Moro nevertheless displays a lucid intelligence which suggests that he does exercise some choices *within* his situation as a prisoner, and he does so in a rational and responsible way.

This rationality is contrasted with the obtuse and repetitive slogans of the *brigatisti*, who have uncritically absorbed the words, rather than the reasons, of others. In representing the *brigatisti* in this way, Bellocchio fails to explore their political motives in any depth. Such an exploration would not have justified the decision to kill a man, but it would at least have constituted an attempt to understand the choices made by the clandestine movement and to work through the grief resulting from those choices. In the film the *brigatisti*'s ability to think independently is almost always replaced by an *esprit de corps*, or 'group thought', which leads them to kill Moro. It is in this desperate group view that Chiara buries her own doubts and uncertainties and in her turn tries to convince a comrade in crisis not to go home to his girlfriend: 'ma noi siamo soldati [...] compagno Ernesto, un po' di entusiasmo rivoluzionario!' [but we are soldiers [...], comrade Ernesto; let's have a little revolutionary enthusiasm!].

8 *Buongiorno, notte*, Press Book (distributed at the screening at the Venice Film Festival, September 2003), 7.
9 See Bernard M.W. Knox, *The Heroic Temper: Studies in Sophoclean Tragedy* (Berkeley and Los Angeles: University of California Press, 1983) (1st edn 1964), 5.

Chiara's doubts and her gradual growth in awareness emerge both through exchanges with her companions and, above all, through the dream sequences. Her dreams form an important element of the film, suggesting what might have been rather than what we know to have occurred. In the first dream, Chiara imagines taking Moro by the hand and leading him towards the exit, but stopping on the threshold after having seen a group of policemen through the spy-hole (this is the one moment in the film which might be interpreted as a reference to the theory of a deliberate collusion by elements in the state to prevent Moro's release by the police). The second dream alludes to an impossible happy ending: Moro gets up and, finding the door of his cell left open and his captors all asleep, walks out of the apartment. We then see him walking down a street in the early morning, smiling.[10] This is followed by a scene back in the hideout where he is taken out to be killed, and then, after an end title, by archive footage of politicians and Pope Paul VI attending the memorial service for the real Aldo Moro, with a return to the fantasy walk to freedom in the very last shot of the film.[11]

These dreams have the function of 'correcting' in fantasy what happened to Moro in reality and at the same time of clarifying the cause of Chiara's suffering. They show the dissolution of Chiara's 'form', the removal of a mask that she replaces on waking, when she acts as if her dreams did not belong to her. Chiara's 'double' is shown at this dream-like level, which is then echoed by her 'double' life: employed at the library of the ministry where, as a guardian of the rules, she ensures that the regulations are respected by the users, while at the apartment-prison where Moro is held captive she acts to subvert the Law.[12] At those moments in which she 'dissolves from form' she is able to be moved by the sight of Moro and recognize in him the human dimension rather than the political symbol to be attacked.

---

10 See Dana Renga's essay in this collection for a discussion of the political significance of the setting of this scene in Rome's EUR district, and its relevance to Italian cinematic history.

11 For a perceptive account of the closing scenes of *Buongiorno, notte*, see Giancarlo Lombardi, 'La passione secondo Bellocchio: gli ultimi giorni di Aldo Moro', *Annali d'italianistica*, 25 (2007), 397–408.

12 On the female double see Sandra M. Gilbert and Susan Gubar, *The Madwoman in the Attic: The Woman Writer and the Nineteenth-Century Literary Imagination* (New Haven and London: Yale University Press, 1979) and Joanne Blum, *Transcending Gender: The Male/Female Double in Women's Fiction* (Ann Arbor: UMI Research Press, 1988).

Fathers and Children

Bellocchio gives particular emphasis in the film to relations between generations. This is expressed both through the conflict between the *brigatisti* and the older Moro, considered as the symbol of a capitalist patriarchal system, and in the sequences dedicated to the memory of the Resistance, which represent the contradiction between the BR's desire for continuity with the Resistance generation, their emulation of the revolutionary and liberationist ideologies of the partisans, and their presumed betrayal of that generation through assassination and dehumanization. Although some critics have seen in Moro the embodiment of the 'father' to be killed, there are others, of the same generation as Bellocchio, such as Anna Calvelli, who have objected:

> Personalmente non mi sento figlia di Moro, né credo che ci si senta la mia generazione che ha vissuto la ribellione nel Sessantotto e che ha avuto dei *maîtres à penser* di ben più alto spessore morale e intellettuale. Non credo neanche che si possa sentire figlia di Moro l'Italia di oggi, che a tutto guarda tranne che alle più elementari regole del codice etico e che, anzi, ha elevato a norma di vita la legge del compromesso e del business.[13]

> [Personally, I don't see myself as a daughter of Moro, nor do I believe that those of my generation see themselves as children of Moro: we lived through the rebellions of 1968 and we looked to *maîtres à penser* of far greater moral and intellectual stature. Moreover, I don't believe that the Italy of today can be seen as the child of Moro, given that contemporary Italy scorns even the most elementary ethics of behaviour and has made a fundamental principle of the law of compromise and business.]

Bellocchio has said, by way of justification of his own position, that he wanted to consider Moro as 'un'identità forte con cui appunto dialogare, scontrarsi, dialettizzarsi' [a strong identity whom one can confront, precisely, and with whom one can converse and dispute].[14]

The theme of the Resistance is tackled in the central scene of the film when Chiara goes to the cemetery with her relatives to commemorate the anniversary of the death of her father, a former partisan. At the restaurant afterwards an ex-partisan friend of her father's declares, 'Anche il tempo più lontano non dimentica il partigiano' [even in the

---

13   Anna Calvelli, 'Dinamiche psicoanalitiche inesistenti', *Cinema sessanta*, 5: 273, 14.

14   E.A. (ed.), 'Marco Bellocchio: le vie dell'inconscio e la libertà del sogno: a colloquio con il regista di *Buongiorno, notte*', *Duel*, 107 (October 2003), 7.

most distant times the partisan will not be forgotten], and breaks into the partisan song 'Fischia il vento' [The Wind Whistles]. He is joined, for the chorus, not only by the members of his own group, but also by a bride and groom celebrating their wedding at a nearby table. The chorus of old and young (even a child sings) is perhaps designed to imply a possible continuity of ideals across the generations. Chiara alone remains silent and looks around in confusion.

The reversal of perspective, the theme of the break in continuity of the tradition of resistance across the generations, continues when Chiara is given a letter by Moro to send to his wife. Moro is by now condemned and knows he will never see his family again. Chiara reads the letter and in Moro's words of resignation and affection she recognizes similarities to the letters that the condemned partisans wrote to their families. Bellocchio here inserts clips from the last episode of Roberto Rossellini's *Paisà* (*Paisan*, 1946), which portrays the partisans condemned to death. In the part of *Il prigioniero* which corresponds to this, Braghetti is reported as saying:

> Lessi alcune di quelle lettere. Mario non ce le nascondeva di certo. Erano terribili. Mio malgrado mi richiamavano alla mente quelle dei condannati a morte durante la resistenza, raccolte in un libro che mio padre teneva in casa e che avevo letto anche a scuola, versando lacrime di rabbia e domandandomi, talvolta, come mi sarei comportata in analoghe circostanze. Adesso il carceriere ero io. Non volevo pensarci. Non dovevo pensarci.[15]

> [I read several of those letters. Mario [Moretti] certainly didn't hide them. They were terrible. They reminded me, against my will, of the letters written by partisans condemned to death during the Resistance, collected in a book that my father kept at home and which I had also read in school, crying tears of anger and asking myself then how I would have behaved in such a situation. Now I was the jailer. I didn't want to think about it. I couldn't think about it.]

The strong implicit assimilation in this part of *Buongiorno, notte* between Moro and the Resistance has been judged by some critics to be excessive.[16] It is unlikely, however, that Bellocchio wanted to show Moro as the direct heir of the Resistance in a political or ideological sense. A more probable explanation of these Resistance

15 Braghetti and Tavella, 108. The reference is to *Lettere di condannati a morte della Resistenza italiana (8 settembre 1943–25 aprile 1945)*, ed. Piero Malvezzi and Giovanni Pirelli (Turin: Einaudi, 1952).
16 See, for instance, Marcello Walter Bruno, '*Buongiorno, notte*. Perché no', *Segnocinema*, 23: 124 (November–December 2003), 60.

memories in the film is that he was seeking to emphasize the figure of the man condemned to death for political reasons, as well as his own wish to oppose violence. In this respect, the allusions to the Resistance may be seen as a hard historical judgement against those who present themselves as revolutionary liberators and yet end up as executioners believing that the end justifies the means. Indeed, in the clip from Paisà of the murder of the partisans, pushed into the Po with their hands tied behind their backs and stones attached to their feet, one can see a clear metaphor of the Resistance betrayed in the present day.[17]

Political Violence and 'Forgiveness': Critiques

In *Buongiorno, notte*, the exposure of the apparent lack of clear political motivation amongst the *brigatisti* may be seen as a severe condemnation of political violence. Despite this, some critics have accused Bellocchio of having adopted an attitude of forgiveness towards them (the stronger, pejorative Italian term used is 'perdonismo'). They claim he has shown their 'human face' and transmitted, albeit unwillingly, to the audience – in particular to young people who did not live through these years – a story in which the cold ferocity of which the BR were capable has been obscured. In an article significantly called 'La tentazione del perdono: cinema e terrorismo' [The Temptation of Forgiveness: Cinema and Terrorism], Aldo Torchiaro accuses both Bellocchio's film and Marco Tullio Giordana's *La meglio gioventù* (2003) 'di rischiare di offrire allo spettatore una visione ingentilita, addolcita, stemperata dei personaggi che quei ruoli rivestivano in quegli anni' [of running the risk of offering to the spectator a gentrified, sweetened and diluted vision of the characters who played those roles in those years].[18] The depiction of an internal rebellion in Chiara (the seed of which is presented in Braghetti's *Il prigioniero*, but in a much weaker form), has also been strongly attacked by some critics, who have interpreted it as another sign of a tendency towards forgiveness on the part of the director.

Bellocchio may indeed have wanted to show the humanity of the *brigatisti*, but it does not follow that he wanted to align himself on the

17   See Alberto Soncini, 'Il sacrificio della ragione', *Cineforum*, 43: 429 (November 2003), 2–4, 5–8.
18   Aldo Torchiaro, 'La tentazione del perdono: cinema e terrorismo', *Italianieuropei: bimestrale del riformismo italiano* (September-October 2003), 239.

side of forgiveness. To 'show the human face' of people who commit criminal acts, of whatever kind, does not amount to a wish to absolve them.[19] Rather, it could be taken as an attempt to demonstrate the complexity of human nature. As Hannah Arendt observed, watching Adolf Eichmann on trial for genocide in Jerusalem in 1961, it is not only monsters who do evil deeds but normal men and women driven by their beliefs or by a misplaced obedience or a mistaken sense of duty.[20] Where Bellocchio is more vulnerable to criticism is in his representation of a lack of reasons among the terrorists. To show them as apparently without motives for their actions, or at any rate not to depict their motives, is actually to pass a harder historical judgement on them than a facile and stereotyped demonization.

The lack of exploration of the political and ideological motives of the *brigatisti* prevents the spectator from identifying politically with them. The only identification left available is at an emotional level, and this makes a genuine absolution, which would have had to appeal to something shared not just on the emotional plane but above all on the rational one, impossible. It is precisely this lack of rational representation that ultimately unites *Buongiorno, notte* with many other texts that represent the period of political violence of the 1970s in Italy.[21] Once one eliminates the political-ideological dynamic that might have constituted the rational *sine qua non* of the group, there remains murder, pure and simple, without any possibility of justification.

Another line of attack on Bellocchio's film was that taken by Giuseppe Ferrara, who had directed in 1986 the first feature film about Moro's incarceration, *Il caso Moro*, discussed below. In his book, *Misteri del caso Moro* [*Mysteries of the Moro Affair*], published in 2003 shortly after *Buongiorno, notte* was released, Ferrara wrote:

---

19 Torchiaro, 243; as Bellocchio himself has stated, 'il film racconta anche la possibilità di un rapporto umano tra Moro e i suoi carcerieri, ma questa contraddizione non va scambiata con uno sguardo indulgente nei confronti dei terroristi' [the film also narrates the possibility of a human rapport between Moro and his captors, but this contradiction should not be mistaken for an indulgent treatment of the terrorists], *Buongiorno, notte* Press Book, 6.

20 Hannah Arendt, *Eichmann in Jerusalem: A Report on the Banality of Evil*, rev. edn (Harmondsworth: Penguin 1976), 25 [orig. (London: Faber, 1963/New York: Viking, 1963)].

21 Among the numerous other examples one could cite are the films *Caro Michele* (Mario Monicelli, 1976), *Caro papà* (Dino Risi, 1979) and *Segreti segreti* (Giuseppe Bertolucci, 1984).

Sposando il punto di vista dei *brigatisti*, Bellocchio si è subito messo nella scia degli 'integrati', degli anticomplottisti, e quindi, forse non scientemente, dalla parte di Cossiga e di Andreotti. E non solo, purtroppo. Accorgendosi dell'imprudenza commessa, il regista continua a dire ad ogni occasione che non ha voluto fare un film storico, e che per la figura di Moro si è ispirato a suo padre. Fandonie. *Buongiorno, notte* è addirittura un film a tesi che racconta per filo e per segno 54 giorni della prigionia di Moro e dei suoi carcerieri. Il cinquantacinquesimo giorno, quello della morte, resta fuori dal film al fine implicito di salvare l'umanità dei *brigatisti*, di non farli apparire troppo crudeli; anzi, al posto dell'assassinio viene messo un 'sogno' della Braghetti, che vorrebbe liberare il prigioniero.[22]

[By adopting the perspective of the *brigatisti*, Bellocchio turns himself into one of those who accept the official line and refuse the conspiracy theories of the kidnap and thereby, perhaps unwittingly, aligns himself with Cossiga and Andreotti. Sadly that's not all. Realizing his mistake, the director never tires of insisting that he did not want to make a historical film, and that the figure of Moro is inspired by his own father. Nonsense. *Buongiorno, notte* is actually a film which presents its own arguable version of the kidnap, and represents in the smallest details the fifty-four days of Moro's imprisonment and that of his jailers. The fifty-fifth day, the day of Moro's death, is left out of the film in order to conform with his implicit intention of asserting the humanity of the *brigatisti*, so as not to make them seem too cruel. Indeed, instead of the assassination we are shown one of Braghetti's 'dreams' in which she expresses her wish to liberate the hostage.]

Ferrara criticizes Bellocchio's film for its elision of the killing of Moro. However, the film in fact ends with archive footage showing the memorial service for Moro organized by the state and the killing is, in any case, clearly suggested in the scene of the *brigatisti* leading the blindfolded Moro out of the 'people's prison', even though the shooting itself is not shown. This 'disappearance of the visible', designed to make the audience think about what has actually taken place, can in certain cases be more effective than the technique of the more overt conspiracy theory accounts – Ferrara's included – which try to make the invisible visible. It does not seem appropriate, therefore, to accuse *Buongiorno, notte* of siding with the state. On the contrary, the film gives a far from positive representation of the ruling class, as the footage of the memorial service shows.

---

22 Giuseppe Ferrara, *Misteri del caso Moro* (Bolsena: Massari, 2003), 20–21.

Bellocchio and Sciascia

Let us now review the ways in which *Buongiorno, notte* picks up and develops those three basic motifs established in Sciascia's *L'affaire Moro*. The first, the dissolution of form, of the external and public mask, is portrayed not only in Moro, where it partly follows the model of the Sophoclean tragic hero, but also in Chiara. The dissolution of Chiara's form is, as we have seen, limited to those moments in which she allows her doubts on what she is doing to surface and in which she recognizes the humanity of her victim after having previously denied it.

As for the second motif, the paradoxical relationship between truth and literature, the film creates a level of metatext or *mise-en-abîme* by drawing attention to the existence of a manuscript entitled *Buongiorno, notte*. This is mentioned for the first time by the *brigatisti* when they open Moro's bags and later by Enzo (Paolo Briguglia), Chiara's colleague at the ministry, who has written a text called *Buongiorno, notte* which he wants her to read. It tells the story of a group of terrorists who have abducted a man. Enzo subsequently lets Chiara know that he has changed the ending of his screenplay. Whereas, in the first draft, the hostage is killed, in the new version the only woman terrorist in the group repents and opposes the logic of political killing 'perché di colpo ha orrore dell'assassinio. Perché non ci crede più. Anzi si infuria con se stessa per essere stata così cieca, così stupida e deve fare qualcosa' [because all of a sudden she is horrified by the idea of the assassination. Because she no longer believes in it. In fact, she is furious with herself for having been so blind, so stupid and she feels she must do something].

Chiara is upset by Enzo's story and manages only to reply that imagination has never been useful for anything – denying in the process one of the slogans of the time, 'l'immaginazione al potere!' [power to the imagination] – while he replies 'l'immaginazione è reale' [imagination is real]. This statement might be taken as encapsulating the intentions of the director who considers it legitimate to challenge the official version of events and who, like Enzo, wants to redeem the woman terrorist.[23] In addition, there are connections here with two of Sciascia's reflections. The first is about the value of history as origin of reality; the second, related to the first, is about the feeling

---

23 See Bellocchio's statement in *Buongiorno, notte* Press Book, 7: 'oggi c'è un'esigenza civile e morale, non solo artistica, di "tradire" la storia, nel senso di non subirla fatalmente' [today, there is a civil and moral, as well as an artistic, need to 'betray' history, in the sense of not being fatally subjected to it].

'che L'affaire Moro fosse già stato scritto' (*L'affaire Moro*, 25) [that the Moro affair had already been written].

The third motif from Sciascia's template, that of light, is taken up in a number of ways in *Buongiorno, notte*. The title of the film, with its juxtaposition of day and night, which perhaps refers to the duplicity of the situation, is an oxymoron inspired by Emily Dickinson's poem 'Good Morning – Midnight'.[24] The motif of light is also taken up quite obviously in the name and nature of the protagonist, Chiara, who represents the conscience of the group, and in the film's repeated use of images of darkness and light, starting with the opening sequence. Here Chiara and Ernesto, pretending to be a couple, are shown around the anonymous bare rooms of the apartment they are going to rent. It is darkened by the lowered shutters. The darkness of the space that will become their hideout and Moro's prison might connote the mental obscurity of the *brigatisti*, but it also suggests the darkness in which we, the spectators of the film, are enveloped, together with the unsuspecting estate agent (the first word we hear spoken is his 'buongiorno'). It is he who says 'vi apro le finestre, così vedete meglio' [I'll open the windows so that you can see better], and who stresses with anticipatory tragic irony the prime characteristics of the apartment, 'sicuro da sguardi indiscreti […] in una zona sicura' [safe from prying eyes […] in a safe area].

Piazza delle Cinque Lune

Released and set in 2003, Renzo Martinelli's film tells the story of Rosario Saracini (Donald Sutherland), the elderly chief prosecutor of Siena who is about to retire and who is sent anonymously an amateur Super8 film. The faded images that he immediately projects on the wall of his apartment show the ambush in Via Fani and the capture of Moro. The magistrate is profoundly shaken by what he sees because it completely departs from the version given by Valerio Morucci and Mario Moretti, the main planners and executors of the ambush.

Martinelli's idea of using as a trigger to memory and historical inquiry a text (here a piece of film), which is presented within the fiction as real, is reminiscent of the famous and much parodied device of the invented historical manuscript in *I promessi sposi* (1840) [*The Betrothed*]. Yet, whereas in Manzoni's novel the discovery and

---

24   Emily Dickinson, *The Complete Poems* (London: Faber, 1975), 203 [orig. in *Further Poems of Emily Dickinson*, ed. Martha Dickinson Bianchi and Alfred Leete Hampson (Boston: Little, Brown, and Company, 1929), 164].

purported transcription of the manuscript was a pretext which at once limited and justified the author's omniscience, in Martinelli's film the faked Super8 film serves as an impetus to new knowledge. Martinelli got the idea after reading a statement made to a journalist by Licio Gelli, master of the P2 Masonic lodge: 'Lei non sarà così ingenuo da pensare che delle persone maniache della documentazione come le BR non abbiano filmato il più clamoroso sequestro di questo secolo?' [You will hardly be so naïve as to think that a group of people as obsessed with documentation as were the BR failed to film the most sensational kidnapping of the century?].[25] After having shot several takes of the ambush scene, Martinelli realized it was not possible to represent or repeat it as the *brigatisti* had described it and he came to the conclusion that their accounts must have been inexact. His Super8 clip consequently shows a version of the ambush which accords with that reconstructed and promoted by Sergio Flamigni and posits the presence of a 'lone hit man' shooting from the right, while the other *brigatisti* come out from a hedge to the left of the cars.[26] Only by the addition of this fifth killer, it appears, can one explain some of the inconsistencies that otherwise would remain unresolved.[27]

The questions posed by Martinelli, via the old magistrate, are about the omissions in the BR account. Why did they never mention the presence of this killer? Who do they still want to cover up for, even after more than a quarter of a century? Who shot from the right?

The device of the Super8 film in *Piazza delle cinque lune* also leads inevitably to a reflection on the relationship between truth and history. In the face of a complex event marked by deception and mystery, by falsehoods or alleged falsehoods, Martinelli decides to show another version of the facts which is both more credible, in his view, and more submerged, using a film which is a fake he himself has created. In this way he may also want to make us reflect on the nature of the images we consume every day and the deception we risk undergoing. The recurrent images of television screens in his film (which link it with both *Buongiorno, notte* and Ferrara's *Il caso Moro*) might also allude to this. The technique he used for the fake film of

---

25 Renzo Martinelli, *Piazza delle cinque lune: il thriller del caso Moro* (Rome: Gremese, 2003), 9.

26 For an outline of both Morucci's and Moretti's testimonies and Martinelli's critique, see Martinelli, 38–39 and 42. Sergio Flamigni, *Convergenze parallele: le Brigate Rosse, i servizi segreti e il delitto Moro* (Milan: Kaos, 1998).

27 Gianluca Floris in his play *Lato destro* (2005), subsequently adapted by him as a novel, *Il lato destro* (Cagliari: CUEC, 2006), actually invents a biography of this fifth man.

the ambush and massacre was to shoot it from a third-floor balcony overlooking Via Fani and then, via a 'degradation' of the image, which otherwise would have been too clean and thus unrealistic, to add fuzzy outlines, moisture stains and a few jumps between frames. The decision to make a thriller may perhaps have drawn more people to see the film and, thus, to become aware of this interpretation of the Moro case. But how many of these spectators then considered the theory of a parallel power to be at least plausible? To expound an unpalatable theory through a format which, by definition, belongs to the realm of mystery, is probably not the most suitable choice, despite the fact that it follows the template of Raymond Chandler's detective novels, where one arrives at a more plausible version of the facts but does not re-establish justice. Even the spectator who has read and accepts Flamigni's theories is likely to be put off by the over-spectacular production, starting with the poster itself, with its bullet hole and trickle of blood, and by these versions of facts which seem to be substantiated by abundant evidence but which, when turned into cinematic spectacle, appear once again to be undermined. Aestheticized shots, digital tricks and rapid camera movements – stylemes typical of action cinema – stretch the audience's attention and patience to the limit and risk swamping them with form.[28]

One is inclined to ask why the historian Flamigni and Moro's family, who collaborated on the film, did not realize that this spectacularization, as well as attracting public opinion to the conspiracy theory, might indirectly end up reinforcing the existing power structure. Furthermore, Martinelli's film seems to announce right from the start the failure of its own intentions. The investigations are in the hands of a capable person who is at the end of his career, betrayed by his friends and assisted by a woman whose family life is threatened by the inquiry itself. A film of accusation thus risks being seen as the drama of one woman's struggle with family life and of an elderly man's loneliness – as the drama, that is, of individuals representative of groups considered socially weak. The other weak character is the *brigatista* who decides to take Saracini to a significant 'memorial' and who is about to die. The political drama, like many other fictional texts about the *anni di piombo*, once again becomes a personal, family drama which sees Saracini, like Moro, succumb.

During Saracini's retirement speech, which he delivers before colleagues and friends in the beautiful Sala del Mappamondo of

---

28 'Styleme' is a term coined (by analogy with 'phoneme') to refer to a recognizable, repeatable feature of an auteur's style. I employ it here to refer to traits found in a genre rather than a director.

the Palazzo Comunale in Siena, the moral calibre of the judge who has spent his life searching for truth and justice emerges clearly: 'Nell'appassionata ricerca della verità, nell'evocazione e nella diffusione della verità, risiede il segreto della vita' [in the passionate search for truth, in the recourse to the truth and in its transmission lies the secret of life]. Saracini is depicted as a classical tragic hero: like Sophocles' Oedipus he allows no obstacle to stop him and sets forth, alone and abandoned by everyone, on his quest for truth. In the course of the film the details of Moro's abduction are obsessively remembered and Saracini now, like Moro twenty-five years before, must pit himself against the ragione di stato (the principle of protecting the state at all costs). However, just as Bellocchio is unable to create a balanced opposition between Moro's reasons and those of his jailers, so Martinelli is unable to create one between the reasons of an honest magistrate in search of the truth and the plots of an inescapable state which remain obscure. What prevents them both from achieving a fully tragic dramatization of the subject matter is once again the lack of any real exploration of the reasons of the antagonists.

Il Caso Moro

Ferrara's film, released in 1986, was based on Robert Katz's 1980 book *Days of Wrath*.[29] It interweaves three narrative strands: the incarceration of the hostage, the negotiations and manoeuvres of the state, and the reactions of the Moro family. Ferrara indicated the possible connections between the abduction and the Italian and foreign secret services. Although he claimed, when the film was released, that he wanted to heighten the Italian public's awareness and urge them towards a search for the truth, it seems that this intention, very similar to that expressed more recently by Martinelli about *Piazza delle cinque lune*, did not have the desired effect.[30] In the harsh judgement of Sandro Zambetti: '*Il caso Moro* non ha dato luogo ad un serio ed ampio dibattito, né, tantomeno, ha "diviso il pubblico" o l'ha "spinto alla ricerca della verità" semplicemente perché strutturato in modo tale da non essere in grado di raggiungere

---

29   Robert Katz, *Days of Wrath: The Public Agony of Aldo Moro* (St Albans: Granada, 1980). With respect to the depiction of the Moro family, Maria Fida Moro stated that she did not recognize herself at all in Ferrara's representation when I interviewed her in Rome on 4 May 2005.

30   Ferrara had a background in committed film-making, with films including *Il sasso in bocca* (1970), *Faccia di spia* (1975) and *Cento giorni a Palermo* (1984).

tali obiettivi' [the reason that *Il caso Moro* has not generated a broad and serious discussion, and still less 'divided the public' or inspired it 'to seek the truth', is that the film is not structured in such a way as to be equipped to reach such goals].[31]

In Ferrara's film, Moro, played by Gian Maria Volonté, is an intense character, a wise person more than a politician (here too he is shown in the 'dissolution of form' mode), a man of great dignity who is aware that only his own family 'recognizes' him and is struggling to get him released. Volonté had also played Signor M in Elio Petri's *Todo modo* [*One Way or Another*] (1976), based on Sciascia's novel of the same name, which was set in other times but was an explicit metaphor for the Moro years. On that occasion, however, he had undermined the figure of Moro:

> Sono le ironie della Storia: dieci anni fa nell'allegorico, grottesco, isterico *Todo modo* di Petri, Volonté aveva fatto del 'signor M' (due parti di Moro, una di Andreotti) un emblema della razza padrona, un Tartufo 'sub specie politica'; oggi mettendo la sordina al suo formidabile mimetismo istrionico, fa di Moro un personaggio di vittima, di mesto e consapevole capro espiatorio, con rispetto e affetto, con una 'pietas' di grande e ben temperata commozione.[32]

> [Such are the ironies of history. A decade ago, in Petri's allegorical, grotesque and delirious *Todo modo*, Volonté played 'Signor M' (two parts Moro to one part Andreotti) as an emblem of the capitalist class, a Tartuffe in a political key. Today, muting his formidable dramatic abilities as a mimic, he plays Moro as a melancholy victim who knows himself to be a scapegoat, in a respectful and empathetic performance infused with compassionate and restrained emotion.]

Ferrara's film also tries to depict, on the basis of the way Moro wrote about them in his letters, Moro's wife, his children and in particular his grandson Luca as having the same dignity and strength. As it proceeds step by step though the events, its use of doubles to play the most important politicians produces a parodic and grotesque effect, as if the intention was to show that they actually are just masks acting on behalf of *ragione di stato*, unable to 'dissolve from form'.

The involvement of a hidden power is clearly indicated by some of the dialogue and also by the sequences with the politicians, who are often shot from above, as if to indicate a superior power

---

31   Sandro Zambetti, 'Ma non era anche un leader della DC?', *Cineforum*, 26: 260 (December 1986), 14.
32   Morando Morandini, 'È la tragedia di un uomo abbandonato', *Il Giorno*, 14 November 1986.

manoeuvring them. Above all, covert American involvement and the operations of the police and experts (graphologists and psychiatrists) are shown in a caricatured manner. Moro is depicted, again, as a character who does not have antagonists of comparable stature to himself. He is surrounded by masks of power and masks of ideology (the motives of the *brigatisti* are not made clear in this film either). The media are also portrayed but, whereas in *Buongiorno, notte* television is the means by which the *brigatisti* are in contact with the reactions and perceptions of the outside world (perceptions which Bellocchio challenges in his portrayal), in Ferrara's film television marks out the progress of the narrative. The way it shows the actions of the terrorists adheres strictly to the way these were reported at the time of the abduction and incarceration of Moro and also shows their contrasting details. Ferrara's movie camera is like the television camera of a journalist who tries to investigate, to follow even those bits of evidence which would open up other possible avenues. Zambetti has said that Ferrara 'si attiene e sostiene la tesi del complotto, ma non la porta avanti, non scava nelle situazioni' [follows and perpetuates the conspiracy version [of the kidnapping], but he does not take it forward, he does not burrow into the events].[33] In other words, *Il caso Moro* delves neither into the reasons why sections of the Italian state or the Americans might have deemed it expedient to sacrifice a senior politician, nor into the question of whether the *brigatisti* acted autonomously or were manipulated or infiltrated by the secret services. Despite Ferrara's intentions of denunciation, therefore, the film, like Katz's source text, retains the nature of a dark political thriller, alluding without explaining.

Conclusion: Erasures of Memory

Buongiorno, notte, and to a lesser extent *Il caso Moro*, follow the narrative and stylistic template established by Sciascia's *L'affaire Moro*. Both films, together with *Piazza delle cinque lune*, also employ elements from established film genres and fit into a wider pattern of retrospective representations of the political violence of the *anni di piombo* which portray it as inexplicable or irrational and thereby empty it of its political motives and meanings. The violence is represented as a deviation from established social and cultural conventions, from traditional norms and roles. For instance, women who refuse to be mothers in order to become terrorists later become

33 Zambetti, 14.

desperate and restless. Chiara, through her dreams, is allowed to manifest uncertainty, a sense of guilt and even a reparative fantasy of liberating Moro. Her maternal inadequacy in the scene where she neglects the baby who is suddenly placed in her care links her to Giulia (Sonia Bergamasco) in *La meglio gioventù*, who renounces the care of her own daughter in favour of politics and discovers too late what she has lost.

The absence of representation of the political reasons of the Red Brigades may be seen as a case of historical erasure. Norman Klein, in another context, has discussed the importance in political history and collective memory both of the image, fixed or stereotyped (the imago), and of erasures around images:

> If we concentrate, the imago seems waiting for us intact: a photo, a document, a table of statistics, an interview. It remains where we put it, but the details around it get lost, as if they were haunted, somewhat contaminated, but empty. Imagos are the sculpture that stands in the foreground next to negative space.[34]

The main erasure in the fictional representations of the left armed struggle is that of the perpetrators' political aims and motives, which are either excluded altogether or alluded to only vaguely. The result is that violence appears as an end in itself. What is missing in most of these representations are precisely those connections that Adriano Sofri has reminded us existed in the late 1970s between the 'moral choice' made by some of those who had entered the extreme left movement, driven by revolutionary aspirations, and the rigorous attractions of a commitment to terrorism:

> La rivoluzione cessava di essere un desiderio, si preparava a diventare un rimorso. Alcuni di loro, che avevano preso le mosse da una scelta morale, [si sentirono] [...] pronti a morire per la causa, per una causa (così infatti fa la sua prima comparsa il tema della violenza nel cuore dei giovani) nel terrorismo diventarono pronti ad ammazzare, finché ammazzare diventò la causa.[35]

> [The revolution ceased to be a desire, it started to become a burden. Some, inspired originally by their moral sense, [came to feel] [...] ready to die for the cause: thus, the matter of violence makes its appearance in the hearts of the young. For the cause they became terrorists ready to kill; ultimately, the killing itself became the cause.]

---

34 Norman M. Klein, *The History of Forgetting: Los Angeles and the Erasure of Memory* (London: Verso, 1997), 4–5.
35 Adriano Sofri, *L'ombra di Moro* (Palermo: Sellerio, 1991), 152.

Where there are allusions in the films to the political determinants of these choices they tend to take the form of generic references to the revolutionary Leninist ideology evoked by the *brigatisti* in their communiqués and other texts and to the military experience of the Resistance.[36]

Such erasures from representation, together with the contents that are then substituted for the erased material, provide important evidence of how a social imaginary works in a given period: what it feels unable to speak about, compelled to turn away from, and what, on the contrary, it feels comfortable speaking about in its place. It is interesting, in this respect, that it is not only writers of fiction who have emphasized the personal factors in retrospectively representing the *anni di piombo*. Valerio Morucci, former brigatista and author of a spy story, *Klagenfurt 3021* (2005), as well as an autobiography, *La peggio gioventù: una vita nella lotta armata* [*The Worst of Youth: A Life in the Armed Struggle*] (2004),[37] has insisted on the need to talk of the *anni di piombo* through fiction, eliminating political language and foregrounding the private dimension:

> Il terreno di spiegazione politica di quello che è avvenuto era ed è totalmente occupato da quelli che non volevano che si spiegasse nulla di quello che era stato e quindi non è quello il terreno su cui si possa riandare a quegli anni. Inoltre sia nel bene che nel male i fatti si conoscono e si conoscevano, sono negli annali della storia del paese. Quello che non si conosceva e che non si conosce sono invece i risvolti emozionali, psicologici, sentimentali e personali di coloro che vi avevano partecipato e lì il linguaggio politico è impotente, lì ci vuole la letteratura. Non c'è altro mezzo e per questo ho cominciato a scrivere. Per l'occupazione di un terreno da parte di altri e l'idea che bisognasse affrontarlo da un altro punto di vista. [...] La fiction per me può avere molto più valore delle ricostruzioni. [...] Non sappiamo affrontare quegli anni perchè abbiamo un approccio troppo politico. [...] L'artista deve parlare un altro linguaggio.[38]

[The domain of political analysis of what happened back then has been and remains monopolized by those who in fact do not want it explained; consequently, to recall those years one cannot have recourse to political analysis. In any case, for better or for worse, we know

36 The formation of the new GAP (Gruppi Armati Partigiani) 'which tried to recreate a partisan organization to fight an expected coup d'état, was an aberration', according to Robert Lumley, *States of Emergency: Cultures of Revolt in Italy from 1968 to 1978* (London: Verso, 1990), 285.

37 Valerio Morucci, *Klagenfurt 3021* (Rome: Fahrenheit 451, 2005); *La peggio gioventù: una vita nella lotta armata* (Milan: Rizzoli, 2004).

38 Author's interview with Valerio Morucci, Rimini, 6 May 2005.

and we have always known what the facts are; they are in the history books of the country. What we did not understand, on the other hand, and what we still do not understand, is the emotional, psychological, sentimental and personal experience of the protagonists. Political language is no help here; here you need literature. Nothing else will do, and that is why I started to write. So that others could inhabit the domain of the past, and because it had to be confronted from a different point of view. [...] Fiction for me can have much greater value in the reconstruction of the past. [...] We don't know how to confront those years because our approach is too political. [...] The artist must speak a different language.]

Sofri's book *L'ombra di Moro* [*The Shadow of Moro*] was written in 1990 shortly after the discovery of letters by Moro in a BR base in Milan. In it he revisits the Moro case (also using Sciascia's template) and discusses the 'Lettera ai brigatisti', an open letter written by Elsa Morante in 1978 but not actually published until ten years later.[39] He draws attention to the fact that Morante never once mentions Moro and that she talks to the *brigatisti* using their own language. This latter fact, he thinks, renders her letter a 'brutto' [ugly] piece of writing.[40] One might suggest that directors and writers, in 'erasing' the political content of left terrorism, were aiming to avoid just this: speaking the language of the terrorists. However, the effect of this avoidance is that the terrorists are left without a voice of their own. Ironically, they are politically and ideologically depersonalized by these representations, just as they depersonalized their own victims.

39   Elsa Morante, 'Lettera alle Brigate Rosse', *Paragone*, 7: 453 (1988), 15–16.
40   Sofri, 82.

8. A Spectre is Haunting Italy: The Double 'Emplotment' of the Moro Affair

Nicoletta Marini-Maio

Some years ago the sociologists Raimondo Catanzaro and Luigi Manconi pointed out that left-wing terrorism was perceived in Italian society as 'una ferita non ancora rimarginata, un dolore collettivo che esplode in forma violenta e lacerante ogni volta che la discussione su quegli anni si riapre' [a wound not yet healed, a collective ache that explodes violently and painfully whenever discussion of those years is rekindled].[1] This observation is still current and particularly true for the most controversial left-wing terrorist act in Italy, namely, the abduction and assassination of the president of the Democrazia Cristiana (DC), Aldo Moro, in 1978 at the hands of the Brigate Rosse (BR). The Moro 'affair' – so-called after Leonardo Sciascia's renowned essay on this subject – has raised many questions about the involvement of the DC, the Partito Comunista Italiano (PCI), the Italian secret services, the CIA, the KGB, criminal groups, and also that significant part of Italian society that voiced its disapproval towards both the BR and the political establishment through the recurrent formula 'né con le Brigate Rosse né con lo Stato' [neither with the BR, nor with the state].[2] The magnitude of the event, the alleged connections among secret, paramilitary or criminal organizations, and the political repercussions of the event, both nationally and internationally, have generated a considerable amount of research and a wide spectrum

---

1   Raimondo Catanzaro and Luigi Manconi, *Storie di lotta armata* (Bologna: Il Mulino, 1995), 7.
2   See Leonardo Sciascia, *L'affaire Moro* (Palermo: Sellerio, 1978). The slogan 'Né con le BR, né con lo Stato' appeared in M. Boato, 'Né con lo Stato né con le BR. Si cerca di prendere l'iniziativa,' in *Lotta continua*, 18 March 1978, 12.

of publications.[3] Since the late 1970s, cultural production on the Moro affair has been incessant. Investigative reports, essays, novels, memoirs, feature films, television programmes and theatrical works have been produced in substantial quantities, and the passage of time has not reduced the rate of production. On the contrary, the list continues to expand and interest continues to grow.

The relevance of the figure of Moro for Italian culture derives from the emblematic force of his assassination. Over the years, Moro has become an icon of martyrdom and has come to encapsulate the anxieties of the Italian public about revolution and violence. Immediately after the event, the political rhetoric on Moro's death suggested metaphors of capitulation, catastrophe and loss, and the sense that an established domain of political and ideological references had come to an end began to circulate.[4] More recently, with a resurgence of terrorism on a global scale, Moro's corpse has acquired the abstract quality of a trope, standing as metonym for the dilemmas regarding the ideological affiliation of Italian left-wing terrorism, the legacies of Marxism in Italian society and the use of political violence in general.[5] In other words, Moro's death has been regarded on a symbolic level as 'part, cause, effect, example', of what

3   It is almost impossible to make an inventory of the publications, cinematic and TV productions, and theatrical works produced on the Moro affair since 1978. A detailed but already dated bibliography may be found in Alan O'Leary, *Tragedia all'italiana: cinema e terrorismo tra Moro e memoria* (Tissi: Angelica, 2007). Many more texts were published to commemorate the thirtieth anniversary of the kidnap in 2008.

4   Former President Giuseppe Saragat, for example, claimed that 'accanto al suo cadavere c'è anche il cadavere della prima repubblica' [beside his corpse there is also the corpse of the First Republic], G. Saragat, *La Repubblica*, May 10, 1978, quoted in Paul Ginsborg, *Storia d'Italia 1943–1996* (Turin: Einaudi, 1998), 477. On a similar note, journalist Eugenio Scalfari argued that after the death of Moro the only way to avoid political collapse and civil war was to work collaboratively towards the common goal of 'rifondare la prima Repubblica' [reestablishing the First Republic] and journalist Luigi Pintor warned that 'ora questa società e questo Stato non possono più restare come erano e come sono, neanche se lo volessero: se non cambieranno in meglio periranno' [now this society and this state can no longer be what they were and what they are, not even if they want to: if they do not change for the better, they will perish]; both citations given in Ginsborg, 477.

5   Ruth Glynn introduced the idea of Moro as metonym in an unpublished paper entitled 'Displaced Confessions: Moro, Metaphor and Metonymy in Female Perpetrator Narratives' presented at the conference 'Remembering Moro', 10–11 November 2006, Institute of Germanic & Romance Studies, London.

took place and what would take place in Italy's past and present.[6] In the collective memory and in its forms of representation – especially film and theatre, arguably the preeminent media of performance and witnessing – Moro's body has assumed the residual, ghostly insistence of a murdered corpse that continues to appear and make its presence felt. Moro has become a remnant, returning to haunt Italian society and to search for justice.

Spectrality and Emplotment

In arguing that Moro has become a spectre in Italian society, I am borrowing Derrida's metaphor on the role of Marxism in contemporary society. Starting from the compelling recurrence of spectral apparitions in Marx's work and interweaving literary tropes with philosophical discourse, Derrida claims that the spectres of Marxism inhabit documents and cultures that are not aware of them. He claims that such spectral presences are figures of 'injunction', which call for responsibility and haunt us as historical subjects, reminding us that 'all the questions concerning democracy, the universal discourse on human rights, the future of humanity, [...] a profound and critical re-elaboration of the concepts of the state, of the nation-state, of national sovereignty and of citizenship [...] would be impossible without vigilant and systematic reference to a Marxist problematic' (97, 98). Derrida emphasizes that the spectres of Marx are endowed with agency: like Hamlet's father they look at us (from the Latin 'speculari'), make us feel looked at and stimulate our reaction (7). Moro's fictional persona is another such paternal figure of injunction. It evokes a literary, Shakespearean fatherly ghost, which rises up from his grave and returns relentlessly to remind us of his death against the background of the political clash of the *anni di piombo*. Because of the ideological shadows its manifold apparitions evoke, the spectre of Moro claims clear reference to a Marxist problematic.

However, this spectre does not seem to solicit a positive reconsideration of the legacies of Marxism, along the lines of Derrida's argument. On the contrary, it highlights the conflict, deeply rooted in Italian history and politics, between the Marxist humanistic principle

---

6   See Jacques Derrida, *Spectres of Marx: The State of the Debt, the Work of Mourning, and the New International*, trans. P. Kamuf (London: Routledge, 1994), xv [orig. *Spectres de Marx: l'État de la dette, le travail du deuil et la nouvelle Internationale* (Paris: Galilée, 1993)].

of social justice and the use of political violence as a means to pursue it. This conflict has been central in left-wing political debates since World War II, when the communist and socialist forces that constituted the largest portion of the partisan Resistance aimed to tear down the old political system and establish in its place a socially just and proletarian-driven country. In the end, communist leader Palmiro Togliatti followed a different set of priorities, namely, liberation from the fascist regime and the establishment of international equilibrium.[7] However, he did not block the revolutionary aspirations of much of his political base, which considered class revolution to be deferred but not annulled. Over the following decades the subsequent manoeuvres of the conservative parties to exclude communists and socialists from government generated strong feelings of resentment and conflict. It was a conflict that the PCI tried to abate by establishing the so-called *compromesso storico* with the DC, setting aside any revolutionary aspiration and finally being able to participate in the decision-making processes of government. However, the abduction and assassination of Aldo Moro, who was its most convinced – if not sole – supporter among both the DC and NATO allies, arguably prevented the compromesso storico from surviving. Moro's body and its phantasmatic traces, therefore, incarnate a spectral presence of the legacies of Marxism, but in a somewhat controversial way. Standing as both victim and accuser, the spectre of Moro appears as the quintessence of the conflict and conjures up an unsettling association between the anti-fascist partisan Resistance and the left-wing armed struggle of the *anni di piombo*.

Drawing upon Derrida's politics of spectrality, this essay examines the theme of the return, the form and the function of the spectral apparitions of Moro in a selection of feature films and television productions. The analysis of these epiphanies, observed in their iconic and photographic consistency, will guide us in the exploration of the different ways in which the collective memory and cultural representations have understood and processed the historical facts in narrative modes or, rather, 'emplotments', in Hayden White's sense of the term.[8] White argues that the means by which a sequence of events is shaped into a story is 'gradually revealed to be a story of particular kind' (7), namely, an emplotment which organizes these events in different narrative modes, such as romance, comedy, tragedy and satire. I would like to apply White's notion of emplotment to

7   See Ginsborg, 46–53 and Claudio Pavone, *Una guerra civile: saggio storico sulla moralità nella Resistenza* (Turin: Bollati Boringhieri, 1991), 313–412.

8   Hayden White, *Metahistory: The Historical Imagination in Nineteenth-century Europe* (Baltimore: Johns Hopkins University Press, 1973), 7.

the analysis of the representation of the Moro case, which claims, so to speak, the entitlement of narrative history, as it shows what White calls the 'deep structure' of the 'poetics' of history (1–2). My discussion will centre on two divergent emplotments that White would consider sub-plots of 'second order',[9] but which, I argue, stand out in the panorama of the cultural productions on the Moro affair, namely, the mystery story, or giallo, and the tragic palinode.[10] In the first emplotment (mystery story) the investigative reading of the event takes the form of crime story and conspiracy plot and assigns to the spectre the instrumental role of the scapegoat, a victim of a political project supposedly designed by arcane puppeteers in control of the world. The second emplotment (tragic palinode) centres on the retraction and the sense of guilt of the protagonists of violence of the *anni di piombo*, particularly for their contribution to the self-destruction of the left-wing *movimento* [movement]. The tone of retraction characteristic of the palinode overlaps with the tragic conflict between controversial interpretations of good and evil. This combination connotes the spectre of Moro as an Oedipal icon, namely, the target of the violence of the rebel children of the *anni di piombo*.[11]

These two emplotments, I argue, imply two underlying political stances on the issues of communism and political violence. The mystery story casts the scenario of the Moro affair as a transnational conspiracy aimed at blocking the rise of communism in Italy. By displacing Moro onto the area pertaining to Yalta power agreements, the mystery story absolves Italian society from direct responsibility in the Moro affair. This emplotment is also instrumental in denying any ideological or political affiliation of the revolutionary stances of the left-wing armed struggle with the PCI which, in fact, firmly rejected any links between the BR and communist culture and politics. In contrast, the tragic palinode emphasizes the protagonists' intellectual and emotional involvement in the terrorist enterprise, their rereading of the facts in the light of the present, their need to admit the responsibility for political violence, their retraction of deeds and ideas and their seeking of collective redemption.

9   Although White admits that history can easily be emplotted in the form of a detective story, he mentions this generic plot only in a collateral fashion with other 'second-order literary genres' like fairy tales (8).
10   A palinode is an ode or song recanting or retracting a view expressed in a former poem. The term comes from the Greek παλιν ('palin', again) and ωδη ('ode', song). In broader terms, a palinode is a re-reading or a retraction of an earlier statement, sentiment, or idea.
11   With regard to the Oedipal configuration of Moro, see also O'Leary, 78–84 and 98.

The bifurcation of the spectre of Moro into a double *figura*, one of mystery and conspiracy and one of retraction and exorcism, is a trope of the 'spectropoetics' I am attempting to retrieve from the analysis of the apparitions of Moro in film.[12] Derrida's notion of spectrality again provides an effective path to elucidate this apparently contradictory phenomenon. In *Spectres of Marx*, he argues that the multiple meanings of the French word *conjuration* (invocation, exorcism and conspiracy) mark the human reactions to spectral manifestations in general and, on a more specifically symbolic level, to Marxism in particular. He points out that such a reaction may in fact be either one of 'magical incantation' (41), which evokes or exorcizes the spirit, or one of conspiracy and secrecy, which 'struggle[s] against a superior power' (40) in the name of a secret oath. The deconstruction of the term is not merely a linguistic game but has a profound figurative value. In the case of the representation of the Moro affair, it mirrors the twofold reaction of Italian society to the *return* of the spectre in collective memory, namely, one of self-absolution (the mystery story) and one of retraction (the tragic palinode).

Examples of the mystery story are particularly abundant in film and rather less plentiful in other cultural productions treating the kidnapping and death of Aldo Moro. In contrast, the tragic palinode is less developed in film – although it has its epitome in Bellocchio's *Buongiorno, notte* – while it dominates, for instance, the theatrical renditions of the event. The emplotments are in some cases hybrid and may show a certain degree of ambiguity, but they are always recognizable and mirror the clash of political and cultural forces still active in Italian society.

The reading of the figure of Moro as a spectre is not completely new. In *L'ombra di Moro*, Adriano Sofri, one of the founders of Lotta Continua, analyses the symbolic and literary implications of the accidental discovery of Moro's memoir in a Milan apartment in 1990 and provides an original interpretation of the impact of Moro's death on Italian culture and politics.[13] Sofri exploits the trope of the 'return' in order to depict the appearance of the memoir as a phantasmatic manifestation of Moro's haunting of Italian politicians and the wider public.[14] He endows the figure of Moro with the tragic rhetoric of a Shakespearean phantom:

---

12 With regard to 'spectropoetics', see Derrida, 10.
13 See Adriano Sofri, *L'ombra di Moro* (Palermo: Sellerio, 1991).
14 For an analysis of Sofri's text, see Max Henninger, 'Recurrence, Retrieval, Spectrality: History and the Promise of Justice in Adriano Sofri's *L'ombra di Moro*', in *Italian Culture*, 22 (2004), 115–36.

La debolezza degli uomini può suggerir loro l'illusione che la morte di chi hanno abbandonato valga a sbarazzarli del rimprovero e del rimorso. Questa illusione è l'antefatto di ogni tragedia. I morti, infatti, tornano. Non hanno forse la forza per spezzare carriere, per togliere dalle facce sorrisi di ordinanza. Non si muovono abilmente fra inchini e colpi bassi di viventi. Si appostano, come il fantasma di Elsinore, di preferenza nelle notti, e rosicchiano i sonni e i sogni. (Sofri, 73)

[Men's weakness may allow them the impression that the death of those they have abandoned will free them from reproach and regret. Such an illusion is the antecedent of every tragedy. In actual fact, the dead always return. Perhaps they lack the strength to ruin careers or to wipe false smiles from faces. The dead do not move with ease amidst the bowing and the low blows of the living. They stalk about, like the ghost at Elsinore, preferably at night, and they gnaw on sleep and dreams.]

Since the Moro affair, as I have argued, encapsulates the conflicting legacies of Marxism in Italian culture, this Shakespearean revenant resurfaces in our political unconscious and urges us to reconsider the sense of his destiny in the light of these legacies.

Photography and the Spectre

The return of the spectre manifests itself in a quantitative fashion through the extraordinary number of works focusing on the Moro affair; there are also certain visual and audio documents that obsessively recur – either in their original forms, as scraps, fictional replicas or symbolic traces – in almost all cultural productions on the Moro affair. The visual documents are very familiar to the Italian audience. These are the two notorious pictures of Moro in the so-called 'people's prison' where Moro was held by the BR (Figs 1 and 2) and the still image of his corpse in a red Renault 4, from the RAI Uno newsreel of 9 May 1978 (Fig. 3). The first two pictures recur in almost all the films on the Moro affair and appear on the great majority of book covers.[15] Indeed, the shelves of Italian bookshops seem to display many versions of the same image, with Moro's face – blurred, distorted, crystallized or pixelated – standing out against the background of the red BR flag. The third picture is a topos of the cinematic and televisual renditions of the event alongside the

---

15   Marco Belpoliti recently published a brief essay in book form in which he examines the communicative power and effects on the media of these two pictures. M. Belpoliti, *La foto di Moro* (Rome: Nottetempo, 2008).

Fig. 1 The notorious image of Aldo Moro in the so-called 'people's prison' delivered to the media by the BR a few days after the abduction.

Fig. 2 The second picture of Moro in the 'people's prison', distributed in response to the counterfeit BR communication announcing Moro's death.

newsreels broadcast by RAI Uno on 16 March 1978, with journalist Paolo Frajese reporting from the scene of the abduction of Moro and the murder of his escort. Equally recurrent are two telephone calls intercepted and recorded by the police: Mario Moretti's ultimatum to Eleonora Moro and Valerio Morucci's call to professor Franco Tritto to announce Moro's death.

Ephemeral though they may be, these audiovisual segments are the only traces of Moro, both alive and dead, that our historical memory has at its disposal in the process of narrative elaboration. The three pictures are particularly evocative. They derive their communicative force from their status as 'indexes', according to the taxonomy of signs elaborated by C. S. Pierce. Indexical signs point to the objects that they denote 'by virtue of being really affected' by such objects, of which they are physical traces and with which they have an existential relation.[16] In the case of the photos of Moro, the nature of that relation is manifold. Like any photographic image, these photos register the presence of an absent object, namely, the

16 See C.S. Peirce, 'Nomenclature and Divisions of Triadic Relations, as Far as They are Determined' [1903], in *The Essential Peirce: Selected Philosophical Writings*, ed. Nathan Houser and Christian Kloesel (Bloomington and Indianapolis: Indiana University Press, 1998), 291–92.

Fig. 3   The photograph of the corpse of Aldo Moro, which was found in Rome on 9 May 1978 (Photograph by Ronaldo Fava. Reproduced with permission).

body of Moro. In addition, they reflect and emphasize the man's trajectory towards his actual death. Therefore, not only do they register 'the return of the departed', as Eduardo Cadava defines the inherently spectral function of photography, but they are themselves spectral remnants and their return takes the form of a haunting.[17] Finally, these photographs represent some discrete moments in the temporal flux, where the camera 'momentarily fixes history in an image' (Cadava, xx). The first two pictures show Moro in the BR 'people's prison': they actually relate to each other, point to Moro's imminent demise, and anticipate the third image (Moro dead in the Renault 4), since they stand as prophetic antecedents to his death.

These pictures exerted a strong effect on the perception of the prisoner's destiny. Immediately after the event, for instance, Leonardo Sciascia wrote that the imprisonment had been for Moro a progressive process of transformation from the status of character to that of 'creature': 'Moro comincia, pirandellianamente, a sciogliersi dalla forma, poiché tragicamente è entrato nella vita. Da personaggio ad "uomo solo", da "uomo solo" a creatura: i passaggi che Pirandello

17   See Eduardo Cadava, *Words of Light: Theses on the Photography of History* (Princeton: Princeton University Press, 1997), 11–12.

assegna all'unica possibile salvezza' [Moro begins, in a Pirandellian manner, to dissolve from form once he has dramatically entered into life. The transitions from stage character to 'solitary man' and from 'solitary man' to creature are those which, according to Pirandello, lead to the only salvation possible].[18] The existential relation – as Pierce would put it – that these images have with Moro and with each other has contributed to the construction of a narrative discourse that connotes Moro as a spectral character. When these images appear as a multimedia commentary within other texts, they bring with them their extradiegetic signification and contaminate such texts, be they feature films, documentaries, television productions, theatrical adaptations, novels, essays or investigative reports.

Imagery and Emplotment

Each individual text manipulates the images of Moro in a particular way, framing them in different aesthetic contexts and endowing them with additional meanings and functions related to how the text has emplotted the Moro affair. In feature films and television productions these images have perhaps the most burdensome role. To provide just a brief list, they appear and have a central function in the feature film *Il caso Moro* (*The Moro Case*, Giuseppe Ferrara, 1986) as well as in the more recent *Buongiorno, notte* (*Good Morning, Night*, Marco Bellocchio, 2003), in the thriller *Piazza delle cinque lune* (*Piazza of the Five Moons*, Renzo Martinelli, 2003) and in the short *A risentirci più tardi* (*Until Later*, Alex Infascelli, 2005). The same is true of almost all the television renditions of the Moro affair, such as the 'La tragedia di Moro' [*The Tragedy of Moro*] section of *La notte della Repubblica* (*The Night of the Republic*, Sergio Zavoli, 1990), the two episodes of the investigative programme *Blu notte: misteri italiani* [*Darkest Night: Italian Mysteries*] entitled *Storia delle Brigate Rosse* [*Story of the Red Brigades*] (2004), written and presented by Carlo Lucarelli, and finally

---

18   Sciascia, *L'affaire Moro*, 72–73. Translation adapted from Leonardo Sciascia, *The Moro Affair*, trans. Sacha Rabinovitch (London: Granta Books, 2002), 55. In his analysis of *Buongiorno, notte*, Bellocchio's controversial film of 2003, Giancarlo Lombardi has powerfully revived Sciascia's interpretation of the figure of Moro as a Pirandellian 'creatura'. See Giancarlo Lombardi, 'La passione secondo Marco Bellocchio: gli ultimi giorni di Aldo Moro,' in *Annali d'Italianistica*, 25 (2007): 397–408.

the two-part mini-series *Aldo Moro: il Presidente* (*Aldo Moro: President*, Gianluca Tavarelli, 2008).[19]

Il caso Moro, which inaugurates the mystery story emplotment in film, stages the abduction of Moro, his segregation inside the people's prison and his assassination. It raises questions and doubts, also discussed by Sciascia, about the ambiguous behaviour of Italian politicians in conducting the search for the hostage and formulates the hypothesis of a political plot at Moro's expense. The questions concern, specifically, the 'hard line' adopted by the DC and the PCI, which refused any negotiation with the BR in the name of the stability and defence of the state. The paradigm followed by Ferrara and the reconstruction of dialogues, characters and events based on documentary evidence place this film in the established Italian tradition of *cinema d'inchiesta* [investigative cinema]. In Ferrara's work, the pictures of Moro from the 'people's prison' materialize through the sympathetic performance of Gian Maria Volonté, the actor who plays the role of the protagonist, whose resemblance to the real Moro is very effective in bringing to life what O'Leary defines as a sense of 'umanità stanca che dà luogo a una verità rassegnata' [a weary humanity that generates a resigned truth].[20] This film captures the indexical load of the original picture and uses it to endow the historical figure of Moro with psychological traits that would then become instrumental to the progressive victimization and, as it were, 'spectralization' of the Italian politician.

Other intertextual references contribute to this process. Sciascia was clearly a very important antecedent in the humanization of the figure of Moro, but Pier Paolo Pasolini, too, played a role in this intense dialogue. Pasolini, who had claimed the right and necessity to place the entire DC on trial on behalf of the Italian citizenry, highlighted several years before Moro's death the latter's partial estrangement from the dirty politics of the late 1960s and 1970s. For him, Moro

19 Interestingly, these audiovisual documents also appear in most of the theatrical productions of the Moro affair: *Rosso Cupo: una donna nelle Brigate Rosse* (Teatrino di Via Pasini: Mestre, 2004) by Antonino Varvarà, the radio drama *Tutti bravi ragazzi: il sequestro Moro e sette testimoni involontari* (Civitella in Val di Chiana: Zona, 2003) by Laura De Luca, *Corpo di stato. Il delitto Moro: una generazione divisa* (Milan: Rizzoli, 2003) by Marco Baliani, and *Aldo Moro: una tragedia italiana* (Teatro Eliseo: Rome, 2007) by Corrado Augias and Vladimiro Polchi.
20 O'Leary, 90. Volonté was also known for a magisterial impersonation of Moro in *Todo modo* (Elio Petri, 1976). In one sequence from *Il caso Moro*, he reproduces Moro's pose and expression in the first picture released by the BR after the abduction (see fig. 1).

was 'colui che appare come il meno implicato di tutti nelle cose orribili che sono state organizzate dal '69 ad oggi, nel tentativo, finora formalmente riuscito di conservare comunque il potere' [Moro is the one who appears to be the least implicated of all in the horrible things that have been perpetrated since '69 in the attempt, so far successful, to retain power under any circumstances].[21]

Another feature film where images play a strong role in the spectralization of Moro is Marco Bellocchio's *Buongiorno, notte*, inspired by Anna Laura Braghetti's memoir, *Il prigioniero* [*The Prisoner*].[22] This film stages the kidnapping and murder of Moro (Roberto Herlitzka) from the internal, claustrophobic scenario of the terrorist hideout, and from the perspective of the female member of the group, who in the film takes the fictional name of Chiara (Maya Sansa). Through the employment of a variety of motifs, *Buongiorno, notte* becomes perhaps the most convincing example of the tragic palinode. These motifs include: firstly, the female terrorist's explicit retraction of the murder; secondly, her progressive consciousness of the BR's abuse of political violence; thirdly, the final reaffirmation of a tragic, spectral finale.

Chiara's process of self-reflection and retraction takes place, so to speak, in images and motion pictures. The first time the apparition of the figure of Moro unsettles her is when she sees him sleeping in the claustrophobic, dark cubicle of his BR cell in a posture that is clearly reminiscent of that of Moro's corpse in the Renault 4 on 9 May 1978. Through this vision Moro appears proleptically dead and his image haunts the spectator's historical memory through Chiara's gaze. Bellocchio's treatment of the images of Moro as well as the compassionate acting style of Roberto Herlitzka are particularly effective in emphasizing the process of humanization of the politician. The close-ups of Moro capture the sense of solitude and impotence delivered also by the use of two original photographs from the 'people's prison'. These close-ups are framed by the spy-hole in the cell door, through which Chiara obsessively views Moro. On the one hand, this perspective makes the spectators aware of the meta-cinematic intention of the director, while, on the other, it surrounds the image of Moro with a phantasmatic aura that transforms it into a dreamlike apparition. *Buongiorno, notte* ends with the spectral image of Moro smiling and walking away from his prison through a Roman

21   Pier Paolo Pasolini, '1 febbraio 1975: l'articolo delle lucciole', in *Scritti corsari* (Milan: Garzanti, 1975), 167.

22   Anna Laura Braghetti and Paola Tavella, *Il prigioniero* (Milan: Feltrinelli, 2003).

suburb to the strains of a Schubert violin sonata, following a parallel montage of the moments preceding his execution by the male members of the BR cell and his counterfactual liberation by Chiara.

This final scene might be interpreted as the projection of Chiara's conciliatory desire for an imagined world from which historical violence is banned. However, the open-air dimension, the high focus of perspective and the juxtaposition of the huge arched building in the background with the squalid, desert-like metropolitan environment (reminiscent of Giorgio De Chirico's metaphysical canvases) produce an uncomfortable feeling of loneliness and disconnection. The Kafkaesque Palazzo della Civiltà Italiana, a remarkable example of fascist imperial architecture, is the visual epitome of political power. In this framing, the Palazzo is haunted by the image of a 'dead man walking', and the symbolic projection of Aldo Moro calls Italian society to admit responsibility not only for his death at the hands of the terrorists, but also for many other 'horrible things' enacted in the *anni di piombo* in name of the dysfunctional principles of power and ideology. The return of the dead Moro who urges us to reconsider his fate in relation to the legacy of Marxism – the main feature of spectrality as theorized by Derrida – is, I would argue, the most relevant stylistic element of *Buongiorno, notte*, a film that has a 'controversa [...] capacità di invocare fantasmi' [controversial [...] ability to invoke ghosts].[23]

Piazza delle cinque lune takes the mystery plot already developed in Ferrara's film to extreme conclusions. In a scenario that combines original documents and fake reconstructions presented as true, this film attempts to deliver an ideological interpretation rooted in an intricate conspiracy theory, which involves the BR and international terrorism, the government, the CIA and clandestine formations of obscure origin. It implicates, in particular, the secret masonic organization P2, and the NATO paramilitary 'stay-behind' organization called Gladio, which had the official aim of countering a possible Soviet invasion through sabotage, propaganda and guerrilla warfare behind enemy lines. According to this interpretation, Gladio, P2, the CIA and Italian intelligence allegedly gave a mandate to the BR to kill Moro in order to undermine the *compromesso storico* and prevent any strategy of openness towards the Soviet Union and

---

23 Luca Bandirali and Stefano D'Amadio, *Buongiorno, notte: le ragioni e le immagini* (Lecce: Argo, 2004), 214. For other stimulating interpretations of the final scene of *Buongiorno, notte*, see Alan O'Leary, 'Dead Man Walking: The Aldo Moro Kidnap and Palimpsest History in *Buongiorno, notte*', *New Cinemas*, 6: 1 (2008), 38–42; Lombardi, 405–7; and Dana Renga's essay in this collection.

communism. This theory considers BR leader Mario Moretti to be an infiltrator hired by the secret services. Both in terms of its plot and its aesthetic choices, *Piazza delle cinque lune* is clearly inspired by *JFK* (Oliver Stone, 1991), a docudrama that stages the assassination of President John F. Kennedy.

Interestingly, when it comes to the pictures of Moro from the 'people's prison' Renzo Martinelli follows the hyper-realistic principle of combining fake and real documents, the same that he applies to the film as a whole. He imagines that, many years after the event, an elderly judge (Donald Sutherland) receives from a former terrorist a super-8 film of the abduction and imprisonment of Aldo Moro. While watching the tape, the judge observes the scene where Moro, apparently alive, is preparing to have his picture taken. In order to shoot this scene, Martinelli superimposed the face of Moro extracted from the original photograph onto the body of an extra (Moro is not the protagonist in this film), and then animated Moro's face using digital techniques. The explicit goal of *Piazza delle cinque lune* is 'di mettere ordine nei fatti, di rintracciare una logica' [to give order to the facts, to find a logic at work], but this hyper-realistic manipulation of the photograph along with an obsessive faith in the conspiracy plot as a rational explanation of the facts offers only an unsettling illusion of reality.[24] The existential relation between the original picture and the figure of Moro, and this picture's spectral reality, are in fact much more meaningful than Martinelli's digital reconstruction. His attempt to 'revive' the body of Moro has instead decapitated the spectre and erased the phantasmatic aura emanating from that body, which has lost its communicative power.

Of great interest for their stylistic features are also certain television productions devoted to or containing a section on the Moro affair: Zavoli's *La notte della Repubblica*, Lucarelli's *Storia delle Brigate Rosse*, Infascelli's *A risentirci più tardi* and Tavarelli's *Aldo Moro: il Presidente*. These television productions often combine fictional aspects with the informative purpose typical of the documentary. Within this group, Zavoli's monumental series *La notte della Repubblica* plays a central role because it is one of the first examples of those programmes claiming an informative role delivered in a partially spectacularized form. *La notte della repubblica* aims to reconstruct the facts by means of different sources and styles of information, including long, poignant interviews with terrorists and witnesses to the events. The specific sections of *La notte della repubblica* concerning Moro have been recently

---

24 Renzo Martinelli, *Piazza delle cinque lune: il thriller del caso Moro* (Rome: Gremese, 2003), 12.

combined and released in the form of an independent, coherent mini-series comprising two videotapes and a book with Moro's corpus of letters written from the 'people's prison'.[25] This section replicates the parent text's alternation of brief but spectacular audio and video segments: newsreel footage, archival and biographical information, songs, interviews, excerpts from documentaries, literary and autobiographical recitations. In *La notte della repubblica* the photographs of Moro and the original newsreels appear several times, with no manipulation. Nevertheless, they acquire a certain degree of fictionalization because of the structure of the programme itself.

Lucarelli's *Storia delle Brigate Rosse* series displays some resemblance to *La notte della repubblica*, but it goes much further in the fictionalization of the event. In fact, this series shapes the history of the BR in the form of a thriller, where the detective-like narrator dissects and reconstructs the events by referring to circumstantial evidence. In addition, Lucarelli accompanies the audiovisual narrative with a number of explicit references to shadows, shards and spectres. For example, he opens and closes the *Storia* with an extended spectral simile:

Ci sono certe storie che, anche se riguardano cose concrete, avvenimenti reali, personaggi in carne ed ossa, sembrano sempre e comunque inquietanti e spaventose storie di fantasmi. Sono le storie di certi misteri italiani. Quelli grandi, quelli che coinvolgono l'intero paese e che si comportano sempre *come fantasmi di un romanzo o di un film dell'orrore*. Fanno paura. E tornano.[26]

[There are some stories that, though they might concern concrete events, real happenings and flesh and blood characters, always resemble disquieting and frightening ghost stories. These are the tales of certain Italian mysteries. The big mysteries, the ones that involve the whole country and that always function *like ghosts in a novel or a horror film*. They frighten us. And they keep coming back.]

Questa è una storia di fantasmi. Ombre nere che escono da quella che Sergio Zavoli, in un programma storico, ha chiamato la notte della Repubblica. Fantasmi che fanno paura. *Come in un film dell'orrore* se ne stanno nascosti nel buio e non basta ignorarli. Non basta chiudere gli occhi e tirarsi il lenzuolo sulla testa perché svaniscano. Questi sono

---

25 Sergio Zavoli, *La notte della Repubblica: il caso Moro* (Rome: Elle U Multimedia, 2000).
26 In this and the following quotation from the programme, the transcription and added emphasis is my own.

fantasmi che non svaniscono. Questi sono fantasmi che esistono, che tornano.

[This is a ghost story. Black shadows that emerge from what Sergio Zavoli, in a historic programme, called the Night of the Republic. They are frightening ghosts. *Just like in a horror film* they hide in the dark and it's not enough simply to ignore them. These are ghosts that do not disappear. These are ghosts that exist, that keep coming back.]

Lucarelli's insistence on the frightening recurrence of phantoms and ghosts is instrumental to the characterization of the *Storia delle Brigate Rosse* as a horror film. This also means that he tends to dramatically fictionalize Italian history, which is the content and context of the series. When the Moro affair is introduced, the spectral allusions become more openly a meta-cinematic commentary. Lucarelli begins the account of the event by comparing the broadcast of the discovery of Moro's body in the red Renault with a typical horror scene, claiming that they have some specific genre elements in common. He does so with rhetorical subtlety, implying the analogy with an extended litotes: '9 maggio 1978. *Se la nostra storia fosse un film dell'orrore non potrebbe iniziare con una scena più agghiacciante di questa*: una macchina ferma in una strada. Una piccola Renault rossa col bagagliaio aperto. E dentro il bagagliaio, il corpo di un uomo' [9 May 1978. *If our story were a horror film, it could not start with a more dreadful scene than this:* a parked car on a street. A small red Renault with the boot open. And inside the boot, the body of a man].

As Lucarelli describes the discovery of Moro's corpse, the scene is shown actually taking place on a television screen set within the frame, so that the event itself is constructed as a narrated object, not as a real document or piece of evidence, in order to allow discussion of the facts. Indeed, the placement of the screen behind the shoulders of the narrator-detective, the black-and-white image that pushes the scene to a distant past and, finally, the meta-narrative comment, 'se la nostra storia fosse un film...' [if our story were a film], suggest that this story is indeed a film, and one that may change depending on the perspective from which one looks at it, or the angle from which one shoots or projects it. In Lucarelli's postmodern aesthetic, the reconstruction of the history of the BR almost eliminates the political context and focuses instead on the clues that could result in the revelation of information that remains hidden. These clues could help, for instance, to name the unidentified members of the terrorist commando that attacked Moro, or to locate an alleged second 'people's prison' that has never been found. The narrator-detective of the *Storia delle Brigate Rosse* dissects and reconstructs the facts by making reference to circumstantial evidence. Following the investigative paradigm, he begins the inquiry by setting up a chronological reversal, that is, he opens with reference to the actions of the 'new' BR in 2003, before tracing this new terrorist formation back to their predecessors of the 1970s.

An alternative form of fictionalization of the Moro affair is provided by Gianluca Maria Tavarelli's two-episode television series, *Aldo Moro: il Presidente*, starring Michele Placido. The series was broadcast on 9 May 2008 by Canale 5, with clear commemorative intentions. *Aldo Moro: il Presidente* attempts to represent the protagonists' inner voices. In this series, all the characters (with the significant exception of Giulio Andreotti) are shown to feel anxious about the kidnapped Moro and to feel some degree of guilt for his fate: Francesco Cossiga, who was one of the most convinced supporters of the 'hard line' policy; Amintore Fanfani and Benigno Zaccagnini, Moro's closest political friends; and even the members of the BR, impassive leader Mario Moretti included.

At the centre of this narrative of guilt stands the figure of Moro, played by Michele Placido. A familiar face in feature films and television series alike, Placido is perhaps most renowned for his appearances in the long-running *La piovra* [*The Octopus*], where he plays the role of the good policeman fighting the mafia.[27] Placido transfers the domestic qualities of his screen persona and his popular acting style to the character of Moro, who acquires a reassuring, paternal demeanour, so that the now canonical image of the first photograph taken from the 'people's prison' is rendered less disturbing when recreated through his face. Even the spectral consistency of the figure of Moro is somewhat domesticated in the series. Towards the end of the drama, Moro dreams that he is on a beach. Here he sees his grandson, Luca, and his wife, Eleonora, but neither of them is able to see him. Further along the strand Moro sees his murdered bodyguards themselves become spectral presences. At the close of the series, the spectre of Moro reappears on the same beach, this time alone. He looks directly at the camera, as if to reinforce the idea that the 'shade', the ghost, of Moro still survives, albeit now in Placido's more friendly, televisual form.

I would like to close this exploration of the cinematic and televisual materializations of the spectre of Moro with a brief mention of Infascelli's short production, *A risentirci più tardi*. This unusual production stages a dramatic encounter between former terrorist

27   Michele Placido played the role of the policeman in the first four series of Damiani's *La piovra*, broadcast by RAI 1 in 1984, 1985, 1987 and 1989.

Adriana Faranda, a member of the BR at the time of the Moro affair, and Francesco Cossiga, former Minister of the Interior, subsequently President of the Italian Republic, and one of the most loathed targets of left-wing radicals. This odd couple talks primarily about the Moro affair, and each one admits full responsibility for the assassination of the statesman:

COSSIGA	Io mi sveglio la notte e penso: ho ucciso Moro.
FARANDA	Anch'io mi sveglio la notte e penso: ho uccisio Moro.
COSSIGA	Sì, ma io più di lei. L'ho ucciso io più di lei.

[COSSIGA	I wake up in at night and think: I killed Moro.
FARANDA	I also wake up at night and think: I killed Moro.
COSSIGA	Yes, but I more than you. I killed him more than you did.]

Archival images (needless to say, the familiar spectral images) interrupt the memories of the conversation every now and then. In addition, as in a reality show, Faranda and Cossiga speak to the camera at regular intervals, individually 'confessing' their feelings, their faces presented in *chiaroscuro*, suggesting that each has only a partial version to offer.

Conclusion

This essay has offered a necessarily brief and preliminary exploration but it has, however, served to identify, on the one hand, the quantitative recurrence of the Moro affair in film and television and, on the other hand, its double 'emplotment'. Drawing upon Derrida's politics of 'spectrality' and Hayden White's notion of metahistory, it has examined the emplotments of the Moro affair in a representative selection of Italian feature films and television productions, and has highlighted the conflict between the revolutionary myths of Italian Marxist tradition and the use of political violence during the *anni di piombo*. This conflict is incarnated in the phantasmatic recurrence of Aldo Moro's body and its spectral traces, a body that turns into a figure of mourning calling for a collective retraction and self-reflection. Particularly in film – the medium of performance and witnessing par excellence – the image of Moro has assumed the residual, ghostly insistence of a murdered body that continues to intrude with its haunting presence. As Adriano Sofri emphasizes, this spectral image is reminiscent of the tragic ghosts of the theatrical tradition: it rises up from its grave, returns relentlessly to remind us of its death, and will not let us go.

9. Moro Martyred, Braghetti Betrayed: History Retold in *Buongiorno, Notte*

Dana Renga

In *Il prigioniero* [*The Prisoner*], the memoir of the only female member of the Brigate Rosse (BR) to live all fifty-four days in Aldo Moro's 'people's prison', Anna Laura Braghetti recounts the complicated process by which she chose to take an active part in a militant terrorist group:

> La mia scelta di entrare in una organizzazione armata è stata il frutto di un lungo, lento corteggiamento, un avvicinamento graduale, passo per passo. [...] Forse il periodo in cui sono stata una spettatrice in platea mi è servito a decidere se farmi o no definitivamente da parte. Era un tempo d'attesa, cercavo un modo per cambiare il mondo e tentavo di capire se le Brigate Rosse fossero o meno uno strumento per far diventare realtà il sogno rivoluzionario.[1]

> [My decision to enter an armed organization was the result of a long, slow courtship, a gradual step by step approach. [...] Perhaps the period in which I was a spectator on the sidelines served to help me to decide once and for all whether or not to join. It was a time of waiting, I was looking for a way to change the world and I was trying to understand whether the BR represented the means to make the revolutionary dream a reality.]

Throughout her memoir, the former *brigatista* repeatedly emphasizes her committed decision. We learn that, during the almost two months when the BR held Moro prisoner, although at times she was scared,

---

1   Anna Laura Braghetti and Paola Tavella, *Il prigioniero* (Milan: Feltrinelli, 2003), 19.

Braghetti never doubted her commitment: 'Io non avevo dubbi morali o politici, avevo paura: è diverso' (42) [I had no moral or political qualms, I was afraid: it's different].

Those familiar with Marco Bellocchio's 2003 film, *Buongiorno, notte* [*Good Morning, Night*], will realize that the director clearly manipulates history in his presentation of Moro's kidnap, imprisonment and eventual execution; he points out, however, that the facts are 'freely adapted' from what is presented in the memoir: 'Sul piano dei fatti il libro della Braghetti ci è stato utile, lì sono descritti alcuni fatti che poi nel film ho liberamente sviluppato e ampiamente tradito. […] Ma la ribellione di Chiara, in parte reale in parte utopistica, nel libro non esiste' [On the level of events, Braghetti's book was useful to us; in the film, I freely developed and fully betrayed some of the events she outlines there. […] But Chiara's partly realistic and partly utopian rebellion doesn't appear in the book].[2] Bellocchio chooses to retell one of modern Italy's most infamous and traumatic moments through the eyes of a woman terrorist. Chiara, the character based on Braghetti, is neurotic and consumed with self-doubt. She is further problematized because she looks to Moro as a father figure and also because Bellocchio, who dedicated the film to his own father, aligns Moro's politics with that of the partisan Resistance. Bellocchio's 'betrayal,' as he puts it, raises a series of questions regarding how Italy in the new millennium deals with the legacy of the kidnap and murder of Moro. For example, what is served by privileging a fictional rebellion over a more historically accurate depiction of events? Is Chiara's wavering meant to condemn violence in extreme terrorist groups, or might it also serve to denounce political parties across the spectrum? What is the end-result of such a dramatic transformation of perspective? And why does Bellocchio choose to recast Moro as a kind and paternal figure who ultimately attains the status of a martyr?

The remoulding of Moro in *Buongiorno, notte* is but one instance of Bellocchio's reworking of the real-world events and individuals that inspire the film. Moro is represented by Bellocchio as a martyr across political lines, in contravention of the construction of him at the time of his kidnap and murder. For example, in *L'affaire Moro* [*The Moro Affair*], a controversial book published just months after the events, Leonardo Sciascia attempts to piece together the details of the case. Interestingly, Sciascia takes issue with the Democrazia Cristiana (DC)

---

2 Federico Chiacchieri, '"Dovevo affermare la mia assoluta infedeltà alla storia," incontro con Marco Bellocchio', *Sentieri selvaggi*, 28 June (2006), www.sentieriselvaggi.it/articolo.asp?sez0=186&sez1=102&art=5513 [accessed 5 August 2010].

and barely deals with the BR. Sciascia opens the book by agreeing with Pier Paolo Pasolini's summation of the DC as 'la pura e semplice continuazione del regime fascista' [the pure and simple continuation of the fascist regime].[3] Sciascia indicts contemporary Italian politics, with Moro as ringleader. By contrast, in *Buongiorno, notte*, Bellocchio repeatedly presents Moro as a Christ-figure and presents his Catholicism as less morally rigid than that of the Vatican.[4] Although Moro was deeply Catholic and attended mass every day, he had been criticized by the Catholic Church because he repeatedly maintained that Church and State should be separate. Nonetheless, Pope Paul VI attempted to intervene after Moro's own party had chosen not to enter into negotiations with the BR in order to prevent Moro's death. As cited in the film, Paul VI famously asked the BR to release Moro 'senza condizioni' [without conditions].[5]

Thus we are presented with two acts of reinvention: firstly that of Moro who, at least in the minds of some, was not the compassionate figure represented in the film.[6] Secondly, there is the reinvention of Braghetti, both through her autobiography, *Il prigioniero*, where she attempts to rewrite and redeem her violent past, and in Bellocchio's film, which acknowledges few of Braghetti's actual transgressions.[7]

3 Pasolini cited in Leonardo Sciascia, *L'affaire Moro* (Palermo: Sellerio, 1978), 15.

4 Giancarlo Lombardi argues that Bellocchio depicts Moro in terms of the sacred, as someone who enters 'nella "prigione del popolo" come un uomo politico amato e odiato da molti [e] ne esce, con la sua morte, una vittima che tutti compiangono' [the 'people's prison' as a man loved and hated by many [and] leaves it, with his death, a victim mourned by all]. 'La passione secondo Marco Bellocchio: gli ultimi giorni di Aldo Moro', *Annali d'italianistica*, 25 (2007), 404.

5 Robin Wagner-Pacifici discusses the Vatican's betrayal of Moro during his kidnapping and states that 'when the clergy refused to acknowledge the Moro of the letters they were, in a sense, dispossessing themselves of one of their own', *The Moro Morality Play: Terrorism as Social Drama* (Chicago: University of Chicago Press, 1986), 256.

6 Richard Drake, in his examination of the documents from the various trials following the Moro assassination, emphasizes the corrupt nature of the Christian Democratic party and scrutinizes several key players who would have been well served by Moro's death. Drake concludes that: 'The continuing controversy of the Moro case, however, does not hinge on the direct responsibility of the *Brigate Rosse* or on actions and motives that have been securely documented. The problem is the government's role in opposing the terrorists', *The Aldo Moro Murder Case* (Cambridge, MA: Harvard University Press, 1995), 249–50.

7 Braghetti was arrested in 1980 after murdering Vittorio Bachelet who, as Vice-President of the Consiglio Superiore della Magistratura (the regulatory body of the Italian magistrature), represented for the BR 'il cuore dello stato' [the heart of the state] (Braghetti and Tavella, 130). Braghetti was subsequently sentenced to life imprisonment, but she has since been released and currently devotes much of her time to assisting women inmates and their families.

While in the memoir Braghetti affirms her sense of political commitment during the Moro kidnap and takes responsibility for her involvement in a militant terrorist group, in *Buongiorno, notte* the character who represents her is depicted as far from revolutionary. In point of fact, Chiara frequently questions her comrades Primo, Mariano and Ernesto (based on Prospero Gallinari, Mario Moretti and Germano Maccari, respectively); is in a state of moral crisis throughout most of the film; and goes so far as to fantasize a complicated scheme by which Moro is liberated.

This was not the case for Anna Laura Braghetti who was, and still is, thought of by many as a 'donna di piombo' [woman of lead] – a play on the expression 'anni di piombo'.[8] Through the narration of her story, Braghetti aims to purge her past actions, all the while accepting responsibility for murder and for terrorism-related offences. In contrast, Bellocchio's film feminizes Braghetti and softens her violent outlook. Responding to that process of feminization, this chapter begins by addressing the various 'myths' associated with women terrorists which Bellocchio seems to be borrowing and then looks closely at how Chiara's recurring dreams do more than simply lend a psychological or oneiric aspect to the film. Chiara's dreamscapes add depth to what could be viewed as the facile appropriation of a worn-out stereotype. More to the point, Bellocchio's recasting paves the way for Moro's martyrdom as Chiara's politically charged fantasies illustrate Moro's *pietas*.

Bellocchio's historical transgression raises some questions regarding the fictionalization of women involved in terrorism, as he is far from alone in creating an emotionally charged depiction. *Buongiorno, notte* sits well with many critical writings that argue that women involved in terrorist organizations do not have a mind of their own, that they frequently doubt their cause, or that they enter into the organization for personal rather than political reasons (following the example of a boyfriend, for example). Why are the political motivations of women terrorists regularly undermined, rewritten or discredited? Several critics maintain that the 'threat' inherent in the embryonic, non-traditional position of the woman terrorist is often downplayed in the media or in popular fiction through a variety of

---

8   I take the expression 'donne di piombo' from Pino Casamassima's *Donne di piombo: unici vite nella lotta armata* (Milan: Francesco Bevevino, 2005), which treats eleven women terrorists, among them Anna Laura Braghetti; ten are from extreme left-wing groups, and one from the extreme right.

strategies including making her more feminine, sexual or domestic. As Beverly Allen argues, 'women on the "terrorist" left are generally represented as being muddle-headed sex objects with well-developed proclivities for doing housework and not speaking out of turn',[9] while Marie Orton remarks: 'Paradoxically, the stereotype of the demonically aggressive terrorist woman simultaneously characterizes her as dependent on her male counterpart: her political involvement is accidental, indirect, or she is seduced into the enterprise by a man, usually a husband or lover, in order to support or further his political pursuit'.[10] Both observations point to Bellocchio's depiction of Chiara as both domesticated and puerile.

Both Allen and Orton, along with Susanne Greenhalgh who has examined representations of women terrorists in modern drama, challenge a whole series of clichés associated with women terrorists in a variety of studies.[11] In 'Woman as Terrorist' (remarkably, the only chapter out of thirty-five that treats women terrorists in *The Criminology of Deviant Women*), H.H.A. Cooper spells out how the woman terrorist is sex-obsessed and incapable of autonomy:

> The female terrorist seems unable to escape male influence in this sphere, either in a personal sense or through involvement with men's movements or objectives. It has been suggested elsewhere that there is a strong connection between terrorism and sex worthy of the closest investigation. [...] The emotional involvement of women terrorists is unusually intense and invariably very personal. It has an obsessive, pathological quality. It is useless to inquire why women became terrorists. It is only productive to ask why this woman or that sought fulfilment through these means. The lines of inquiry invariably lead back to men in general or to some man in particular. [...] Indeed, it has been advanced that a primary cause of female terrorism is erotomania. [...] Clearly, the sexual relationships of women terrorists have considerable influence on what they do and why they do it. The key to female terrorism undoubtedly lies hidden in their complex sexual nature.[12]

---

9 'Terrorism Tales: Gender and the Fictions of Italian National Identity', *Italica*, 69:2 (1992), 170.

10 'De-Monsterizing the Myth of the Terrorist Woman: Faranda, Braghetti and Mambro', *Annali d'italianistica*, 16 (1998), 283.

11 Susan Greenhalgh, 'The Bomb in the Baby Carriage: Women and Terrorism in Modern Drama', in *Terrorism and Modern Drama*, ed. John Orr and Dragan Klaic (Edinburgh: Edinburgh University Press, 1990), 150–57.

12 'Woman as Terrorist', in *The Criminology of Deviant Women*, ed. Freda Adler and Rita James Simon (Boston: Houghton Mifflin Company, 1979), 154.

Robin Morgan joins Cooper in the categorization of women terrorists as dependent, apolitical beings solely motivated by libido, as she casts the woman as 'sexual lure' and various male terrorists as Casanova figures who ensnare females with their charm.[13] Daniel E. Georges-Abeyie almost avoids the critical trap of stereotyping women terrorists by contextualizing them within a feminist perspective. I say 'almost', however, because Georges-Abeyie argues that women terrorists commonly exhibit masculine qualities and 'seek success in some non-feminine realm, by displaying aggression, unadorned faces and bodies, toughness, or other masculine qualities'.[14] The 'taming' of the woman terrorist might be achieved by a variety of means, for example, as Beverly Allen points out, through such tactics as creating binary oppositions between the neo-fascist, aggressively sadistic male and a non-violent 'newly feminist' female.[15] Here and elsewhere, the woman terrorist is often stereotyped as 'bed and kitchen'; she is presented as safe: a clichéd sex object who is overly dependent upon a male other. Also, her political engagement is frequently downplayed as she 'happens' onto the political scene by following a partner, and without much forethought.

Bellocchio matches several of these attitudes as he stresses Chiara's disquiet with the militarism of the group, a position the director associates with her gender difference: in various scenes, we see her cooking, cleaning, ironing or holding a baby, whereas in *Il prigioniero*, it is affirmed that domestic tasks are mostly performed by Prospero who 'ha una vita di maschilismo da farsi perdonare' (Braghetti and Tavella, 79) [who has a life of sexism behind him to atone for]. Furthermore, on one occasion Chiara faints when a priest comes to bless the house in which Moro is kept captive, which suggests that she cannot bear her role as jailer. At a later stage, in a key and particularly striking scene in which Moro asks his captors for their advice on a letter he is drafting to the Pope, Moro begins by asking if

13 Morgan argues that women can be coerced into joining the world of terrorism with emotional and sexual lures. 'Equally pernicious and far more common is the use of sex and "love" to enmesh women – and, in turn, the use of women's sexuality to further the cause. This form of coercion – recruitment by romance – is what the Demon Lover's message is all about', Robin Morgan, *The Demon Lover: On the Sexuality of Terrorism* (New York and London: W.W. Norton & Co., 1989), 201.
14 'Women as Terrorists', in *Perspectives on Terrorism*, ed. Lawrence Zelic Freedman and Yonah Alexander (Wilmington: Scholarly Resources Inc., 1983), 82.
15 Beverly Allen, 'Terrorism, Feminism, Sadism: The Clichéing Experience in the Brand-Name Novel', *Art and Text*, 33 (1989), 78.

there is a woman among his captors; he can tell, he explains, by 'come sono ripiegate le calze' [the way the socks have been folded]. He then proceeds to read out the letter he has drafted, and in doing so reduces Chiara to tears. She is crying, she explains, because the letter is cold, lacking in emotion, but her visual representation belies her words and the director conveys grief and concern as feminine qualities.

Anna Laura Braghetti is not so easily pigeonholed. In *Il prigioniero*, Braghetti seeks to penetrate the roots of her political involvement and contextualize her actions, relationships and decisions. Through writing the self, Braghetti merges her current identity as an activist and social worker with past associations of murderer and terrorist (she freely admits that she is guilty of murder), all the while discrediting some of the aforementioned common 'myths' of the terrorist woman. Official history in *Il prigioniero* is time and again interwoven with the personal realm; chapters alternate between recounting the details of Moro's kidnap and imprisonment and details of Braghetti's life before and after the Moro kidnap. For example, in chapter 18, Braghetti details a chance encounter with Roberto Benigni in a bar in Rome in 1980, while in the following chapter we are back in 1978, in the apartment in Via Montalcini, where the BR learn of a letter falsely announcing the death of Moro. All told, out of the twenty-one chapters of the memoir, eleven of them focus on Moro's incarceration (beginning with the morning of his abduction on 16 March and concluding with his assassination on 9 May) while in the other ten Braghetti uncovers her public and private history, from her early captivation with leftist politics to her arrest and years spent in prison. Braghetti narrates the particulars of her family life, the sacrifices made for her family after the death of her parents, her various love interests, the development of her political engagement, the hardships suffered as a result of several years in prison, and so on. Ruth Glynn persuasively argues that the dual structure of *Il prigioniero* represents a way for Braghetti to construct a 'post terrorist identity' as, in the memoir, she 'takes responsibility for her violence without apologizing for her politics'.[16] Chiara, on the other hand, is never depicted as insurrectionary, and her politics are, at best, in the nascent stages of formation.

Unlike Chiara or the protagonists of so many films and novels that feature female terrorists devoid of a political formation, we learn early on in the chronicle that Braghetti was politically engaged at the young

---

16   Ruth Glynn, 'Through the Lens of Trauma: The Figure of the Female Terrorist in *Il prigioniero* and *Buongiorno, notte*', in *Imagining Terrorism: The Rhetoric and Representation of Political Violence in Italy, 1969–2006*, ed. Pierpaolo Antonello and Alan O'Leary (Oxford: Legenda, 2009), 68.

age of fourteen: 'Anche se ero impegnata in politica da quando avevo quattordici anni – le lotte a scuola, poi due anni a Lotta Continua, un breve passaggio nel PCI – ormai lavoravo otto ore al giorno, e [...] sapevo che, mentre tutti discutevano di violenza rivoluzionaria, già c'era chi la praticava' (Braghetti and Tavella, 17) [Although I was politically engaged from the age of fourteen – school protests, then two years in Lotta Continua, a brief period in the PCI – I was now working eight hours a day, and [...] I knew that, while others talked of revolutionary violence, there were those who were already practising it]. All told, Braghetti's committed position underscores the commitment of the brigatisti as a whole: the movement came before all else, and many, upon entering the organization, gave up all contact with their family. Moreover, unlike many of the woman protagonists of various terrorist novels, Braghetti left her partner, Bruno Seghetti, in order to participate in the Moro kidnap.

Ultimately, Braghetti questions the gender stereotypes that Bellocchio will later exploit. It remains to be seen, however, if writer and director have the same ends in view. On the surface, Bellocchio follows the trend to de-politicize women terrorists, and to displace their deviance into the sexual and/or emotional realm. In doing so, he succeeds in reworking Braghetti's memoir and shifting the narrative focus from that of a woman committed to the BR's ideological agenda to someone incapable of decisive action. Bellocchio problematicizes the challenging notion of the deviant female in that Braghetti, recast as Chiara, is portrayed as a fearful woman who has serious misgivings about the moral certainty of her mission. Chiara's doubts have considerable repercussions in terms of how Moro is viewed: he comes off as a soft-spoken, kind and family-oriented man who is martyred as a result of a corrupt political system, and his death recalls the sacrifices made by members of the partisan Resistance some thirty years earlier.

The Oneiric and the Political

Bellocchio's drastic transformation of perspective is first evident in the title of the film, borrowed from Emily Dickinson's poem 'Good Morning – Midnight' (1862):

> Good Morning – Midnight –
> I'm coming Home –
> Day – got tired of Me –
> How could I – of Him?

Sunshine was a sweet place –
I liked to stay –
But Morn – didn't want me – now –
So – Goodnight – Day!

I can look – can't I –
When the East is Red?
The Hills – have a way – then –
That puts the Heart – abroad –

You – are not so fair – Midnight –
I chose – Day –
But – please take a little Girl –
He turned away![17]

Clear in the chiasmus of lines 1 and 8 (Good Morning / Midnight, Goodnight Day), the poetic narrator unambiguously turns towards night as she has been rejected by day, representative of a 'normal life,' or involvement in the symbolic order (a reference to Dickinson's probable agoraphobia). The choice is made for her, not by her. Unlike Braghetti, who acknowledges her moral certainty, both the poetic narrator and Bellocchio's Chiara are infantilized, and have no such autonomy. Dickinson's midnight is Chiara's night, lived out in the labyrinthine and claustrophobic apartment-prison, which might call to mind the shadowy, atemporal atmosphere of Gaetano Previati's painting *Il giorno sveglia la notte* [*Day Wakes the Night*] (1905). Parallels continue between Dickinson's poem and Bellocchio's film in that, as expressed in the third stanza, an additional psychological space is present – that of the oneiric, represented as aurora. Temporality is a key thematic in both the film and the poem (note eight references to day, night, morn, etc.). These clearly demarcated indicators of mortality are inconsistent with what is implied in the third stanza: a dream space associated with madness, between sleeping and waking. Palpable in Bellocchio's film is a constant tension between the political and the personal, the 'struggle' of the brigatisti that has as its end a change of the political landscape and Chiara's persistent and regressive dreaming and daydreaming. No such space exists in Braghetti's memoir; here, instead, the protagonist lives her life in only two worlds, 'impiegata di giorno e di notte rivoluzionaria, assassina, regina della casa del terrore' (Braghetti and Tavella, 30) [an employee

---

17   Emily Dickinson, *The Complete Poems of Emily Dickinson* (London: Faber, 1975), 203.

by day and by night a revolutionary, assassin, queen of the house of terror].

The oneiric space introduced in Bellocchio's film is rich in fictionality and intertextual references. Attempting to wake Chiara from her dreaming is Enzo Passoruolo, the author of a screenplay (which is about a fictional kidnap and entitled *Buongiorno, notte*) which Moro is reading when he is abducted. Bellocchio's intertextual reference does not stop here. Enzo acts as Chiara's conscience; he denounces the BR, whose members, he maintains, are 'pazzi e stupidi' [crazy and stupid] and tells Chiara, in a key scene, that he has changed the screenplay's ending. Among the jailers in his fictionalized kidnap, he claims, is a woman who must decide whether or not to save the political prisoner. In his revised ending, Enzo explains to Chiara, the woman terrorist stops believing in the cause and becomes enraged with herself for having been so misguided.[18] But Enzo serves another purpose: he also embodies the ethos of the partisan Resistance in that he accompanies Chiara's family on a Sunday outing to visit her parents' graves and then, at lunch, joins in the singing of the Resistance ballad, 'Fischia il vento' [The Wind Whistles], whose concluding stanzas are as follows:

E se ci coglie la crudele morte
dura vendetta verrà dal partigian
ormai sicura è già la dura sorte
del fascista vile traditor

Cessa il vento, calma è la bufera
torna a casa il fiero partigian
sventolando la rossa sua bandiera
vittoriosi, e alfin liberi siam!

[And if cruel death should take us
The partisan will mete out a harsh revenge
By now the harsh fate of the Fascist
Vile traitor, is certain

The wind ceases, the storm is calm
The proud partisan returns home
Waving his red flag
Victorious, and finally free, are we!]

---

18 Ruth Glynn discusses this scene in terms of a 'compensation fantasy' that functions in relation to Bellocchio's 'victimized revisiting of the trauma of the *anni di piombo* in an attempt to win a victory over the perpetrators' (71).

All generations (those present in the scene include elderly partisans, a couple fresh from their wedding and young children) join in the nostalgia of recalling the fascist as a 'vile traitor' while the partisans aspire to victory and liberty. Chiara is the only one ill-at-ease here for, as in many other moments in the film, she is involved in questioning her role as jailer and in equating the BR with fascism while aligning Moro with the wronged partisans; this is the recurrent leitmotif woven through Chiara's fantasy world.

Dreams occupy a central position in the film, and Chiara's dreams or daydreams are peppered with images and scenes from both Roberto Rossellini's seminal neorealist film, *Paisà* [*Paisan*] (1946), and Dziga Vertov's *Three Songs About Lenin* (1934). Bellocchio explains that the excerpts from Vertov's film on Lenin's virtues signify that Chiara is envisaging the beginning of the end of the BR: 'È come se la neve, la panchina dove sedeva Lenin, è come se lei sentisse, proprio nei giorni del trionfo, con Moro nelle loro mani, come se improvvisamente tutto si fosse raggelato, come se fosse l'inizio della loro fine' (Chiacchiari, para. 20) [It's as if the snow, the bench where Lenin sat, it's as if she could feel in those days of triumph, with Moro in their hands, that everything had suddenly frozen, that it was the beginning of the end for them]. These *mises-en-abîme* articulate Chiara's sublimated connection to the 'morally intact' commitment of the Resistance, or to the origins of communism or, in the simple terms of the ballad, to the concept of a clearly identifiable enemy. Her daydreams of revolution and execution of the innocent allude to her sense of revolutionary principle, while her final fantasy of liberating Moro reinforces her moral ambiguity. Chiara's nocturnal wanderings connect Moro, a shadowy political figure to say the least, to a decisive historical moment, the Resistance, and reinforce the awkward conceit of Moro as martyr.

Cinema History and Political Ambiguity

A rather problematic aspect of *Buongiorno, notte* is the political jumble that it presents. What are the implications of wedding the politics of both Moro and the BR to that of the anti-fascist partisan struggle? A close look at the scene in which Chiara reads Moro's letter of farewell to his wife Eleonora (Noretta) illustrates the thematics of political ambiguity frequently aligned with Chiara's perspective. Several subject positions are presented, and each one is associated with a distinct narrative perspective – respectively that of: Moro in his cell; Mariano, Primo and Ernesto who watch him; Chiara in her bedroom;

the footage of insurrection and executions (some from *Paisà*); and finally, family members mourning the dead. As Moro's voice-over of his final letter to his wife, delivered on 5 May – 'Amore mio, sentimi sempre con te e tienimi stretto. Bacia e carezza Fida, Demi, Luca' [My love, feel that I am always with you and keep me close. Kiss and hug Fida, Demi, Luca] – is replaced by that of a letter written by Resistance fighter Pedro Ferreira to his fiancé, Chiara's discomfiture is externalized. Moro's heart-wrenching farewell to his wife and grandchildren fades into the opening lines of Ferreira's letter, which announces his imminent execution: 'Amore mio, Domattina all'alba una plotone d'esecuzione della guardia repubblicana fascista metterà fine ai miei giorni' [My love, tomorrow morning at dawn, an execution squad of the republican fascist guard will put an end to my life]. This letter comes from *Lettere di condannati a morte della resistenza partigiana* [*Letters of Italian Resistance Fighters Sentenced to Death*], a book that Chiara keeps by her bed, alongside Marx and Engels' *The Holy Family*.[19]

At this point in the film's narrative, Moro has just been sentenced to death by the BR. As Bellocchio conveys it, the decision does not sit well with Chiara. This portrait of events contrasts with the reality outlined by Braghetti in *Il prigioniero*. Explaining why she did not leave the apartment before Moro was killed, Braghetti simply states: 'Semplicemente, ci credevo. La fede rivoluzionaria, unita all'autodisciplina e alla necessità di mettere le mie emozioni al secondo posto, sperimentate fin dall'infanzia, erano più forte di qualunque altra' (182) [I simply believed. My revolutionary faith, combined with self-discipline and the need to relegate my emotions to second place, something I had experienced ever since childhood, were stronger than any other consideration]. In Bellocchio's film, however, the short scene in which Chiara reads Moro's final letter to his wife incorporates frequent close-ups of Chiara (there are five segments focusing on her, four that have as their subject matter scenes of revolution or partisan executions and three that focus on Moro and his captors). Chiara's dreamscape externalizes her psychic disarray, a dimension not present in Braghetti's memoir, and reveal Bellocchio's uneasy construction of martyrdom for Moro. As Moro's writings are rendered interchangeable with those of the condemned members of the Resistance in Chiara's mental landscape, Chiara herself is infantilized and robbed of political autonomy.

---

19 *Lettere di condannati a morte della resistenza partigiana*, ed. Piero Malvezzi and Giovanni Pirelli (Turin: Einaudi, 1952).

The inclusion of footage from Rossellini's film is a slippery issue, however. In both *Paisà* and *Roma città aperta* [*Rome, Open City*] (1945), 'fascist/Nazi' signified corruption and amorality, both in terms of gender and politics, while 'anti-fascist/partisan' occupied the moral high ground. Rossellini's revolutionary films painted a morally sound and heroic picture of the Resistance, foregrounding hope for the future and the eventual triumph of good over evil. Right and wrong are not so strongly differentiated in the film, however, as, in a second letter (the most detailed one in a compilation of one hundred), Ferreira tells his party members that he is not dying in vain: 'Muoio soddisfatto e contento di aver compiuto fino al supremo sacrificio il mio dovere verso la Patria e verso me stesso' (Malvezzi and Pirelli, 110) [I die satisfied and content in the knowledge that I have made the supreme sacrifice, in carrying out my duty to my country and to myself]. Ferreira's sentiments are echoed in the spoken words of Pink Floyd's 'The Great Gig in the Sky' which accompany the scene:

And I am not frightened of dying, any time will do, I
Don't mind. Why should I be frightened of dying?
There's no reason for it, you've gotta go sometime.
I never said I was frightened of dying.

Also in this second letter, partisan Ferreira details for his comrades how certain fascist officials involved in his trial should be treated in the new Italy: 'Con la massima considerazione ed il massimo rispetto esaminando il bene che hanno fatto come uomini' (Malvezzi and Pirelli, 110) [With the greatest consideration and the greatest respect, examining the good that they have done as men]. One fascist, Ferreira explains, 'è un avversario leale, onesto e d'onore' (111) [is a loyal, honest and honourable adversary], a statement that shares the ethos of Captain Bellodi's conversation with Mafioso Don Mariano in Leonardo Sciascia's *Il giorno della civetta* [*The Day of the Owl*].[20] Do the BR, Bellocchio might be asking, deserve the same compassion that Ferreira desires for his executioners? Through the oneiric rendition of this letter, Bellocchio implies that Chiara's wish is for Moro to forgive

20   Following his Nietzschean discourse on the nature of 'man', mafia boss Don Mariano tells Captain Bellodi: 'Lei, anche se mi inchioderà su queste carte come un Cristo, lei è un uomo' [Even if you nail me to these documents like Christ to His cross, you're a man] and Bellodi, who has previously loathed Mariano, responds: 'Anche lei' [So are you]. Leonardo Sciascia, *Il giorno della civetta* (Turin: Einaudi, 1961), 100. Translation from Leonardo Sciascia, *The Day of the Owl* in *The Day of the Owl/Equal Danger*, trans. by Archibald Colquhoun (London: Paladin, 1984), 102.

his captors, as Ferreira pardons the fascists. A further implication is that Chiara has confused Moro with her own dead father, a member of the Resistance, and cannot bear the guilt, prompted by Enzo, that she feels for having betrayed his ideals.

In the final sequence of the film, Chiara fantasizes her ultimate betrayal; she imagines drugging her comrades during a 'last supper' – complete with the sign of the cross – in order to abet Moro's escape. In her dream, Moro walks free at dawn towards the most iconic and controversial structure of the fascist period: the Palazzo della Civiltà Italiana, located in the Esposizione universale di Roma, or EUR. As it was originally conceived, the EUR served a variety of functions: above all, its inauguration would celebrate fascism's *ventennio nero* [twentieth anniversary], as it was to be the setting for the World's Fair. It was thereby meant to reaffirm the place of fascism in the global arena, celebrating and legitimizing colonial conquests (at the time the project was conceived, Italy had recently invaded and occupied Ethiopia). But EUR was also conceived differently from any other World's Fair in that the majority of the structures were meant to be permanent. In this context, the *mise-en-scène* of Moro's imagined escape might suggest that Bellocchio is interested in critiquing the persistence of fascist mentalities in contemporary politics, social relations and economic structures. However, it also begs to be read in light of Rossellini's revolutionary film, *Roma, città aperta*, as the Palazzo is present there in the celebrated cinematic escape of partisan Francesco from the Fascists and Nazis.

The escape scenes in both films contrast with the final, memorable vision of Rossellini's film when pairs of Italian boys march towards St. Peter's after witnessing Don Pietro's execution at the hands of the fascists: the dome of St. Peter's is a beacon for the new generation of Italian youth, while the Palazzo is out of place with both the iconography of this scene and the Baroque architecture of the city's largest dome. The children in *Roma, città aperta*, veritable sons of partisans, march towards the famous church after Don Pietro's death at dawn as Moro walks towards the Palazzo della Civiltà Italiana in Bellocchio's film.[21] In replacing the spiritual seat of Catholicism

21 Alan O'Leary draws a narrative parallel between Moro's fictionalized escape and the inclusion of the famous scene from *Paisà* where partisans are drowned in the Po: 'Within its episode, the martyrdom of the partisans in *Paisà* is a disgusting and useless loss; "outside" the film, we know that the partisans' cause was victorious and that the sacrifice was not in vain – but we need this knowledge to make thematic sense of the story. The counterfactual representation of Aldo Moro's escape in the penultimate sequence of *Buongiorno, notte* is akin to the death of these partisans in *Paisà*, not so much because Moro is "like" the

by historical fascism's most evident physical tribute, is Bellocchio suggesting that the death and martyrdom of Don Pietro, Manfredi and countless partisans was in vain? Or rather, that the revolutionary principles held so dear by members of the Partisan Resistance only served as fodder for the BR? If so, Bellocchio is positing that Rossellini's ideological position, his Catholic humanism and belief in the 'possibility of man', a conceit reiterated in *Buongiorno, notte* by both Moro and Enzo, was futile. Without a doubt, allusions to the finale of *Roma, città aperta* in Moro's spectral walk through Rome cogently align him with the Partisan Resistance. In Rossellini's film, the protagonists, Don Pietro and Manfredi, die as Christ figures, martyrs to a new Italy that is both Catholic and Communist, and Rossellini's future partisans represent an Italy that might one day be healed from the trauma of the *ventennio nero*. Moro, however, was put to death while neither church nor party came to his aid, so that, more than thirty years on, Rossellini's message has come full circle.

The story does not end here, as the impossible dream of Moro's liberation is immediately contradicted by a shot of him being taken out of his prison, moments before his execution. Violence is not fictionalized and Moro's death is relegated off-screen, its aftermath only allowed to creep into the closed quarters of the apartment through the television which screens documentary footage of his funeral. In downplaying the violence and focusing on the human enigma, however, Bellocchio makes new martyrs. The DC turned their back on Moro, the party's metaphorical father, claiming not to recognize him any more, and Moro's execution is a direct response to the DC's refusal to negotiate (to save Moro's life the BR asked for an exchange of political prisoners). Here and elsewhere, Bellocchio, like Rossellini before him, underlines the connection between religion, politics and sacrifice. Mariano, the character based on Mario Moretti, explains that members of an armed movement must be willing to undergo any sacrifice, even that of killing their own mother. Matricide is a common thematic in Bellocchio's opus. In his first feature film, *I pugni in tasca* [*Fists in the Pocket*] (1965), protagonist Ale kills his mother by pushing her off a cliff, while in *L'ora di religione* [*The Religion Hour*] (2002), the mother's murder by a mentally unstable son precipitates her martyrdom and eventual canonization. Both these films bitterly critique Catholic moralism and the middle class, the direct targets of the BR; but in *Buongiorno, notte*, Bellocchio turns

partisans (as Chiara believes), but because it is not the "real" end of the film or story', 'Dead Man Walking: The Aldo Moro Kidnap and Palimpsest History in *Buongiorno, notte*', *New Cinemas*, 6:1 (2008), 42.

his attention from matricide to parricide in order to underscore the DC's obstinate moralism.

In 'Lost in Transition', Ida Dominijanni argues that Bellocchio presents Moro as Italy's last father, and that his death, essentially, implies the death of the Italian state:

> Italy has been fatherless since Moro's assassination, not because the fathers of the Republic have all died […] but because their deaths have not been worked through. Removed in death, their spirits still hang over the collective unconscious and nobody can take their place. The tragic death of Moro, assassinated by terrorists but left to be murdered – according to Bellocchio (and this is also my interpretation) – by the 'hard line' adopted by the State, is subjected to this removal process in a distinctive manner.[22]

This 'distinctive manner' is foregrounded in the final scene of the film, which comprises the footage of the state funeral (Moro's body absent) attended by his party members, those to whom Moro, the party President, in his final letter attributed 'full responsibility' for his death:

> Vorrei restasse ben chiara la piena responsabilità della D.C. con il suo assurdo ed incredibile comportamento. Essa va detto con fermezza così come si deve rifiutare eventuale medaglia che si suole dare in questo caso. È poi vero che moltissimi amici (ma non ne so i nomi) o ingannati dall'idea che il parlare mi danneggiasse o preoccupati delle loro personali posizioni, non si sono mossi come avrebbero dovuto.[23]

> [I would like to make quite clear that full responsibility lies with the DC, and with its absurd and incredible behaviour. This must be firmly stated, just as the medal that is generally awarded in these cases must be rejected. It is true that many, many friends (but who, precisely, I do not know) – whether deluded by the idea that to speak out would damage me or worried about their own personal position – were not moved to act as they should have been.]

Thus, the Christian Democratic party is held responsible, not the BR. The footage of the funeral is accompanied by Pink Floyd's 'Shine on You Crazy Diamond', a song that expresses the impotent political and social climate of the 1970s and often accompanies Chiara's dreams

---

22 'Lost in Transition', in *Across Genres, Generations and Borders: Italian Women Writing Lives*, ed. Susanna Scarparo and Rita Wilson (Newark: University of Delaware Press, 2004), 202.

23 Sergio Flamigni, *'Il mio sangue ricadrà su di loro': gli scritti di Aldo Moro prigioniero delle BR* (Milan: Kaos edizioni, 1997), 202.

and fantasies.[24] The interplay of shadow and light in the song recalls both Dickinson's poem and the apartment-prison, while mention of 'martyrs', 'prisoners' and 'legends' evoke Moro's new status. Certainly, by transferring the blame for Moro's death from the BR to Moro's own party, Bellocchio is dialoguing with and compensating for Chiara's sense of guilt. His recasting has gone one step further: not only has he succeeded in utterly abrogating Braghetti's sense of political commitment, he has also created an apologia for Chiara's betrayal of both the personal and the political (her two fathers). Although Chiara's politics come through as deeply ambivalent, her insightful and inveterate dreams engender a critique of violence, and point towards a much more thorough indictment of Moro's executioners.

24   The lyrics we hear are: 'Come on you target for faraway laughter / Come on you stranger, you legend, you martyr, and shine! [...] / Threatened by shadows at night, and exposed in the light / Shine on you crazy diamond [...] / Come on you raver, you seer of visions, / Come on you painter, you piper, you prisoner, and shine! / Nobody knows where you are, how near or how far...'

Section 4
Terrorism and Ethics

10. Ethics of Conviction vs Ethics of Responsibility in Cinematic Representations of Italian Left-Wing Terrorism of the 1970s[1]

Leonardo Cecchini

The *Anni di Piombo* beyond Conflicting Discourses

The *anni di piombo* still represent an open wound in Italian collective memory. Unlike other countries that have emerged from bloody internal conflicts and outbreaks of war among the various groups that constitute the nation, Italy has proved to be unable to establish a Commission for Truth and Reconciliation aimed at reaching a shared consensus on re-imagining the past. After the fall of the Berlin Wall and the collapse of the political system that had prevailed in Italy during the Cold War, all the factors necessary for overcoming the 'period of emergency' (as the *anni di piombo* are also termed) and for reaching some form of reconciliation among the parties involved seemed to be in place. Instead, to date, it has not been possible to effect a collective working through of the experience of political violence.

On the one hand the left – having abandoned in jail those who had chosen armed struggle, and had seen themselves in the revolutionary tradition that views violence as the midwife of history – has liquidated the revolutionary tradition as an outmoded instrument of the twentieth century, forgetting just how many terrorists emerged from its own 'family album'.[2] On the other hand, the right-wing

---

1   Translated by Kate Mitchell and the editors.
2   The expression is Rossana Rossanda's in her article 'Il discorso sulla DC', *Il Manifesto*, 28 March 1978.

neo-fascists of the Movimento Sociale Italiano, who for a long time had flirted with the violence of the neo-nazi and neo-fascist extremist groups, have today refashioned themselves into the more respectable Alleanza Nazionale, and prefer to construct themselves first and foremost as the victims of the political violence of those years.[3] Finally, we must not forget the responsibilities of a number of high-level state figures for the so-called 'strategy of tension' and stragismo, responsibilities that remain unpunished and that those same individuals would like to erase from public memory. In the absence of a path towards reconciliation and healing, these factors still have negative repercussions on civic life in Italy today.

This results in a schizophrenic oscillation in Italian public discourse on the *anni di piombo* between a constant attempt at repression and oblivion and intermittent political exploitation of the past in accordance with the contingent interests of today's various political formations. It should not surprise us then if the historical memory of younger generations is pervaded not by simple ignorance but by the 'divisiveness' – i.e., the practice of systematic delegitimization of the discourse of the Other – that many observers have identified as one of the most harmful characteristics of Italy's political culture.[4] One such example is provided by the organization of the various associations of the relatives of the victims of the *anni di piombo* along political lines, with the victims of 'black' terrorism on one side and those of 'red' terrorism on the other. This tendency to acknowledge only the suffering of the fallen on one's own side can be understood on a human level, but on the level of civic life and of the country's collective memory its effects can only be harmful. It is also an expression of the 'factional memory' that still afflicts public debate on the *anni di piombo*.[5]

In the absence of an institutional response from the state and public opinion alike, the task of representing and reimagining the *anni di piombo* in collective memory has been transferred to memoir and fiction. Especially since the 1990s, Italy has witnessed a revisiting of those years within the field of cultural production (film, television, narrative, memoir) which has assumed the task of attempting to

---

3   See Anna Cento Bull, *Italian Neofascism: The Strategy of Tension and the Politics of Nonreconciliation* (New York: Berghahn, 2008).

4   Loreto Di Nucci and Ernesto Galli Della Loggia, *Due nazioni: legittimazione e delegittimazione nella storia dell'Italia contemporanea* (Bologna: Il Mulino, 2003).

5   Barbara Spinelli, *Il sonno della memoria: l'Europa dei totalitarismi* (Milan: Mondadori, 2001), 218–20.

compensate for the absence of political will and of providing Italian society with a means for reflection.

It is now widely recognized that every historical narration is a reconstruction of memory which is inherently linked to the conditions of its interpretation. History and collective memory ought not to be considered as opposing categories (with one transmitting 'truth', the other the values and ethical norms of a given social group) but should instead be conceived of as two complementary modalities of remembrance.[6] Narration changes the very event that is narrated. It acts upon the narrated action, and in changing what is being narrated, changes itself in the act of narration. To express this another way, fictional representations are positioned along a continuum at the other end of which one finds the events. These determine how they are represented and, at the same time, cannot be interpreted independently of their representation.[7] In this way, fiction comes to play an important role in the reconstruction of the past and thus in the relationship between memory and identity.

In this chapter I reflect upon the dialectic between history and narration in a section dedicated to the analysis of interpretative categories of the actions and motivations of some of the protagonists of the *anni di piombo*. This is followed by a second section in which I examine a series of works in order to identify representations which are potentially useful for understanding, reimagining and overcoming the choices that led to those tragic events, while contributing to the construction of a shared memory and, perhaps, to a form of reconciliation.

Accidental Heroes

In the first half of the 1980s, public debate on left-wing terrorism – which was nearing defeat but still raging – revolved essentially around two poles: a demonization of the terrorists as monstrous, and a historico-political analysis of the mechanisms that had generated 'compagni che sbagliano' [errant comrades]. Umberto Eco contributed to the debate with two journalistic pieces that, in

6   Aleida Assmann, *Ricordare: forme e mutamenti della memoria culturale* (Bologna: Il Mulino, 2002) [orig. *Erinnerungsräume: Formen und Wandlungen des kulturellen Gedâchtnisses* (München: Beck, 1999)]; Paul Ricœur, *Ricordare, dimenticare, perdonare: l'enigma del passato* (Bologna: Il Mulino, 2004) [orig. *La mémoire, l'histoire, l'oubli* (Paris: Seuil, 2000)].
7   Alan O'Leary, *Tragedia all'italiana: cinema e terrorismo tra Moro e memoria* (Tissi: Angelica, 2007), 53–55.

accordance with his customary dialogical procedure, attempted to blur the lines between the two camps.[8] As an implicit reply to those, especially on the left, who claimed a moral lawfulness of violence as a motor for change but who saw in the violence of the Brigate Rosse (BR) first and foremost a political error, Eco on the one hand invites a priori suspicion of any and all mysticisms of violence and, on the other, insinuates that heroes and dangerous adventurers may have more in common than we are prone to believe. And yet, faced with the risk of winding up with a single melting-pot of Christian martyrs, supporters of Garibaldi, the BR and partisans, Eco makes a crucial distinction: 'Il problema è di sapere, di capire, come non tutti i sacrifici, non tutto il sangue, sia speso per gioco. Ma è una dura vicenda di ragionevoli discriminazioni' (Eco, 121) [The challenge is to know, to understand, that not all sacrifices, not all blood, is shed for fun. But making such well-founded choices is a difficult task].

The discriminating factor that Eco immediately proposes is a simple one: 'Gli eroi veri, coloro che si sacrificano per il bene collettivo, e che la società riconosce come tali, [...] sono sempre gente che agisce malvolentieri. [...] L'eroe vero è sempre eroe per sbaglio, il suo sogno sarebbe di essere un onesto vigliacco come tutti' (122) [True heroes, those who sacrifice themselves for the good of the people, and whom society recognizes as such, [...] are always people who act unwillingly. [...] The true hero is always a hero by accident; his or her dream is to be an honest coward like everyone else]. What Eco therefore proposes is a type of 'involuntary hero' who takes action and chooses violence because he or she cannot do anything else, yet who is primarily motivated not by grand ideals or universal utopias but by a sense of responsibility to him- or herself and to others.

The essence of Eco's formula seems to me fully compatible with the more elaborated categories developed by Tzvetan Todorov who, building on Mikhail Bakhtin's theories of dialogism, searches for a secular ethics adequate to the individual faced with extreme situations and decisions, such as those that frequently presented themselves during the last century. Todorov's research represents an enquiry into totalitarian thought (and into the totalitarianisms of the twentieth century). For Todorov, totalitarian thought radically

---

8   Umberto Eco, ' La voglia di morte', *La Repubblica*, 14 February 1981, and 'Perché ridono in quelle gabbie?', *La Repubblica*, 16 April 1982. Both articles have been reprinted in Eco, *Sette anni di desiderio* (Milan: Bompiani, 1995), 119–22 and 123–25 respectively.

denies alterity and thus does not allow for plurality.[9] The *forma mentis* of totalitarian thought not only characterizes the historical totalitarianisms (Fascism, Nazism and Stalinism) with which Todorov's analysis is principally concerned, but is also present within every monologic public discourse in the Bakhtinian sense of the term. The grammar of totalitarian discourse, argues Todorov, recognizes only the existence of two groups: an 'us' which elides the differences between individuals and a 'them' which comprises all those who must be fought and defeated (39). Todorov also reflects at length upon a tragic human misconception that he calls the 'temptation of the good', that is, an inclination to accept the bad with the intention of producing a superior good. For the purposes of an absolutist good of humanity projected into the future, excessive horrors and cruelties simply do not exist and the moral quality of actions is judged not by the means utilized but by the 'legitimate' ends that come to justify everything.

For example, in examining life and death decisions and actions taken by members of the resistance movement in the Warsaw Ghetto during the uprising of April 1943, or in Nazi-occupied France, Todorov suggests that one should recognize within those decisions the inspiration of two value systems which, though fundamentally different, are both worthy of respect. These are: an *ethics of conviction* driven by the imperative to do what is right 'at all costs' (including the renouncement of individual interests and happiness); and an *ethics of responsibility* which forces the individual to weigh up first and foremost the consequences of an action for the collective. Todorov is especially attracted to the latter category; this does not mean that for him convictions are irrelevant, but that an ethics of conviction intrinsically tends to avoid that principle of dialogism which, following Bakhtin, is a cornerstone of Todorov's system of thought and values. Moreover, such an ethics tends to privilege the quality of the ends over and above that of the means.

Todorov's thought and categories are useful because, on the one hand, they help us to understand the assumptions and values of those who kill for a purpose; on the other hand, they give us the means to criticize these values from the point of view of one's responsibility, not only towards oneself but, above all, towards others. The values proposed by Eco as well as his predilection for 'involuntary' heroes seem to concur with Todorov's considerations on altruism – a key

---

9   Tzvetan Todorov, *Hope and Memory: Reflections on the Twentieth Century*, trans. by David Bellos (London: Atlantic Books, 2003), 34 [orig. *Mémoire du Mal, Tentation du bien: Enquête sur le siècle* (Paris: Robert Laffont, 2000)].

category in Todorov's consideration of ethics – since they raise awareness in the individual of the Other that is in themselves.

Ends and Means of the Armed Struggle

Can Eco's and Todorov's considerations help us to distinguish between violence that is justifiable and violence that is unjustifiable? Beyond the obvious distinctions of historical context, is there a moral difference between killing a prison guard in cold blood in Italy in 1978, and shooting a Nazi official in the back in 1944? What are the value systems and principles that persuade us that the violence practised by partisans in the anti-Nazi and anti-fascist struggle was justifiable and justified, while the armed struggle of the subversive movements of the 1970s is perceived as unjustifiable?

It may seem incongruous to compare the actions of the partisans during the Resistance movement with those of the fighters of the armed organizations during the *anni di piombo*. Yet there are two main reasons why this comparison is relevant. Firstly, organizations of armed struggle in Italy themselves considered their actions a continuation of the ideals of the Resistance movement. Undoubtedly, for the militants of the armed groups of the 1970s, the Resistance movement represented an important founding myth; this is documented by the statements of many ex-terrorists (and by the 'blessing' granted by ex-partisans to the BR).[10] Secondly, on the level of the classification of actions, it cannot be denied that the murders and injuries inflicted by armed groups in the 1970s strongly resemble attacks against leading Nazi-fascists during the Resistance movement.

In both cases, a clandestine group condemns a person to death, after an investigation, and enforces the sentence; the victim is taken by surprise, and is unable to defend him- or herself. The people involved in the action share a moral responsibility, even if the attacker has not necessarily taken part in the decision to kill, or if the person who has made the decision has not taken part in the action. It is not surprising therefore that the accounts of the psychological cost borne by those involved in the process of killing another human being in cold blood are almost identical in memoirs written by former terrorists of the 1970s and those provided by survivors of the Resistance movement.

---

10   Renato Curcio, for example, recalls the solemnity of the occasion in which weapons used by former partisans were entrusted to him and the nascent BR, marking their inheritance of the 'betrayed resistance movement', *A viso aperto: vita e memoria del fondatore delle Brigate Rosse* (Milan: Mondadori, 1993), 71.

Anna Laura Braghetti, for example, describes as follows her reactions after having fired eleven pistol shots at Vittorio Bachelet, the elderly Vice-President of the Consiglio Superiore della Magistratura (the regulatory body of the Italian magistrature):

> Dopo l'azione provai un senso di vuoto assoluto. Per uccidere qualcuno che non ti ha fatto niente, che non conosci, che non odi, devi mettere da parte l'umana pietà, in un angolo buio e chiuso, e non passare mai più di lì con il pensiero. Devi evitare sentimenti di qualsiasi tipo, perché sennò, con le altre emozioni, viene a galla l'orrore.[11]

> [After the action I felt a sense of utter emptiness. To kill someone who has done nothing to you – whom you do not know, whom you do not hate – you have to put human compassion to one side in a dark and enclosed corner, and never return there in your thoughts. You have to avoid having feelings of any kind, because if you do, along with other emotions, horror sets in.]

In an interview with Carla Mosca and Rossana Rossanda, Mario Moretti, the leader of the BR during the Moro kidnapping, does not hide the fact that the decision to 'justifiably execute' Moro in cold blood (Moretti still judges his actions 'justifiable', following the thinking of the BR at that time) did not leave him morally and psychologically indifferent:

> - Sei stato tu?
> Sì.
> - Si è detto che era Gallinari?
> No. Non avrei permesso che lo facesse un altro. Era una prova terribile, uno si porta la cicatrice addosso per la vita. [...]
> Nella sentenza è scritto che due [colpi] sono senza silenziatore. Tutti e nove col silenziatore. Guarda che stai riaprendo una ferita tremenda, Carla.[12]

> [- Was it you?
> Yes.-
> It has been suggested that it was Gallinari.
> No. I wouldn't have allowed another person to do it. It was a terrible

---

11   Anna Laura Braghetti and Paola Tavella, *Il prigioniero* (Milan: Mondadori, 1998), 122. The passage immediately following this one tells of another *brigatista* who, when he had to kill, was not able to hide his nausea and his shock at having confronted, not an armed and resolute man, but an unarmed person who had allowed himself to be killed without protest.
12   Mario Moretti, Carla Mosca and Rossana Rossanda, *Brigate Rosse: una storia italiana* (Milan: Anabasi, 1994), 167, 169.

ordeal; the scars remain for the rest of your life. [...]
In the sentence it states that two [shots] were fired without a silencer.
All nine were fired with a silencer. Listen, Carla, you are opening up
a terrible wound.]

We can usefully compare these accounts with testimonial accounts
from members of the Gruppi Armati Patriottici (GAP), squadrons of
partisans (mostly belonging to the PCI) who fought in the occupied
cities carrying out attacks and murders on Nazis, fascists and their
functionaries.[13] It is, of course, necessary to point out the obvious
differences concerning the historical context. Firstly, the partisans
presented themselves as the only 'true' representatives of a country
occupied by foreign troops (even if these troops were also assisted by
native collaborators); secondly, at the time of the events, and according
to collective historical memory, the partisans enjoyed the active
recognition and support of the population. None of these conditions
can be applied to members of the various militant organizations
active in Italy in the 1970s, regardless of their identification with
the ranks of the 'oppressed' and despite institutional tendencies to
underestimate the following that they enjoyed.

And yet, for the partisans, an intimidatory and therefore
terrorist means was not uncommonly employed against those who
collaborated with the occupying army. Their actions are therefore
comparable to the equally terrorist aims of the kneecappings and
murders carried out by the militants of the armed struggle in the
1970s. The decisive difference, in my opinion, concerns the different
value systems underlying the two phenomena. In the Resistance
movement, the moral reason for the killing of informers was not
primarily rooted in the beliefs of the fighter who has to kill his or her
enemies but in an ethics of responsibility according to which, even if
killing a person is wrong, it may be necessary in order to save the lives
of others.[14] Reading partisan testimonials, it becomes clear that the

---

13   See Manlio Calegari, *La sega di Hitler* (Milan: Selene, 2004), and Alessandro
Portelli, *L'ordine è già stato eseguito: Roma, le Fosse Ardeatine, la memoria* (Rome:
Donzelli, 1999), 157–66.

14   My argument here is informed also by my reading of testimonies by WWII
Danish partisans who, during the German occupation (1940–1945), took part
in the so-called *stikkerlikvideringer*, the killing of Danish informers (around 400
people). Interviewed by the Danish journalist Peter Øvig Knudsen, veterans of
the Danish Resistance describe the doubts they experienced before carrying out
planned killings; they describe the upset and feeling of emptiness following the
event, the awareness that it was an extreme choice that remains 'for the rest of
one's life': 'We were killers [...] and of the worst kind, because we planned [the
murders] [...] It is a fact that we have had to live with ever since', *Efter Drabet*

fact of taking the life of another person in cold blood is experienced as the assumption of a responsibility that one would prefer not to have on one's shoulders, but that one assumes nonetheless, against one's will, for collective reasons (the liberation of the country, the safety of companions) that at the time were perhaps not perceived as 'right' by the entire collective, but that later became the property of the national collective memory.

In short, it seems to me that Todorov's distinction helps us to understand better the dramatic choices of these people. At the same time, I am aware that abstract principles, if applied too schematically, can often become instruments of political and ideological struggle rather than instruments of understanding. Alessandro Portelli is right to argue against those who today apply *a posteriori* the distinction made by Todorov between ethics of conviction and ethics of responsibility to the choices made at the time by the fighters of the Resistance movement. For Portelli, it seems that in a situation of world war, it is not possible to abstractly set a 'good' ethics (of responsibility) against a 'bad' ethics (of conviction) and to attribute to them two *separate and contrasting* subjects – 'the good' (those who did not want resistance actions in Rome in order to avoid harming civilians) against 'the bad' (the partisans of the GAP) who carried out the actions.[15] However, in the case of the armed struggle of the 1970s, it seems to me that one can only speak of war in Giorgio Bocca's terms: as a war declared and carried forward unilaterally by a single party and with 'nemici inventati che non sapevano neppure di esserlo' [invented enemies who were not even aware of being enemies].[16]

(Copenhagen: Gyldendal, 2001), 176; see also 54, 159, 163, 176, 330. Knudsen cites the testimony of Frode Jakobsen, the founder of the *Frihedsråd* (the wartime Committee for Freedom): 'the Nazi supporters who [...] were killed and injured were not attacked *because of their beliefs*, but merely because they accepted, for payment, the role of identifying their compatriots who were active in the struggle for freedom and of handing them over to the Gestapo. It was not *in order to punish* that these informers were rendered incapable of harming, but because they caused the imprisonment and the execution of many people, and to prevent them from continuing their activity of collaboration which put others at risk' (33, my emphasis).

15   Portelli, 441. As Portelli affirms on the same page, 'erano proprio *tutti* necessari i bombardamenti alleati sulle città tedesche e italiane? O non avevano un fine *terroristico*?' [were *all* the allied bombings on the Italian and German cities strictly necessary? Or did they not have a *terroristic* intent?]. Todorov confronts this very question when he discusses the 'morality' of the Hiroshima and Nagasaki atom bombings (249–57).

16   Giorgio Bocca, 'La nostra orribile stagione di sangue', *La Repubblica*, 20 March 2004.

Italy in the 1970s was not an occupied nation and, although its democracy may have been limited in many ways, nor was it a dictatorship. It is undoubtedly the case that certain sectors of the state connived with the strategy of tension and contributed to bombs exploding in public places, killing unarmed people in order to weaken the democracy. Yet this could not (and did not) justify a declaration of unilateral war against the forces of order and the judiciary. Moreover, it seems to me that in the moment of taking the life of another human being there is a tendency among militants of the armed struggle to act according to the principle that the moral qualities of the action depend not on the means used but on the 'legitimate' ends that come to justify everything. They act, therefore, according to an ethics of conviction.

In Sergio Zavoli's television documentary, *La notte della repubblica*, a review of the history of the *anni di piombo* presents many interesting examples of the process of re-elaborating the ethical and ideological value systems advanced by the ex-militants of the armed struggle after their defeat. In a language that is often schizophrenic and which reflects the contrast in identity between the 'I' of then and that of today, many ex-terrorists affirm that the decision to kill (and to die) was, in the great majority of cases, based on an abstract ideal of social purification rather than on reasoned distinctions between ends and means.[17] Here, too, it is not about juxtaposing *a priori* the two ethics, condemning the 'bad' (those who embraced political violence) and absolving 'the good' (for example, the left-wing democrats who did not). Instead, it is about pointing out the dangers (and the costs) of a violent choice made by subordinating every other value to ideology, in accordance with the ideals of 'the temptation of the good' outlined by Todorov.

Questions of Representation and the *Anni di Piombo*

I would now like to turn to the field of representation in order to analyse a number of films on the *anni di piombo*. In doing so, I will attempt to answer the following questions: does cinematographic fiction on the *anni di piombo* help to illuminate in some way the

17 See for example the interview with Silveria Russo transcribed in Sergio Zavoli, *La notte della repubblica* (Milan: Mondadori, 1992), 374. For an analysis of this interview, see Francesco Caviglia and Leonardo Cecchini, 'A Quest for Dialogism: Looking Back at Italian Political Violence in the '70s', in *Constructing History, Society and Politics in Discourse: Multimodal Approaches*, ed. Torben Vestergaard (Aalborg: Aalborg University Press, 2009), 127–48.

Todorovian dilemma between an ethics of responsibility and an ethics of conviction? Can a young public that has not lived through those events learn something from these films regarding the value systems of those who participated in the armed struggle? Are these films capable of representing the climate of those times, and what contribution do they give to the creation of a shared memory of the past?

One thing that is noticeable in the large majority of films on the *anni di piombo* is the absence of any 'represented' or 'recounted' violence. The directors who approach the period are reluctant not only to bring the attacks, the woundings and the almost daily murders of those years directly to the screen, but even to make their protagonists recount such episodes. This reluctance to represent violence is best exemplified by Mimmo Calopresti's *La seconda volta* (*The Second Time*, 1996): during the editing process, the director decided to cut the original film-script scene in which the ex-terrorist Lisa recounts in detail to Alberto the action that should have led to his death (Alberto still has the bullet embedded in his head).[18] In these films, violence is neither represented nor told, but is instead relegated to the zone of the unspoken, of the implicit, of ellipsis, all evidence of the director's anti-documentary choices. Like *La seconda volta*, Wilma Labate's *La mia generazione* (*My Generation*, 1996), Franco Bernini's *Le mani forti* (*Strong Hands*, 1996) and Marco Turco's *Vite in sospeso* (*Belleville*, 1998) can be defined as 'posthumous' films for they are not so much interested in terrorism and its ideology as in 'post'-terrorism and its legacy – the victims and their families, the (ex-)terrorists, and implicitly the whole of Italian society twenty to thirty years later.

The Ethics of Assassination

There is, nevertheless, a significant exception to this rule, and it is Gillo Pontecorvo's film, *Ogro* (*Operation Ogre*, 1979). One could reasonably point out that Pontecorvo's film is not a film on the *anni di piombo* but a reconstruction of the attack on the designated heir to the Spanish dictator Francisco Franco, Admiral Carrero Blanco, who was killed by ETA in a targeted bomb blast in Madrid on 12 December 1973. Yet as Pontecorvo himself confirms, there is no doubt that the film, which

---

18   Scene 86 in the unpublished script of *La seconda volta*, provided courtesy of the script-writer Francesco Bruni. For an analysis of this film in terms of its dialogic staging of the perspectives of the victim and perpetrator, see Caviglia and Cecchini.

was made in 1978 at the moment when the BR were kidnapping and killing Aldo Moro, is intended as a commentary upon the events in Italy at the time, and therefore is also an oblique work on the political violence of Italy during those years.[19]

Pontecorvo's original intention for the film (based on the book of the same title by Julien Aguirre, who had participated in the attack) was to describe an episode in the struggle for liberation against the Spanish dictatorship that would come to an end with the death of Franco (1975). He wanted to create, together with *La battaglia di Algeri* (*The Battle of Algiers*, 1966) and *Queimada* (*Burn!*, 1969), a kind of trilogy on the struggle for liberation against colonial and/or authoritarian oppression. Pontecorvo originally intended ETA's attack against Carrero Blanco to be considered a legitimate action of struggle against an important figure within a cruel dictatorship, an action that was not very different from acts that Pontecorvo himself had carried out during the Resistance. However, in the context of the political violence of those years in Italy, that concept now risked being read as an exaltation of the BR's armed struggle against the democratic state born of the Resistance, an armed struggle that Pontecorvo saw as a dangerous political error. For that reason, Pontecorvo admitted that he had developed a 'guilty conscience' (Bignardi, 162) with respect to the film as originally conceived.

In order to absolve that guilty conscience, Pontecorvo altered the film's structure to include a frame narrative designed to contain and contextualise the central account of the attack on Carrero Blanco. The frame narrative screens an imaginary political debate, set in the Basque country in 1978 (and therefore in post-Franco Spain), on the legitimate use or otherwise of violence in political action. This debate figures as a third-party address to the Italian BR. In the first flash-forward to that post-Franco period, two members of the assault team who killed Carrero Blanco (Txabi and his wife Ayamore) are shown discussing the problem of political violence in Bilbao in 1978. Unlike his wife and the comrades who participated in the 1975 attack, Txabi has continued the armed struggle against the democratic Spanish state and, during an ambush on a civil guard, has been mortally wounded. At the end of the film, we return to the scene of the initial flash-forward where Txabi, the 'errant comrade', lies on his death-bed and asks his former comrades – who had, together with him, eliminated Carrero Blanco – to understand his decision to continue the armed struggle in the name of an ideal conviction even after the end

19 Irene Bignardi, *Memorie estorte ad uno smemorato: vita di Gillo Pontecorvo* (Milan: Feltrinelli, 1999), 174.

of the dictatorship. However, while grieving for the imminent death of their friend, Txabi's former comrades are united in condemning his actions as irresponsible.

Ogro is almost didactic in juxtaposing a legitimate use of violence (the struggle for freedom and against Franco's dictatorship) and an illegitimate use of violence (the armed struggle against the representatives of a democratic system). It therefore distinguishes between those who choose violence on the basis of an ethics of responsibility – after a close investigation of the relationship between the means and the ends (not only Ayamore but also the head of the Esarra regiment and the priest, Joseba) – and those who choose violence on the basis of an ethics of conviction (Txabi). In addition to members of the BR, the film seems to address all those who (entrenched in the ideology of violence as the midwife of history) exalted the use of violence and identified *tout court* with the anti-colonial struggles described in *La battaglia di Algeri* without considering the differences in the two historical and political contexts. It is this perhaps that explains the outmodedness of *Ogro*: it is a film that seeks to address and explain everything to a viewer who no longer exists today.[20]

The Moro Kidnap: Conspiracy and Psychology

In 2003 *Piazza delle cinque lune* (*Piazza of the Five Moons*, Renzo Martinelli) and *Buongiorno, notte* (*Good Morning, Night*, Marco Bellocchio) were released within three months of one another; both were dedicated to what was surely the most traumatizing episode of the *anni di piombo*: the kidnapping and murder of Aldo Moro by the BR. If the subject matter is the same, the approach to the events differs radically. While *Buongiorno notte* approaches the events from a psychological and ethical point of view, *Piazza delle cinque lune* treats them from the point of view of conspiracy.

The Moro affair lends itself particularly well to being revisited through this type of narration and, in fact, Martinelli's film raises one of the most common conspiracy theories relating to Moro's kidnapping and murder: that the BR were influenced by the CIA and by an anticommunist apparatus embedded within the institutions of

---

20   See for example the interview where Fausto Bertinotti, the former leader of the left-wing party Rifondazione Comunista, underlines how he once fully identified with the Algerian terrorists in *La battaglia di Algeri*, but no longer does so. Fausto Bertinotti, 'Questo movimento è nuovo', *La Repubblica*, 2 November 2003.

the Italian state. This is a theory which has been codified in *La tela del ragno* [*The Spiderweb*] by Sergio Flamigni, a former PCI-listed senator and the historical adviser to the scriptwriter of *Piazza delle cinque lune*. The film contains several familiar *topoi* of the conspiracy film: the existence of secret 'proof' (a Super8 film of the Moro kidnapping filmed by an eye-witness whose identity remains unknown); an enquiry carried out by the main protagonist (the ex-magistrate, Saracini); the 'friend' (Saracini's bodyguard) who is revealed at the end to be part of the conspiracy; and the negative ending in which the hidden powers triumph over the honest investigator.

While it is beyond the scope of this essay to dwell on the many unexplained events of the Moro affair, a crucial event in Italy's history, it is doubtful that Martinelli's approach can contribute in any way to overcoming the divisions of the 'period of emergency'. Indeed, the opposite appears to be true. By rendering the BR unwitting puppets in the hands of powers greater than them, Martinelli's film implicitly reduces their responsibility for the events. It seems to me that this is a dangerous simplification because the judgement on the moral quality of the BR's actions becomes secondary (a suggestion supported by the fact that several ex-BR members have enthusiastically accepted the idea that they had been conditioned by external forces) and their responsibility is thus subordinated to that of other mysterious actors (whose 'superior' aims justify the use of any means). Consequently, the socio-political conflict of the *anni di piombo* – of which armed struggle was but one aspect – disappears from history. But above all it seems to me that the effect produced by conspiracy-theory narratives on public opinion is genuinely harmful, because rather than throwing new light on the events, it makes them even more difficult to interpret, and instils a sense of distrust in the wider public.

Buongiorno, notte, on the other hand, takes a different route.[21] At the centre of Bellocchio's film lies the relationship between Aldo Moro and Chiara, the young female terrorist whose point of view structures much of the narrative. Bellocchio's Chiara was inspired by *Il prigioniero* [*The Prisoner*], the autobiographical account, published in 1998, of the ex-*brigatista* Anna Laura Braghetti who, in addition to detailing the fifty-four days of the Moro kidnapping, also recounts how she found herself involved with the BR. I say 'found herself' because on reading the book one is left with the disconcerting feeling

---

21 From here on, my argument is based on material I have developed in my essay 'Rappresentazioni degli anni di piombo', in *Atti del VII Congresso degli Italianisti Scandinavi: Mémoires de la Societé Néophilogique de Helsinki*, LXVIII, ed. Enrico Garavelli and Elina Suomela-Härmä (Helsinki: Societé Néophilogique, 2005), 299–310.

of a person who has joined the armed struggle without knowing quite why; or rather, who is unsure whether she made the choice according to private or emotional motivations or because of political and ideological beliefs.[22] Braghetti is periodically faced with a choice that ever more inevitably takes her down the path of armed struggle for personal rather than political reasons.[23]

More than once in the book she repeats that she had neither sufficient experience nor sufficient political talent to sustain an autonomous political position against the BR during the kidnapping. She asserts that she tried nonetheless to convince Mario Moretti and Prospero Gallinari to save Moro's life. And yet at the end of the book the ideological reasons re-emerge: 'Perché rimasi? Me lo sono chiesto tante volte, e mai ho trovato una risposta. O forse, oggi non mi basta la risposta che mi diedi quella notte. Semplicemente, ci credevo' (Braghetti and Tavella, 170) [Why did I stay? I've asked myself that so many times, and never found an answer. Or maybe it's just that today the answer I gave myself that night no longer suffices. I simply believed]. She goes on to add, however, that: 'E poi avevo fiducia in Moretti e Prospero. La contestazione che mi ero permessa poche ore prima era il mio massimo' (170) [Besides, I had faith in Moretti and Prospero. The protest I had allowed myself a few hours earlier was as much as I could muster]. This is where the unresolved contradiction between Anna Laura, the revolutionary woman, and Anna Laura, the woman *belonging to* the revolution, appears in all its clarity.

What in Braghetti's book is presented as a continuous shift between private desire and political justification of her actions becomes in Bellocchio's film an ethical conflict between humanitarian and ideological motivations, between the principles of an ethics of responsibility which forbids the killing of an unarmed and imprisoned person and those of an ethics of conviction which bestows values so absolutist in political terms as to justify even the killing of a hostage. In the claustrophobic atmosphere of the apartment where Moro was held captive, Chiara's internal conflict arises from the fact that she partakes, on the one hand, of the utopian vision for which the BR finally killed Moro but cannot, on the other, accept the murder of a mild and defenceless man who in her eyes has all the characteristics of a father.

---

22 My reading of this aspect of Braghetti's account is different from the interpretation provided by Dana Renga in this collection, where it is suggested that *Il prigioniero* paints Braghetti as a conscious political subject.
23 See for example Braghetti and Tavella, 13–15 and 49–50.

And yet, if we are to believe the testimony of Adriana Faranda, who also participated in the Moro operation and who was one of only two BR members to oppose the death sentence on *political* grounds, it is simply not credible that considerations of a humanitarian kind could play a role in the decisions of the BR, who subordinated every other value to ideology. Interviewed after seeing the film, Faranda declared: 'È impensabile che Anna Laura dicesse: salviamo Moro perché è un uomo: o si traduceva in una linea politica, oppure era come non dirlo' [It's unthinkable that Anna Laura would have said: let's save Moro because he's a human being; either she would have had to translate the idea into political terms, or it would have been as if she had not spoken at all].[24]

However, the psychological approach chosen by Bellocchio, because it avoids a minutely documentary representation of the Moro affair, serves a socio-pedagogical function. That function is particularly pertinent to the younger audience who did not live through the events depicted, because it foregrounds the question of the terrorists' value systems and the ethical, psychical and human consequences of those values. The fundamentalist discourse of ideology is potentially oppressive and destructive not only for others but also for the terrorists themselves, as Chiara's internal conflict demonstrates, because it subordinates the identification of humanity as the other (the ethical) to political utopia (the ends).

Conclusion: *La Meglio Gioventù*

I will now make some concluding remarks by drawing on *La meglio gioventù* (*The Best of Youth*, Marco Tullio Giordana, 2003). Although *La meglio gioventù* is not a film on the *anni di piombo* but a six-hour TV serial made for RAI in 2002, it was released as a film in two parts after winning an award at Cannes in 2003 (and was finally broadcast by RAI in December 2003 to an audience of eight million viewers). Interweaving the public and the private, Giordana (and his screenwriters Sandro Petraglia and Stefano Rulli) tells the story of the Italian Republic from the mid-1960s to the turn of the century through the events experienced by two brothers, Nicola and Matteo,

---

24 'Intervista ad Adriana Faranda', http://materialiresistenti.blog.dada.net/post/26627/Intervista+a+Adriana+Faranda [accessed 5 August 2010].

and their family, and offers a portrait of the so-called '68 generation which is at the centre of this story.[25]

Alongside other crucial events of recent Italian history, space is dedicated to the armed struggle, which in the film is represented by the character of Giulia, Nicola's partner. Nicola falls in love with Giulia in Florence upon hearing her play the piano in the wake of the floods of 1966; together they take part in the 1968 student riots in Turin where their daughter, Sara, is later born. Over the course of the film, Nicola studies medicine, becomes a psychiatrist and tries to improve the conditions in which the mentally ill are held in Italy. Giulia, on the other hand, chooses the armed struggle: she abandons Nicola, Sara and the piano, and goes underground. Thus, the film presents the different choices which that generation found itself making with regard to civic and political commitment.

Giordana shows great sympathy for the male protagonist, Nicola, who is in effect the representative of the reformist tendency of the 1968 movement. In the figure of Nicola, Giordana presents the successes and defeats of all those who, during those years, chose to reform the system from within, in spite of all the difficulties. However, I would contend that the film does not so convincingly explain the 'extremist' choice made by Giulia.[26] And yet, in their different choices, one can clearly see the value systems that spur them on. If we apply Todorov's terminology here, Giulia is the representative of an ethics of conviction that prefers the ideal to the real, the abstract to the concrete. For a godlike ideal (social justice, the Revolution), she sacrifices concrete human values: maternal love, her love for Nicola and her own creativity. Nicola, on the other hand, represents altruism and an ethics of responsibility, a secular and non-violent ethics. His actions are not heroic – there is nothing extraordinary about them – but they require a profound faith in humankind and an awareness of the relationship between ideals (ends) and ethics (means).

The spectator is never in doubt as to where the director's sympathies lie; nor is she unaware of his identification with the values represented by Nicola and his reformist itinerary, which allegorically

---

25   The absence of any reference to the strategy of tension and the *stragismo* of the right (and of the state) is, arguably, a serious defect in a film that aspires to an epic portrayal of the Italian Republic's recent history.

26   In the one scene in which Giulia voices her motivations (a dialogue with Nicola), she rejects the validity of discussion in favour of responding to violence with violence. Giulia's character seems to be inspired by the biography of Adriana Faranda. See Silvana Mazzocchi, *Nell'anno della tigre: storia di Adriana Faranda* (Milan: Baldini and Castoldi, 1994).

is also that of Italy. Nevertheless, the film communicates sincere regret for the waste that Giulia's choice has implied both for herself (the theme of suppressed creativity returns several times) and for those dear to her. While displaying no understanding of her decision to participate in armed struggle, Giordana appears to forgive Giulia and request that she be forgiven. It is Nicola at the end of the film who expresses the point of view of the filmmakers when, with the words, 'Sei felice? Allora è arrivato il momento d'essere generosi' [Are you happy? Well, then, the time has come to be generous], he strongly encourages a reconciliation between Sara and Giulia, who has now been released from jail. The film's intention to offer a collective and shared representation of the history of a generation is evident, as is its intention to settle the accounts and make peace with the past, not only in an individual sense (as evinced in the various life stories of the film's characters) but also in a collective sense.

It may be that Giordana's aim is rather sentimental, and yet, in spite of its limitations, it seems to me that *La meglio gioventù* has considerable social and pedagogical importance. I believe it represents a largely successful attempt to explore how one should approach the relationship between memory, the past, forgetting and forgiveness. The object of Sara's forgiveness, insofar as she represents younger generations, is not the past event, that is to say a criminal action (the mistaken choice of her mother and many others), but its meaning and place in relation to the present and the future. It is not so much about cancelling a debt as about unravelling the knots of the past; it is not a question of forgetting the events themselves, which must, on the contrary be accurately preserved, but of erasing blame, which paralyses memory and impedes the formation of a collective identity. The everyday challenge of collective living may be reduced to the use one makes of the relationship between memory and forgetting when what is at stake is the construction of a collective memory and, therefore, identity.

Unfortunately, it seems that there is little desire in Italy to set out on the path towards the construction of a shared memory. The predominant practice in public opinion is to declare one's own ideas as absolute instead of retaining those ideas while also trying to interrogate and understand those of the Other. Moreover, there is little will to eliminate the practice of political exploitation of the past. Instead of working through one's past and moving on without forgetting it, as Rusconi suggests, it seems that the Italian preference is for 'a past that will not pass', which is capable of conditioning and controlling the present.[27]

---

27   Gian Enrico Rusconi, *Germania: un passato che non passa. I crimini nazisti e l'identità tedesca* (Turin: Einaudi, 1987).

Glossary

Anni di piombo	Period of activity of left and right wing terrorist organizations in Italy (c. 1969–83)
7 aprile	Day in which, in 1979, Piero Calogero issued warrants for the arrest of far left activists, forcing many of them into exile. The date has also come to stand for the long series of trials that followed.
Autonomia Operaia	Italian extra-parliamentary leftist movement, particularly active in the late 1970s
Brigate Rosse (BR)	Left-wing terrorist organization founded in 1969, and more or less disbanded in the late 1980s
Brigatista (pl. –i)	Member of the Brigate Rosse (BR)
Carabinieri	Italian national gendarmerie. A member of this organization is known as a *carabiniere*.
Cinema d'autore	Auteur cinema
Cinema d'impegno	Politically or socially committed cinema
Cinema d'inchiesta	A form of Italian cinema, particularly prevalent in the late 1960s and 1970s, which investigated mysterious events, whether in a documentary or semi-fictionalized manner
Commedia all'italiana	subgenre of Italian comedy dating from 1959. It is marked by a bitter infusion of social critique. In English, referred to as 'comedy Italian style'.
Compromesso storico	The 'historical compromise' between the two largest Italian political parties, the PCI and the DC, during the 1970s. Promoted by Aldo Moro and Enrico Berlinguer, this compromise

	was to be sealed through the creation of a government of national solidarity, led by a DC Prime Minister and officially sponsored by all members of the PCI.
Democrazia Cristiana (DC)	Christian Democrat party, founded in 1942 and active until 1993. Throughout its existence, it continued to secure the highest number of votes at all elections, and participated in all governments of the First Republic.
Gruppi d'Azione Partigiana (GAP)	'Groups of Partisan Action': a left-wing para-military organization founded by Giangiacomo Feltrinelli in 1970, and active until 1972, shortly after his death.
Gruppi Armati Patriottici (GAP)	'Groups of Patriotic Action': Anti-fascist Resistance groups (mostly allied to the PCI) who fought in the occupied cities carrying out attacks and murders on Nazis, fascists and their functionaries in 1943–45.
Gladio	Covert paramilitary apparatus founded in the 1950s with the support of the USA and sponsored by the Italian Secret Services. Its function was to intervene and stage a coup in the case of the electoral victory of the PCI.
Lotta armata	Armed struggle; term with which members of terrorist organizations identified their activity.
Lotta Continua	Extra-parliamentary group of the extreme left, active from 1969 to 1982
Movimento	Term used to refer to the broad leftist social and student movement with its origins in 1968 but which continued until the late 1970s
Movimento Sociale Italiano (MSI)	Italian Social Movement, a far right party, heir of the Fascist party after WWII
Nuove Brigate Rosse	New Red Brigades, active from 1998 to 2003
Partito Comunista Italiano (PCI)	Italian Communist Party, founded in 1921 and active until 1991, when, after the Fall of the Soviet Union, it was dismembered into three different parties: Democratici di Sinistra (DS), Rifondazione Comunista (RC), and Comunisti Italiani (CI). It was Italy's second largest party

until the end of the First Republic, though it never participated in any of its governments.

Pentito/a (pl. –i) — Apprehended terrorists who decided to 'collaborate' with the judiciary, receiving considerable reduction in sentences in return. The phenomenon was known as *pentitisimo*.

Poliziottesco — Also called 'Poliziesco all'italiana', the Italian variation of the 'cop film' genre, characterized by an exuberant use of action and extreme violence

Propaganda Due (P2) — Masonic lodge, active since the end of the nineteenth century, and operating illegally, in the attempt to influence or control the state, from 1976 to 1981

RAI — Radiotelevisione Italiana: Italian public broadcasting corporation, formerly Radio Audizioni Italiane.

Rifondazione Comunista (RC) — One of the three political parties which emerged from the splintering of the PCI

Sessantotto — 1968, the year of widespread worker protest and student revolts which spilled over into 1969 and influential for much of the ideological tumult of the 1970s

Stragismo — A tactic of large scale indiscriminate bombings employed by right-wing terrorist organizations

Strategia della tensione — 'Strategy of tension': refers to a concerted effort by authoritarian elements close to the Italian state, including its Secret Services, to control and manipulate left- and right-wing terrorist organizations in order to spread panic among the population, and thus keep the PCI away from power.

Bibliography, Filmography and Theatrical Production

Bibliography

Allen, Beverly, 'Terrorism, Feminism, Sadism: The Clichéing of Experience in the Brand-Name Novel', *Art and Text*, 33 (1989), 75-80

—, 'Terrorism Tales: Gender and the Fictions of Italian National Identity', *Italica* 69: 2 (Summer 1992), 161-76

Ang, Ien, *Watching Dallas* (London: Methuen, 1985)

—, *Watching Television* (London: Routledge, 1991)

Arcagni, Simone, 'Diavolo in corpo', in *Le forme della ribellione: il cinema di Marco Bellocchio*, ed. Luisa Ceretto and Giancarlo Zappoli (Turin: Lindau, 2004), 117-21

Arendt, Hannah, *Eichmann in Jerusalem: A Report on the Banality of Evil*, rev. edn (Harmondsworth: Penguin 1976) [orig. (London: Faber, 1963/New York: Viking, 1963)]

Argentieri, Mino, 'La commedia e la storia d'Italia', in *Commedia all'Italiana: angolazioni controcampi*, ed. Riccardo Napolitano (Rome: Gangemi Editore, 1986), 95-111

Assmann, Aleida, *Ricordare: forme e mutamenti della memoria culturale* (Bologna: Il Mulino, 2002) [orig. *Erinnerungsrâume: Formen und Wandlungen des kulturellen Gedâchtnisses* (München: Beck, 1999)]

Baliani, Marco, *Corpo di stato. Il delitto Moro: una generazione divisa* (Milan: Rizzoli, 2003)

Bandirali, Luca and Enrico Terrone, 'L'uomo che sapeva troppo', *Segnocinema*, 24: 125 (2004), 4-7

Bandirali, Luca and Stefano D'Amadio, *Buongiorno, notte: le ragioni e le immagini* (Lecce: Argo, 2004)

Bartali, Roberto, 'The Red Brigades and the Moro Kidnapping: Secrets and Lies', in *Speaking out and Silencing: Culture, Society and Politics in Italy in the 1970s*, ed. Anna Cento Bull and Adalgisa Giorgio (Oxford: Legenda, 2006), 146-60

Behan, Tom, 'Allende, Berlinguer, Pinochet … and Dario Fo', in *Speaking Out and Silencing: Culture, Society and Politics in Italy in the 1970s*, ed. Anna Cento Bull and Adalgisa Giorgio (Oxford: Legenda, 2006), 160-71

Bellocchio, Marco, *Buongiorno, notte* (Press Book distributed at the screening at the Venice Film Festival, September 2003)

Belpoliti, Marco, *La foto di Moro* (Rome: Nottetempo, 2008)

Bertinotti, Fausto, 'Questo movimento è nuovo', *La Repubblica*, 2 November 2003

Bertolucci, Giuseppe, 'Intervista', in *Segreti segreti* [DVD] (Rome: Istituto Luce, 2004)

Bignardi, Irene, *Memorie estorte ad uno smemorato: vita di Gillo Pontecorvo* (Milan: Feltrinelli, 1999)

Blum, Joanne, *Transcending Gender: The Male/Female Double in Women's Fiction* (Ann Arbor: UMI Research Press, 1988)

Boato, Marco, 'Né con lo Stato né con le BR: si cerca di prendere l'iniziativa', *Lotta continua*, 18 March 1978

Bocca, Giorgio, *Il caso 7 aprile* (Milan: Feltrinelli, 1980)

—, 'La nostra orribile stagione di sangue', *La Repubblica*, 20 March 2004

Bolla, Luisella, *Incantesimi: Alice nel paese della fiction* (Florence: Vallecchi, 2004)

Borghini, Fabrizio, *Mario Monicelli: cinquantanni di cinema* (Pisa: Edizioni Master, 1985)

Braghetti, Anna Laura and Paola Tavella, *Il prigioniero* (Milan: Mondadori, 1998; repr. Milan: Feltrinelli, 2003)

Brunetta, Gian Piero, *Storia del cinema italiano*, ii: *Dal 1945 agli anni ottanta* (Rome: Editori Riuniti, 1982)

Bruni, David, '*Colpire al cuore* di G. Amelio: lo sguardo discreto', in *Schermi opachi: il cinema italiano degli anni '80*, ed. Lino Miccichè (Venice: Marsilio, 1998), 237-47

Bruno, Giuliana, *Atlas of Emotion: Journeys in Art, Architecture and Film* (New York: Verso, 2002)

Bruno, Marcello Walter, '*Buongiorno, notte*: perché no', *Segnocinema*, 23: 124 (November-December 2003), 60

Buonanno, Milly, *Cultura di massa e identità femminile: l'immagine della donna in televisione* (Turin: ERI, 1983)

—, ed., *Sceneggiare la cronaca: la fiction italiana, l'Italia nella fiction. Anno Terzo*, ed. Milly Buonanno (Turin: VQPT Nuova Eri, 1992)

—, *Narrami o diva: studi sull'immaginario televisivo* (Naples: Liguori, 1994)

—, ed., *Il bardo sonnacchioso: la fiction italiana, l'Italia nella fiction. Anno Quinto* (Turin: ERI/VQPT, 1994)

—, *La piovra: la carriera politica di una fiction popolare* (Genoa-Milan: Costa & Nolan, 1996)

—, *Indigeni si diventa: locale e globale nella serialità televisiva* (Milan: Sansoni, 1999)

—, *Le formule del racconto televisivo: la sovversione del tempo nelle narrative seriali* (Milan: Sansoni, 2002)

Burns, Jennifer, 'A Leaden Silence? Writers' Responses to the *anni di piombo*', in *Speaking out and Silencing: Culture, Society and Politics in Italy in the 1970s*, ed. Anna Cento Bull and Adalgisa Giorgio (Oxford: Legenda, 2006), 81-94

Cadava, Eduardo, *Words of Light: Theses on the Photography of History* (Princeton: Princeton University Press, 1997)

Calabrese, Omar, *Neo-Baroque: A Sign of the Times*, trans. by C. Lambert (Princeton: Princeton University Press, 1992)

Caldwell, Lesley, 'Is the Political Personal? Fathers and Sons in Bertolucci's *Tragedia di un uomo ridicolo* and Amelio's *Colpire al cuore*', in *Speaking Out and Silencing: Culture, Society, and Politics in Italy in the 1970s*, ed. Anna Cento Bull and Adalgisa Giorgio (Oxford: Legenda, 2006), 69-80

Calegari, Manlio, *La sega di Hitler* (Milan: Selene, 2004)

Calvelli, Anna, 'Dinamiche psicoanalitiche inesistenti', *Cinema sessanta*, 5: 273 (2003), 14

Calvi, Gabriele and Massimo Martini, *L'estremismo politico: ricerche psicologiche sul terrorismo e sugli atteggiamenti radicali* (Milan: Franco Angeli, 1982)

Camerini, Claudio, 'I critici e la commedia all'italiana: le occasioni perdute', in *Commedia all'Italiana: angolazioni controcampi*, ed. Riccardo Napolitano (Rome: Gangemi Editore, 1986), 179-81

CARI (Committee Against Repression in Italy), 'April 7: Repression in Italy', *Semiotext[e]*, 3: 3 (1980), 172-7

Carocci, Enrico, 'Il terrorismo e la "perdita del centro": cineasti italiani di fronte alla catastrofe', in *Schermi di piombo: il terrorismo nel cinema italiano*, ed. Christian Uva (Soveria Mannelli: Rubbettino, 2007), 115-32

Casamassima, Pino, *Donne di piombo: undici vite nella lotta armata* (Milan: Bevivino, 2005)

Catanzaro, Raimondo, 'Subjective Experience and Objective Reality: An Account of Violence in the Words of its Protagonists', in

The Red Brigades and Left-wing Terrorism in Italy, ed. Raimondo Catanzaro (London: Printer Publishers, 1991), 174-203

Catanzaro, Raimondo and Luigi Manconi, *Storie di lotta armata* (Bologna: Il Mulino, 1995)

Caviglia, Francesco and Leonardo Cecchini, 'A Quest for Dialogism: Looking Back at Italian Political Violence in the '70s', in *Constructing History, Society and Politics in Discourse: Multimodal Approaches*, ed. Torben Vestergaard (Aalborg: Aalborg University Press, 2009), 127-48

Cecchini, Leonardo, 'Rappresentazioni degli anni di piombo', in *Atti del VII Congresso degli Italianisti Scandinavi: Mémoires de la Société Néophilologique de Helsinki*, ed. Enrico Garavelli & Elina Suomela-Härmä (Helsinki: Société Néophilologique, 2005), 299-310

Cento Bull, Anna, *Italian Neofascism: The Strategy of Tension and the Politics of Nonreconciliation* (New York: Berghahn, 2008)

Cento Bull, Anna and Adalgisa Giorgio, eds, *Speaking Out and Silencing: Culture, Society, and Politics in Italy in the 1970s* (Oxford: Legenda, 2006)

Chiacchiari, Federico, '"Dovevo affermare la mia assoluta infedeltà ai fatti e alla Storia", incontro con Marco Bellocchio', *Sentieri selvaggi*, 28 June 2006, www.sentieriselvaggi.it/articolo. asp?sez0=186&sez1=102&art=5513 [accessed 5 August 2010]

Ciment, Michel, 'Bernardo Bertolucci Discussing *Tragedy of a Ridiculous Man*', *Film and Filming*, 328 (1982), 12-16

Consolo, Vincenzo, *Lo spasimo di Palermo* (Milan: Mondadori, 1998)

Conti, Antonio and Andrea Tiddi, 'Gli anni Ottanta: le generazioni dell'esilio', *DeriveApprodi*, 7: 16 (1998), 19-20

Cooper, H.H.A., 'Woman As Terrorist', in *The Criminology of Deviant Women*, ed. Freda Adler and Rita James Simon (Boston: Houghton Mifflin Company, 1979), 150-57

Crowdus, Gary, 'Personalizing Political Issues: An Interview with Francesco Rosi', *Cineaste* 12: 2 (1982), 42

Cuddon, J.A., *The Penguin Dictionary of Literary Terms and Literary Theory*, 3rd edn (Harmondsworth: Penguin, 1991)

Curcio, Renato, *A viso aperto: vita e memoria del fondatore delle BR. Intervista di Mario Scialoja* (Milan: Mondadori, 1993)

Curti, Roberto, *Italia odia: il cinema poliziesco italiano* (Turin: Lindau, 2006)

D'Agostini, Paolo, 'L'incontro Maestri della regia: Francesco Rosi', *La Repubblica Domenica*, 18 February 2007

Dalle Vacche, Angela, *The Body in the Mirror: Shapes of History in Italian Cinema* (Princeton: Princeton University Press, 1992)

D'Amico, Masolino, *La commedia all'italiana: il cinema comico in Italia dal 1945 al 1975*, 2nd edn (Milan: Il Saggiatore, 2008)

De Cataldo Giancarlo, *Romanzo criminale* (Turin: Einaudi, 2004)

De Franceschi, Leonardo, 'L'attore negli anni della crisi', in *Storia del cinema italiano*, xiii: *1977-1985*, ed. Vito Zagarrio (Venice: Marsilio, 2005), 303-15

Deleuze, Gilles, *Cinema 1: The Movement Image*, trans. by H. Tomlinson and R. Galeta (London: The Athlone Press, 1992) [*L'Image-mouvement* (Paris: Editions de Minuit, 1983)]

Della Casa, Stefano, *Mario Monicelli* (Florence: Il Castoro/La Nuova Italia, 1986)

De Luca, Laura, *Tutti bravi ragazzi: il sequestro Moro e sette testimoni involontari* (Civitella in Val di Chiana: Zona, 2003)

Deriu, Fabrizio, '*La tragedia di un uomo ridicolo* di B. Bertolucci: il complesso di Crono', in *Schermi opachi: il cinema italiano degli anni '80*, ed. Lino Miccichè (Venice: Marsilio, 1998), 273-82

Derrida, Jacques, *Spectres of Marx: The State of the Debt, the Work of Mourning, and the New International*, trans. by P. Kamuf (London: Routledge, 1994) [orig. *Spectres de Marx: l'État de la dette, le travail du deuil et la nouvelle Internationale* (Paris: Editions Galilée, 1993)]

Dickinson, Emily, 'Good Morning - Midnight', in *The Complete Poems* (London: Faber, 1975), 203 [orig. in *Further Poems of Emily Dickinson*, ed. Martha Dickinson Bianchi and Alfred Leete Hampson (Boston: Little, Brown, and Company, 1929), 164]

Di Nucci, Loreto and Ernesto Galli della Loggia, *Due nazioni: legittimazione e delegittimazione nella storia dell'Italia contemporanea* (Bologna: Il Mulino, 2003)

Doane, Mary Ann, *Femmes Fatales: Feminism, Film Theory, Psychoanalysis* (New York and London: Routledge, 1991)

Dogliotti, Miro and Luigi Rosiello, eds, *Lo Zingarelli 1996: Vocabolario della lingua italiana*, 12th edn (Bologna: Zanichelli, 1996)

Dominjanni, Ida, 'Lost in Transition', in *Across Genres, Generations and Borders: Italian Women Writing Lives*, ed. Susanna Scarparo and Rita Wilson (Newark: University of Delaware Press, 2004), 192-209

Drake, Richard, *The Aldo Moro Murder Case* (Cambridge, MA: Harvard University Press, 1995)

E.A., 'Marco Bellocchio: le vie dell'inconscio e la libertà del sogno. A colloquio con il regista di *Buongiorno, notte*', *Duel*, 107 (2003), 7

Eco, Umberto, 'Fenomenologia di Mike Bongiorno', in *Diario minimo* (Milan: Bompiani, 1963), 30-35

—, 'La voglia di morte', *La Repubblica*, 14 February 1981, repr. in *Sette anni di desiderio* (Milan: Bompiani, 1995), 123-26

—, 'Perché ridono in quelle gabbie?', *La Repubblica*, 16 April 1982, repr. in *Sette anni di desiderio*, (Milan: Bompiani, 1995), 119-22

Eitinger, Leo, 'The Concentration Camp Syndrome and its Late Sequelae' in *Survivors, Victims and Perpetrators: Essays on the Nazi Holocaust*, ed. Joel E. Dimsdale (London: Taylor and Francis, 1980), 127-62

Elsaesser, Thomas, 'Postmodernism as Mourning Work', *Screen*, 42: 2 (2001), 193-201

Fantoni Minella, Maurizio, *Non riconciliati: politica e società nel cinema italiano dal neorealismo a oggi* (Turin: UTET, 2004)

Faranda, Adriana, 'Intervista ad Adriana Faranda', http://materialiresistenti.blog.dada.net/post/26627/Intervista+a+Adriana+Faranda [accessed 05 August 2010]

Fenster, Mark, *Conspiracy Theories: Secrecy and Power in American Culture* (Minneapolis and London: University of Minnesota Press, 1999)

Fenzi, Enrico, *Armi e bagagli: un diario delle Brigate Rosse* (Genoa-Milan: Costa & Nolan, 1998)

Ferrara, Giuseppe, *Misteri del caso Moro* (Bolsena: Massari, 2003)

Ferraù, Alessandro, 'Il pubblico è sovrano', *Giornale dello Spettacolo*, 7 (1971), 11

Fink, Guido, '*La tragedia di un uomo ridicolo*', in *In viaggio con Bernardo: il cinema di Bernardo Bertolucci*, ed. Roberto Campari & Maurizio Schiaretti (Venice: Marsilio, 1994), 102-11

Fiske, John, and John Hartley, *Reading Television* (London: Methuen, 1978)

Flamigni, Sergio, *La tela del ragno* (Milan: Kaos, 1993)

—, *Il mio sangue ricadrà su di loro: gli scritti di Aldo Moro prigioniero delle BR* (Milan: Kaos, 1997)

—, *Convergenze parallele: le Brigate Rosse, i servizi segreti e il delitto Moro* (Milan: Kaos, 1998)

—, *Trame atlantiche: storia della loggia masonica segreta P2* (Rome: Kaos, 2005)

Floris, Gianluca, *Il lato destro* (Cagliari: CUEC, 2006)

Foot, John, *Milan since the Miracle: City, Culture, Identity* (Oxford: Berg, 2001)

Freud, Sigmund, *Totem and Taboo*, in *The Standard Edition of the Complete Psychological Works of Sigmund Freud*, ed. James Strachey in collaboration with Anna Freud assisted by Alix Strachey and Alan Tyson; trans. by James and Alix Strachey, 24 vols (London: Hogarth Press and the Institute for Psycho-analysis, 1953-1974), xiii (1953), 1-162 [*Totem und Tabu* (Leipzig and Vienna: Heller, 1913)]

—, 'From the History of an Infantile Neurosis' in *The Standard Edition of the Complete Psychological Works of Sigmund Freud*, ed. James Strachey in collaboration with Anna Freud assisted by Alix Strachey and Alan Tyson; trans. by James Strachey, 24 vols (London: Hogarth Press and the Institute of Psycho-analysis, 1953-74), xvii (1955), 1-122 ['Aus der Geschichte einer infantilen Neuroes', in *Sammlung kleiner Schriften zur Neurosenlehre*, 5 vols (Leipzig and Vienna: Deuticke, 1906-22), iv (1918)]

—, 'Beyond the Pleasure Principle', in *The Standard Edition of the Complete Psychological Works of Sigmund Freud*, ed. James Strachey in collaboration with Anna Freud and assisted by Alix Strachey and Alan Tyson, trans. by James Strachey, 24 vols (London: Hogarth Press and the Institute for Psycho-analysis, 1953-74), xviii (1955), 7-64 [*Jenseits des Lustprinzips* (Vienna: Internationaler Psychoanalytischer Verlag, 1920)]

Gaggi, Silvio, 'Navigating Chaos', in *New Punk Cinema*, ed. Nicholas Rombes (Edinburgh: Edinburgh University Press, 2005), 113-25

Galli, Giorgio, *Piombo rosso: la storia completa della lotta armata in Italia dal 1970 a oggi* (Milan: Baldini, Castoldi, Dalai, 2004)

Georges-Abeyie, Daniel E., 'Women as Terrorists', in *Perspectives on Terrorism*, ed. Lawrence Zelic Freedman and Yonah Alexander (Wilmington: Scholarly Resources, Inc., 1983), 71-84

Giacovelli, Enrico, *La Commedia all'Italiana*, 2nd edn (Rome: Gremese Editore, 1995)

Gilbert, Sandra M. and Susan Gubar, *The Madwoman in the Attic: The Woman Writer and the Nineteenth-Century Literary Imagination* (New Haven and London: Yale University Press, 1979)

Gilmore, Leigh, *The Limits of Autobiography: Trauma and Testimony* (Ithaca: Cornell University Press, 2001)

Ginsborg, Paul, *A History of Contemporary Italy 1943-88* (Harmondsworth: Penguin, 1990)

—, *Storia d'Italia 1943-1996* (Turin: Einaudi, 1998)

—, *Italy and its Discontents: Family, Civil Society, State 1980-2001* (New York: Palgrave, 2003)

Ginzburg, Natalia, *Caro Michele* (Milan: Mondadori, 1973)

Glynn, Ruth, 'Through the Lens of Trauma: The Figure of the Female Terrorist in *Il prigioniero* and *Buongiorno, notte*', in *Imagining Terrorism: The Rhetoric and Representation of Political Violence in Italy, 1969-2009*, ed. Pierpaolo Antonello and Alan O'Leary (Oxford: Legenda, 2009), 63-76

—, 'Displaced Confessions: Moro, Metaphor and Metonymy in Female Perpetrator Narrative' (Unpublished paper presented at the 'Remembering Moro' conference, Institute of Germanic & Romance Studies, London, 10-11 November, 2006)

Greco, Michela, *Il digitale nel cinema italiano: estetica, produzione, linguaggio* (Turin: Lindau, 2002)

Greenhalgh, Susanne, 'The Bomb in the Baby Carriage: Women and Terrorism in Modern Drama', in *Terrorism and Modern Drama*, ed. John Orr and Dragan Klaic (Edinburgh: Edinburgh University Press, 1990), 150-57

Guazzini, G. '*Caro papà*', *Cinema Nuovo*, 28: 261 (1979), 53-4

Günsberg, Maggie, *Italian Cinema: Gender and Genre* (Basingstoke: Palgrave, 2005)

Hall, Stuart, 'Encoding/Decoding', in *Culture, Media, Language* ed. Stuart Hall and others (London: Hutchinson/Centre for Contemporary Cultural Studies, 1980), 128-38

Harvey, Sylvia, 'Woman's Place: The Absent Family of Film Noir', in *Women in Film Noir*, ed. E. Ann Kaplan, rev. edn (London: British Film Institute, 1998), 35-46

Hegel, Georg Wilhelm Friedrich, *Lectures on the Philosophy of History*, trans. by J. Sibree (London: G. Bell, 1910 [1840])

Henninger, Maximilian, 'Recurrence, Retrieval, Spectrality: History and the Promise of Justice in Adriano Sofri's *L'ombra di Moro*', in *Italian Culture*, 22 (2004), 115-36

Herman, Judith, *Trauma and Recovery: From Domestic Abuse to Political Terror* (London: Pandora, 2001)

Friedrich Hölderlin, *Sämtliche Werke*, 6 vols (Stuttgart: Kohlhammer, 1965-66), ii (1965)

Jacobson, Brooke, '*The Tragedy of a Ridiculous Man*', *Film Quarterly*, 37: 3 (1984), 58-9

Jameson, Fredric, *The Political Unconscious: Narrative as a Socially Symbolic Act* (Ithaca, NY: Cornell University Press, 1981)

Jamieson, Alison, *The Heart Attacked: Terrorism and Conflict in the Italian State* (London and New York: Marion Boyars 1989)

Kaplan, E. Ann, ed., *Women in Film Noir* (London: British Film Institute, 1998)

Katz, Robert, *Days of Wrath: The Ordeal of Aldo Moro, the Kidnapping, the Execution, the Aftermath* (St Albans: Granada, 1980)

Klein, Norman M., *The History of Forgetting: Los Angeles and the Erasure of Memory* (London: Verso, 1997)

Kline, T. Jefferson, *Bertolucci's Dream Loom: A Psychoanalytic Study of Cinema* (Amherst: University of Massachusetts Press, 1987)

Knox, Bernard M.W., *The Heroic Temper: Studies in Sophoclean Tragedy* (Berkeley and Los Angeles: University of California Press, 1983)

Knudsen, Peter Øvig, *Efter Drabet* (Copenhagen: Gyldendal, 2001)

Lacan, Jacques, *The Seminar of Jacques Lacan*, i: *Freud's Papers on Technique 1953-1954*, trans. by John Forrester (Cambridge: Cambridge University Press, 1988) [*Le Séminar de Jacques Lacan*, i: *Les Écrits techniques de Freud 1953-1954* (Paris: Editions du Seuil, 1975)]

Lenci, Sergio, *Colpo alla nuca* (Rome: Editori Riuniti, 1980)

Levantesi, Alessandra, 'Memorie di un recensore militante: il cinema italiano', in *Schermi opachi: il cinema italiano degli anni '80*, ed. Lino Miccichè (Venice: Marsilio, 1998), 89-98

Lombardi, Giancarlo, 'Unforgiven: Revisiting Political Terrorism in *La seconda volta*', *Italica* 77: 2 (2000), 199-213

—, 'Virgil, Dante, *Blade Runner*, and Italian Terrorism: The Concept of *Pietas* in *La seconda volta* and *La mia generazione*', *Romance Languages Annual*, 11 (2000), 191-96

—, 'Terrorism, Truth, and the Secret Service: Questions of Accountability in the Cinema of the *stragi di stato*', *Annali d'Italianistica*, 19 (2001), 285-302

—, 'Parigi o cara: Terrorism, Exile, and Escape in Contemporary Italian Cinema and Theatre', *Annali d'Italianistica*, 20 (2002), 403-24

—, 'La passione secondo Marco Bellocchio: gli ultimi giorni di Aldo Moro', *Annali d'italianistica*, 25 (2007), 397-408

Loshitzky, Yosefa, *The Radical Faces of Godard and Bertolucci* (Detroit: Wayne University Press, 1995)

Lumley, Robert, *States of Emergency: Cultures of Revolt in Italy from 1968 to 1978* (London: Verso, 1990).

Malvezzi, Piero and Giovanni Pirelli, eds, *Lettere di condannati a morte della Resistenza italiana (8 settembre 1943-25 aprile 1945)* (Turin: Einaudi, 1952)

Marcus, Millicent, 'Beyond *Cinema Politico*: Family as Political Allegory in *Three Brothers*', in *Poet of Civic Courage: The Films of Francesco Rosi*, ed. Carlo Testa (Trowbridge: Flicks Books, 1996), 116-37

Martinelli, Renzo, *Piazza delle cinque lune: il thriller del caso Moro* (Rome: Gremese, 2003)

Martini, Emanuela, ed., *Gianni Amelio: le regole e il gioco* (Bergamo: Lindau, 1999)

Mast, Gerald, *The Comic Mind: Comedy and the Movies* (New York: Random House, 1976)

Matrone, Maurizio, 'Police Film Festival: un festival per i poliziotti' in *3° Police Film Festival: Anni '70. Il poliziotto tra fiction e realtà,* ed. Anna Di Martino, Maurizio Matrone, and Massimo Moretti (Cineteca di Bologna, 1997), 6

Mazza, Antonio, 'Vogliamo i colonnelli', *Rivista del Cinematografo*, 5 (1973), 213-14

Mazzocchi, Silvana, *Nell'anno della tigre: storia di Adriana Faranda* (Milan: Baldini & Castoldi, 1994)

Mereghetti, Paolo, *Dizionario dei film 2002* (Milan: Baldini & Castoldi, 2002)

Micciché, Lino, *Cinema italiano degli anni '70* (Venice: Marsilio, 1980)

—, 'Gli eredi del nulla per una critica del giovane cinema italiano', in *Una generazione in cinema: esordi e esordienti 1975-85*, ed. Franco Montini (Venice: Marsilio, 1988), 251-8

—, *Filmologia e filologia: studi sul cinema italiano* (Venice, Marsilio, 2002)

Morandini, Morando, 'È la tragedia di un uomo abbandonato', *Il Giorno*, 14 November 1986

—, 'Rapporti critici', in *Gianni Amelio*, ed. Gianni Volpi (Turin: Scriptorium, 1995), 27-32

Morante, Elsa, 'Lettera alle Brigate Rosse', *Paragone*, 7: 453 (1988), 15-16

Moretti, Mario, Carla Mosca, and Rossana Rossanda, *Brigate Rosse: una storia italiana* (Milan: Anabasi, 1994)

Morgan, Robin, *The Demon Lover: On the Sexuality of Terrorism* (New York & London: W.W. Norton & Co., 1989)

Morley, David, *The 'Nationwide' Audience* (London: British Film Institute, 1980)

—, *Interpreting Audiences* (London: Sage, 1993)

Morucci, Valerio, *La peggio gioventù: una vita nella lotta armata* (Milan: Rizzoli, 2004)

—, *Klagenfurt 3021* (Rome: Fahrenheit 451, 2004)

Mullen, Anne, *Inquisition and Inquiry: Sciascia's Inchiesta* (Market Harborough: Troubadour, 2000)

Mulvey, Laura, 'Visual Pleasure and Narrative Cinema', *Screen*, 16: 3 (Autumn 1975), 6-18

Napolitano, Riccardo, ed., *Commedia all'italiana: angolazioni controcampi* (Rome: Gangemi Editore, 1986)

Natalini, Fabrizio, 'Diavolo in corpo', in *Marco Bellocchio: il cinema e i film*, ed. Adriano Aprà (Venice: Marsilio, 2005), 185-9

Ndalianis, Angela, *Neo-Baroque Aesthetics and Contemporary Entertainment* (Cambridge, MA and London: MIT Press, 2004)

Neroni, Hilary, *The Violent Woman: Femininity, Narrative and Violence in Contemporary American Cinema* (Albany: SUNY University Press, 2005)

O'Leary, Alan, 'Film and the *Anni di Piombo*: Representations of Politically-Motivated Violence in Recent Italian Cinema', in *Culture, Censorship and the State in Twentieth-Century Italy*, ed. Guido Bonsaver and Robert S.C. Gordon (Oxford: Legenda, 2005), 168-78

—, *Tragedia all'italiana: cinema e terrorismo tra Moro e memoria* (Tissi: Angelica, 2007)

—, 'Dead Man Walking: The Aldo Moro Kidnap and Palimpsest History in *Buongiorno, notte*', *New Cinemas*, 6: 1 (2008), 33-45

—, 'Moro, Brescia, Conspiracy: The Paranoid Style in Italian Cinema', in *Imagining Terrorism: The Rhetoric and Representation of Political Violence in Italy 1969-2009*, ed. Pierpaolo Antonello and Alan O'Leary (Oxford: Legenda, 2009), 48-62

O'Rawe, Catherine, '"I padri e i maestri": Genre, Auteurs, and Absences in Italian Film Studies', *Italian Studies*, 63: 2 (2008), 173-94

Orton, Marie, 'De-Monsterizing the Myth of the Terrorist Woman: Faranda, Braghetti and Mambro', *Annali d'italianistica*, 16 (1998), 281-96

—, '"Terrorism" in Italian Film: Striking the One to Educate the Hundred', *Romance Languages Annual*, 11 (2000), 306-12

Paget, Derek, 'Codes and Conventions of Dramadoc and Docudrama' in *The Television Studies Reader*, ed. Robert C. Allen and Annette Hill (London: Routledge, 2004), 196-208

Pasolini, Pier Paolo, '1 febbraio 1975: l'articolo delle lucciole', in *Scritti corsari* (Milan: Garzanti, 1975), 160-68

—, *Lettere luterane* (Turin: Einaudi, 1976)

Pavone, Cesare, *Una guerra civile: saggio storico sulla moralità della resistenza* (Turin: Bollati Boringhieri, 1991)

Peirce, C.S., 'Nomenclature and Divisions of Triadic Relations, as Far as They are Determined' [1903], in *The Essential Peirce: Selected Philosophical Writings*, ed. The Peirce Edition Project (Bloomington and Indianapolis: Indiana University Press, 1998), 291-92

Pergolari, Andrea, 'La fisionomia del terrorismo nero nel cinema poliziesco italiano degli anni '70', in *Schermi di piombo: il terrorismo nel cinema italiano*, ed. Christian Uva (Soveria Mannelli: Rubbettino, 2007), 159-72

Pillitteri, Paolo, *Cinema come politica: una commedia all'italiana* (Milan: Franco Angeli, 1992)

Place, Janey, 'Women in Film Noir', in *Women in Film Noir*, ed. E. Ann Kaplan (London: British Film Institute, 1998), 46-68

Portelli, Alessandro, *L'ordine è già stato eseguito: Roma, le Fosse Ardeatine, la memoria* (Rome: Donzelli, 1999)

Project for Excellence in Journalism, *The State of the News Media, 2004: An Annual Report on American Journalism* (Washington, DC: Project for Excellence in Journalism, 2005) www.stateothemedia. org/2004/ [accessed 5 August 2010]

Ricœur, Paul, *Ricordare, dimenticare, perdonare: l'enigma del passato,* trans. by N. Salomon (Bologna: Il Mulino, 2004) [orig. *La mémoire, l'histoire, l'oubli* (Paris: Seuil, 2000)]

Rimanelli, Marco, 'Italian Terrorism and Society, 1940s-1980s: Roots, Ideologies, Evolutions, and International Connections', in *Italy,* ed. Mark Donovan (Dartmouth: Ashgate, 1998), 223-70

Riviere, Joan, 'Womanliness as Masquerade' (1929), in *Formations of Fantasy,* ed. Victor Burgin, James Donald, and Cora Kaplan (London: Methuen, 1986), 35-44

Rossanda, Rossana, 'Il discorso sulla DC', *Il Manifesto,* 28 March 1978

Rossi, Nerino, *La voce nel pozzo* (Venice: Marsilio, 1990)

Rusconi, Gian Enrico, *Germania: un passato che non passa: i crimini nazisti e l'identità tedesca* (Turin: Einaudi, 1987)

Sciascia, Leonardo, *Il giorno della civetta* (Turin: Einaudi, 1961)

—, *Pirandello e la Sicilia* (Caltanissetta: Sciascia, 1961)

—, *Pirandello e il pirandellismo* (Caltanissetta: Sciascia, 1953)

—, *L'affaire Moro* (Palermo: Sellerio, 1978; repr. Milan: Adelphi, 1994)

—, *The Day of the Owl/Equal Danger,* trans. by Archibald Colquhoun and Arthur Oliver (London: Paladin, 1984)

—, *The Moro Affair,* trans. by Sacha Rabinovitch (London: Granta Books, 2002)

Sedgwick, Eve Kosofsky, *Between Men: English Literature and Male Homosocial Desire* (New York: Columbia University press, 1985)

Segal, Naomi, *Narcissus and Echo: Women in the French 'récit'* (Manchester: Manchester University Press, 1988)

Sesti, Mario, ed., *Regia di Gianni Amelio* (Naples: Edizioni scientifiche Italiane, 1992)

Showalter, Elaine, *The Female Malady: Women, Madness, and English Culture, 1830-1980* (New York: Pantheon, 1985)

Smith, Murray, *Engaging Characters: Fiction, Emotion, and the Cinema* (Oxford: Oxford University Press, 1995)

Sofri, Adriano, *L'ombra di Moro* (Palermo: Sellerio, 1991)

Sola, Piero, 'La tragedia di un uomo ridicolo', *Rivista del Cinematografo,* 54: 12 (1981), 679

Soncini, Alberto, 'Il sacrificio della ragione', *Cineforum,* 43: 429 (November 2003), 2-4, 5-8

Sorlin, Pierre, *The Film in History: Restaging the Past* (Oxford: Basil Blackwell, 1980)

Spinelli, Barbara, *Il sonno della memoria: l'Europa dei totalitarismi* (Milan: Mondadori, 2001)

Tardi, Rachele, *Representations of Italian Left Political Violence in Film, Literature and Theatre (1973-2005)* (Unpublished doctoral dissertation, University of London, University College, 2005)

Tilgher, Adriano, *Studi sul teatro contemporaneo* (Rome: Libreria di Scienze e Lettere, 1923)

Todorov, Tzvetan, *Hope and Memory: Reflections on the Twentieth Century*, trans. by D. Bellos (London: Atlantic Books, 2003) [orig. *Mémoire du Mal, Tentation du bien: Enquête sur le siècle* (Paris: Robert Laffont, 2000)]

Torchiaro, Aldo, 'La tentazione del perdono: cinema e terrorismo', *Italianieuropei: bimestrale del riformismo italiano* (September-October 2003), 233-44

Traina, Giuseppe, *Leonardo Sciascia* (Milan: Bruno Mondadori, 1999)

Ussher, Jane, *Women's Madness: Misogyny or Mental Illness?* (New York: Harvester Wheatsheaf, 1991)

Uva, Christian, ed., *Schermi di piombo: il terrorismo nel cinema italiano* (Soveria Mannelli: Rubbettino, 2007)

Uva, Christian and Michele Picchi, eds, *Destra e sinistra nel cinema italiano: film e immaginario politico dagli anni '60 al nuovo millennio* (Rome: Edizioni Interculturali, 2006)

Venturelli, Renato, 'Intervista a Paola Tavella, coautrice di *Il prigioniero*' www.feltrinelli.it/IntervistaInterna?id_int=1193 [accessed 5 August 2010]

Wagner-Pacifici, Robin E., *The Moro Morality Play: Terrorism as Social Drama* (Chicago: University of Chicago Press, 1986)

Wheeler, Elizabeth A., *Uncontained: Urban Fiction in Postwar America* (New Brunswick: Rutgers University Press, 2001)

White, Hayden, *Metahistory: The Historical Imagination in Nineteenth-Century Europe* (Baltimore and London: Johns Hopkins University Press, 1973)

—, *Tropics of Discourse* (Baltimore and London: Johns Hopkins University Press, 1978)

Williams, Raymond, *Television: Technology and Cultural Form* (London: Wesleyan University Press, 1974)

Wood, Mary, 'Francesco Rosi: Heightened Realism', in *Projections 8*, ed. J. Boorman & W. Donohue (London: Faber and Faber, 1998), 272-95

—, *Italian Cinema* (Oxford: Berg, 2005)

—, 'Italian Film Noir', in *European Film Noir*, ed. Andrew Spicer (Manchester: Manchester University Press, 2007), 237-72

Wright, Steve, *Storming Heaven: Class Composition and Struggle in Italian Autonomist Marxism* (London: Pluto Press, 2002)

Zagarrio, Vito, 'Dopo la morte dei padri: dagli anni della crisi agli arbori della rinascita', in *Storia del cinema italiano*, xiii: *1977-1985*, ed. Vito Zagarrio (Venice: Marsilio, 2005), 3-39

Zambetti, Sandro, 'Ma non era anche un leader della DC?', *Cineforum*, 26: 260 (1986), 13-18

Zavoli, Sergio, *La notte della repubblica* (Milan: Mondadori, 1992)

Filmography

A ciascuno il suo, dir. by Elio Petri (Cemo Film, 1967)

Aldo Moro: il Presidente, dir. by Gianluca Maria Tavarelli (Taodue, 2008)

A risentirci più tardi, dir. by Alex Infascelli (Wilder, 2005)

Attacco allo stato, dir. by Michele Soavi (Taodue, 2006)

La battaglia d'Algeri, dir. by Gillo Pontecorvo (Casbah Film, 1966)

Un borghese piccolo piccolo, dir. by Mario Monicelli (Auro Cinematografica, 1977)

Buongiorno, notte, dir. by Marco Bellocchio, (Filmalbatros, 2003)

Cadaveri eccellenti, dir. by Francesco Rosi (Les Productions Artistes Associés, 1976)

Caro Michele, dir. by Mario Monicelli (Flag, 1976)

Caro papà, dir. by Dino Risi (AMLF, 1979)

Colpire al cuore, dir. by Gianni Amelio (Intea, 1982)

Diavolo in corpo, dir. by Marco Bellocchio (Film Sextile, 1986)

Donne armate, dir. by Sergio Corbucci (Italian International Film, 1990)

Una fredda mattina di maggio, dir. by Vittorio Sindoni (Bravo Production, 1990)

I nuovi mostri, dir. by Mario Monicelli, Dino Risi, Ettore Scola (Dean Film, 1977)

Il caso Mattei, dir. by Francesco Rosi (Verona Produzione, 1972)

Il caso Moro, dir. by Giuseppe Ferrara (Yarno Cinematografica, 1986)

Il cinico, l'infame e il violento, dir. by Umberto Lenzi (Dania Film, 1977)

Il terrorista, dir. by Gianfranco De Bosio (22 Dicembre, 1963)

Indagine su un cittadino al di sopra di ogni sospetto, dir. by Elio Petri (Vera Films, 1970)

L'istruttoria è chiusa: dimentichi, dir. by Damiano Damiani (Fair Film, 1975)

La notte della Repubblica: il caso Moro, dir. by Sergio Zavoli (Elle U Media, 2000)

La meglio gioventù, dir. by Marco Tullio Giordana (BiBiFilm, 2003)

La mia generazione, dir. by Wilma Labate (Compact, 1996)

La polizia accusa: il servizio segreto uccide, dir. by Sergio Martino (Dania Film, 1975)

La polizia ringrazia, dir. by Stefano Vanzina (Dieter Geissler Filmproduktion, 1972)

La seconda volta, dir. by Mimmo Calopresti (Banfilm, 1995)

Le mani forti, dir. by Franco Bernini (ACHAB Film, 1996)

Maledetti vi amerò, dir. by Marco Tullio Giordana (Coop. Jean Vigo, 1979)

Mordi e fuggi, dir. by Dino Risi (Champion, 1973),

Nucleo Zero, dir. by Carlo Lizzani (Diamante Films, 1984)

Ogro, dir. by Gillo Pontecorvo (Action Film, 1979)

Parole e sangue, dir. by Damiano Damiani (RAI, 1980)

Per non dimenticare, dir. by Massimo Martelli (Istituto Luce,1992)

Piazza delle cinque lune, dir. by Renzo Martinelli (Blue Spice Film, 2003)

Poliziotti violenti, dir. by Massimo Tarantini (Staff, 1976)

Roma a mano armata, dir. by Umberto Lenzi (Dania Film, 1976*)*

Romanzo criminale, dir. by Michele Placido (Cattleya, 2005)

Segreti segreti, dir. by Giuseppe Bertolucci (A.M.A. Film, 1985)

Todo modo, dir. by Elio Petri (Cinevera, 1976)

Tre fratelli, dir. by Francesco Rosi (Iterfilm, 1981)

Vite in sospeso, dir. by Marco Turco (RAI, 1998)

Vogliamo i colonnelli, dir. by Mario Monicelli (Dean Film, 1973)

Theatrical Productions (Unpublished)

Augias, Corrado and Vladimiro Polchi, *Aldo Moro: una tragedia italiana* (Teatro Eliseo: Rome, 2007)

Varvarà, Antonino, *Rosso Cupo: una donna nelle Brigate Rosse* (Teatrino di Via Pasini: Mestre, 2004)

Index

CPSIA information can be obtained at www.ICGtesting.com
Printed in the USA
LVOW10s2329220714

395594LV00011B/292/P